Praise for
Shattered Dreams

"It has been a delight to watch Larry Crabb continue his journey down the path toward a mature and honest spirituality. I look on him as an advance scout in places I have yet to venture."

—PHILIP YANCEY
author of *Reaching for the Invisible God* and *What's So Amazing About Grace?*

"I've lost count of how many times God has used Larry Crabb to tinker with my interior world. Five pages into this book I muttered to myself, 'Here we go again.'"

—BILL HYBELS
senior pastor of Willow Creek Community Church

"Believing that true human joy is ultimately 'the discovery of who and what we were each created to be, and that the One who made us is committed to our fruitfulness and fulfillment in being and becoming that,' I am pleased to recommend Larry Crabb's work. His commitment to bringing practical guidance and personal passion to the table, enabling others to find and grow in God's best purposes for their lives, makes me thankful for his writings and work."

—JACK W. HAYFORD
founding pastor of The Church on the Way and chancellor of The King's College and Seminary

"Anyone who knows Larry Crabb knows he's on an extraordinary journey, deep into the soul. And through his recent books—especially this one—we readers are privileged to tag along as Larry brings us to yet another level. He shows us a place where we are sure to encounter the core of our being. And it's here that he teaches us to connect with each other and with God more meaningfully than we ever imagined possible. Through *Shattered Dreams,* Larry skillfully guides us on a transforming journey toward joy—a journey you surely do not want to miss."

> —LES PARROTT, PH.D.
> author of *When Bad Things Happen to Good Marriages*

"With typical clarity, Dr. Larry Crabb has again tackled a thorny issue of Christian doctrine that others have either passed by or addressed with vocabulary and theology that doesn't match human experience. In *Shattered Dreams,* Dr. Crabb gently removes the broken pieces of our human dreams until at last he uncovers a loving, wise, and infinitely compassionate God whose ways we may not understand but whose heart we can always trust."

> —DAVE DRAVECKY
> president of Dave Dravecky's Outreach of Hope National
> Cancer Ministry

SHATTERED DREAMS

God's Unexpected
Path to Joy

LARRY CRABB

Eight-Week Workbook Included

WATERBROOK
PRESS

SHATTERED DREAMS

All scripture quotations, unless otherwise indicated, are taken from the Holy Bible, New International Version®, NIV®. Copyright ©1973, 1978, 1984 by Biblica, Inc.™ Used by permission of Zondervan. All rights reserved worldwide. www.zondervan.com. Scripture quotations marked (MSG) are taken from The Message by Eugene H. Peterson. Copyright © 1993, 1994, 1995, 1996, 2000, 2001, 2002. Used by permission of NavPress Publishing Group. All rights reserved. Scripture quotations marked (NLT) are taken from the Holy Bible, New Living Translation, copyright © 1996. Used by permission of Tyndale House Publishers Inc., Wheaton, Illinois 60189. All rights reserved.

Italics in Scripture quotations reflect the author's added emphasis.

Trade Paperback ISBN 978-0-307-45950-3
eBook ISBN 978-0-307-82266-6

Copyright © 2001 by Lawrence J. Crabb, Jr., PhD, PA
Workbook copyright © 2001 by Lawrence J. Crabb, Jr., PhD, PA

Published in association with Yates & Yates, LLP, Literary Agent, Orange, California.

All rights reserved. No part of this book may be reproduced or transmitted in any form or by any means, electronic or mechanical, including photocopying and recording, or by any information storage and retrieval system, without permission in writing from the publisher.

Published in the United States by WaterBrook, an imprint of the Crown Publishing Group, a division of Penguin Random House LLC, New York.

WATERBROOK® and its deer colophon are registered trademarks of Penguin Random House LLC.

Library of Congress Cataloging-in-Publication Data
Crabb, Lawrence J.
    Shattered dreams : God's unexpected pathway to joy / by Larry Crabb.—1st ed.
        p. cm.
    1. Spiritual life—Christianity. 2. Christian life. I. Title.
    BV4501.3 .C73 2001
    248.8'6—dc21
                                                00-054084

Printed in the United States of America
2016

10 9

SPECIAL SALES
Most WaterBrook books are available at special-quantity discounts when purchased in bulk by corporations, organizations, and special-interest groups. Custom imprinting or excerpting can also be done to fit special needs. For information, please e-mail specialmarketscms@penguinrandomhouse.com or call 1-800-603-7051.

CONTENTS

THOUGHTS FROM
TEN YEARS LATER

I wrote this book in 2000. A year earlier, in the church that was my church home at the time, I spent eight consecutive Sunday school hours teaching the book of Ruth to about sixty adults. On a few Sundays, the number swelled to nearly one hundred. Something was happening in that class. The thoughts that were later organized into *Shattered Dreams* came to life in my mind and soul during those eight weeks.

The publishing house that had contracted to print my next book turned down the manuscript. "Too negative," they said. "Nobody would buy a book titled *Shattered Dreams*. People want to be happy." I'm grateful to the folks at WaterBrook Press for taking a risk on what many might see as an unnecessarily negative message.

I was in my midfifties when the book first released. The road I'm walking seems narrower now, and strangely more appealing. A deeper, muffled, more subtle dream is in the process of being shattered. And a new kind of happiness is slowly releasing, a kind that the sort of shattered dreams I had in mind when I wrote the book cannot destroy. That seems clearer now.

At the time, I was a two-year cancer survivor, a cancer that came within hours of claiming my life. Now, the cancer is back—a very slow-growing kind, I'm told, and nonmetastasizing. By the time you read this, that assurance may have been proven false or it might be confirming the hope that I won't need surgery until I'm pushing one hundred.

I'd prefer to get a phone call today telling me that the radiologist misread my scan, that the concerning spot is no longer concerning. That preference has been a prayer, one of many not answered according to my preferences. And I have no biblical guarantee that my dream of symptom-free living till I'm one hundred will not be shattered. The cracks are already visible.

The dream of good health is an obvious one; it's visible and measurable, like dreams of a great marriage, fulfilling vocation, or sufficient income. And obvious difficulties call for obvious responses to manage the problem, to make it go away or to keep your sanity if it doesn't. Get a second opinion, find a good counselor, train for a new job. Obvious shattered dreams keep alive the hope that there are ways to manage the crisis and get through without falling apart with something that will help you feel better, at least for a season.

Perhaps this is a dream only those of advancing years have, but in my midsixties I'm aware of a deeper dream than good health, relationships, employment, and finances. I think it's a core dream that's at the center of every human being, subtle, and so imbedded in our makeup that we experience it as an entitlement, a *given* of how things should be. It's a dream we don't believe *might* come true, but one that we think *should* if there really is a God.

It's the dream to be truly happy, to feel excited about life, to wake up every morning full of energy to tackle the adventure and seize the opportunity that lies before us, and ultimately, to encounter God's palpable presence in every dark night.

Since I wrote *Shattered Dreams,* that common human dream has spawned new Christian approaches (I use the term *Christian* loosely here) that are designed to pursue it coming true. Health-and-wealth gospel has devolved into a gospel of wish-fulfillment. The true gospel that repairs brokenness and heals wounds has morphed into a pop spirituality that offers feel-good transcendent experiences in any circumstance of life. Morning quiet times have developed into turnkey disciplines for more deeply "sensing" God. And kingdom theology has forgotten the promise of future glory in heaven for the here-and-right-now kingdom we can bring fast through social and political activism.

As I see it, one unintended effect of all this is the de-emphasizing and even denial of the ongoing battle against sin that self-aware believers face. As a result, our ability to wait is weakened, our self-discipline is reduced, and our longing for the coming world is all but destroyed. And the loss of our longing is especially damaging.

Paul made it crystal clear that Christians who won't wait for the satisfaction they want are worthy of pity: "And if our hope in Christ is only for this life, we are more to be pitied than anyone in the world" (1 Corinthians 15:19, NLT). When Jesus' followers dream of feeling here and now what no one will completely or enduringly feel until heaven, the result can be heresy and addiction. Whatever seems to provide spiritual fulfillment in this life seems both right (risk of heresy) and necessary (risk of addiction).

And what I'm seeing more clearly now than when I wrote this book is that *the mother of all shattered dreams is the pursuit of shatterproof hope in the here and now.* Listen to Paul again, speaking to the Colossian Christians.

"For we have heard of your faith in Christ Jesus and your love for all of God's people, *which come from your confident hope of what God has reserved for you in heaven*" (Colossians 1:5, NLT).

Our job as spiritually forming Christians is to believe God when He promises to work both everything that happens in our lives and everything that happens in our souls for the good of people who love God and who surrender to however He wants to use them in this life (see Romans 8:28). That's *faith.* Spiritually forming Christians neither use other people to make them feel better nor isolate themselves from people who might hurt them, but instead give whatever is alive and good within them for the sake of the other's blessing, even when the personal cost is high. That's *love.*

Faith and love, Paul tells us, come from hope, and that hope is not for full satisfaction now but rather for what God promises to provide when we get home. Until what's coming sustains us in what's currently going on—death, disease, starvation, all kinds of discouragement and evil—we will cling to the false hope that the happiness we were created to enjoy is available here and now. And that hope can become a demand, a narcissistic, obsessive quest for the spiritual fulfillment we assume we're entitled to. We will deny the truth that our deepest desires remain unsatisfied every day, and that our greatest dream of fully felt union with God lies shattered and unfulfilled every moment of this life.

Yet when the hope of what God has reserved for us in heaven sustains us, our dream of energetic passion and complete satisfaction in life shifts from a demand to a surrendered, patient longing. And our confidence in God's promise of what lies ahead frees us to share in the kind of happiness Jesus knew while He lived in this difficult world, the kind that comes from serving God's purposes in any circumstance, that kept Him anchored in His calling and passionate for God's vision, even during Gethsemane and on Golgotha.

Jesus believed God with absolute trust in His Father's goodness. Jesus loved God (and us) at any cost to Himself. His *faith* and *love* were sustained by His *hope* in what He knew lay ahead. The happiness that anchors our soul and keeps alive our passion for God's vision comes from the faith and love that spring from *that* hope. And this is why in Jesus, spiritual fruit was always ripe—"love, joy, peace, patience, kindness, goodness, faithfulness, gentleness and self-control" (Galatians 5:22–23).

Imagine yourself

- *loving* a rejecting spouse, a prodigal child, a critical or pushy friend.
- radiating *joy* in a cancer ward, as a patient.
- knowing *peace* during a financial catastrophe.
- exhibiting *patience* in the most trying circumstance at work.
- being *kind* to a needy neighbor when you'd rather do anything but.
- releasing the *goodness* of God's nature when your nature is screaming for someone to be good to you.
- *faithfully* following your call to serve when your only results are more weeds.
- *gently* responding to someone who undermines or demeans you.
- exercising *self-control* by not succumbing to a temptation after a severely disappointing day.

When the dream of experiencing now what is reserved for us in heaven is decisively shattered and when the shattering is embraced and not fought, either we'll sink into despair or we will hope in God, and wait as faith becomes a firmer foundation and godly love a way of life.

The shattering of our deepest dream of fulfillment in the present becomes the unexpected pathway to the happiness Jesus knew during His life on earth: the happiness of trusting God, serving others, and confidently waiting for complete happiness in being reunited with God in paradise forever.

That's some fresh thought from this midsixties Christian living with an assortment of terrific blessings and uncertain challenges. It all leaves me feeling pretty good a lot of the time, though I'm often weary and sometimes unmotivated to do much of anything. But I want truth to move me through my ups and downs on the pathway to life. I want the truth of hope, sometimes unfelt, to keep me faithful and loving.

And as these thoughts slowly mature into convictions through time in the Bible, in prayer, in worship and community, I think I'll have a better chance of finishing well and not letting weariness paralyze me or futility overwhelm me. I'll have a better shot at agreeing with Paul that "everything else is worthless when compared with the infinite value of knowing Christ Jesus my Lord" (Philippians 3:8, NLT), of knowing Him as my Savior from sin, as the model of my vision for helping people and our culture for good, and as my strength as I walk the narrow road of faith and love that comes from the hope of heaven.

And that happiness, that joy, is available now. And it's enough to last me till then.

DR. LARRY CRABB, founder and director of NewWay Ministries
August 2010

A NEW WAY

Three ideas fill my mind as I write this book. The first is this: *God wants to bless us.*

At a time when every blessing the Jews expected to enjoy was taken from them, God spoke of a coming day when "I will never stop doing good to them.... I will rejoice in doing them good" (Jeremiah 32:40-41).

That day has come. God is now dealing with us in a new way. Our badness is no longer the obstacle to blessing. Nor is our goodness the condition for blessing.

In God's new way, He blesses us just because He loves—because we're His beloved children and He wants to reveal Himself through us. That idea fills more than my mind. It fills my heart. Let me put it even more clearly.

> *There's never a moment in all our lives, from the day we trusted Christ till the day we see Him, when God is not longing to bless us. At every moment, in every circumstance, God is doing us good. He never stops. It gives Him too much pleasure. God is not waiting to bless us after our troubles end. He is blessing us right now, in and through those troubles. At this exact moment, He is giving us what He thinks is good.*

There, of course, is the rub. He gives us what *He* thinks is good, what He *knows* is good. *We* don't always agree.

We have our own ideas about what a good God should do in the middle of our circumstances, ideas that stretch all the way from opening a space in a crowded parking lot near the mall's entrance to funding our ministry dreams to straightening out our kids to giving us a negative biopsy report.

It's those ideas that get in the way of our realizing what goodness really is. Like children, we believe a loving parent would give us ice cream without first making us eat spinach. Goodness is ice cream. It certainly isn't spinach.

But our problem is worse than that. Not only do we want what immediately feels good and often dislike what in fact is good for us, but we're also out of touch with what would bring us the most pleasure if it were given to us. There *is* a heavenly ice cream with the nutritional value of spinach. And it's available now, in this life.

That introduces the second idea that drives me as I write:

> *The highest dream we could ever dream, the wish that if granted would make us happier than any other blessing, is to know God, to actually experience Him. The problem is that we don't believe this idea is true. We assent to it in our heads. But we don't feel it in our hearts.*

We can't stop wanting to be happy. And that urge should prompt no apology. We were created for happiness. Our souls therefore long for whatever we think will provide the greatest possible pleasure. We just aren't yet aware that an intimate relationship with God is that greatest pleasure.

Without knowing it, we yearn for an encounter with God that creates an experience far more intimate than any bride and groom have ever enjoyed on their wedding night, an experience with more satisfying depth than the happiest couple in history has celebrated on their fiftieth anniversary. But in our foolishness we look for that experience in all the wrong places. To use biblical language, we dig broken cisterns to satisfy our thirst and walk right by the fresh spring of water that is God.

Feel the Embrace

God wants to bless us. That's the first idea. Because He can't resist giving us the highest good, He's determined to give us an encounter with Himself. It's the greatest blessing He can think of. It's the highest dream the self-aware human soul envisions.

But we're not self-aware. We're out of touch with the central longing of our hearts. *An encounter with Him is what we want, but we don't know it.* That's the second idea. Let me develop it a little further.

We dream lower dreams and think there are none higher. We dream of good marriages, talented kids, enough health and money to enjoy life, rewarding work, and an opportunity to make a difference in the world.

All good things. Of course we want them. But we think they're the *best* things. That's what God means when He calls us foolish.

In the old way, when God was remote and inaccessible, it would have been difficult to imagine anything better than the blessings of life, than all those lower dreams that are legitimate goods.

But in the new way (what theologians call the New Covenant), God is present and available. He is here and now. When Jesus cried, "It is finished," the unapproachable God of intimidating holiness opened His arms and invited us to feel His embrace.

The greatest blessing is no longer the blessing of a good life. It never was. It is now the blessing of an encounter with God. It always has been. But now, in the new way, the greatest dream is available.

But we don't view things that way. So God goes to work to help us see more clearly. One way He works is to allow our lower dreams to shatter. He lets us hurt and doesn't make it better. We suffer and He stands by and does nothing to help, at least nothing that we're aware we want Him to do.

In fact, what He's doing while we suffer is leading us into the depths of our being, into the center of our soul where we feel our strongest passions.

It's there that we discover our desire for God. We begin to feel a desire to know Him that not only survives all our pain, but actually thrives in it until that desire becomes more intense than our desire for all the good things we still want. Through the pain of shattered lower dreams, we wake up to the realization that we want an encounter with God more than we want the blessings of life. And that begins a revolution in our lives.

That's the third idea. Let me express it this way:

Our shattered dreams are never random. They are always a piece in a larger puzzle, a chapter in a larger story.

Pain is a tragedy. But it's never only a tragedy. For the Christian, it's always a necessary mile on the long journey to joy.

The suffering caused by shattered dreams must not be thought of as something to relieve if we can or endure if we must. It's an opportunity to be embraced, a chance to discover our desire for the highest blessing God wants to give us, an encounter with Himself.

This book is an invitation to taste and see that the Lord is good even when the bottom falls out of your life. Let me repeat those three ideas that this invitation builds on:

1. *God wants to bless you.* He gets a kick out of making His children happy. He feels much the same way parents feel on Christmas morning as they anticipate watching their kids unwrap presents amid squeals of delight.

2. *The deepest pleasure we're capable of experiencing is a direct encounter with God.* In God's new way of dealing with people, He does us the most good by making Himself available to be enjoyed and by seeing to it that we seek an encounter with Him with more energy than we seek anything else.

But we almost always mistake lesser pleasures for this greatest pleasure and live our lives chasing after them. We're not in touch with our appetite for God.

3. So the Holy Spirit awakens that appetite. *He uses the pain of shattered dreams to help us discover our desire for God,* to help us begin dreaming the highest dream. Shattered dreams are not accidents of fate. They are ordained opportunities for the Spirit first to awaken then to satisfy our highest dream.

That's what's on my mind as I write *Shattered Dreams.*

What I say in this book strikes me as a Spirit-arranged and therefore fitting launch of God's call on the rest of my life. I think you'll profit more from this book if you understand the call that it begins to answer.

My Call

God's Spirit has instructed me to focus my life and ministry around three words: *encounter, community,* and *transformation.*

I sense God's call to *encounter* Him in a way that fills my soul with more joy than any other experience and to lead others toward a similar encounter. Because I cannot arrange for that encounter to take place, I find myself pleading more these days for sovereign mercy than for well-used competence.

I sense God's call to develop and participate in a *community* where no one remains unknown, unexplored, undiscovered, or untouched; where we discover our true selves; where we realize that we really are passionate followers of Jesus; where people become spiritual friends. I want to help people across the world enjoy that kind of community. Again, in view of the enormity of the task, I am reduced to prayer more than I am prompted to strategize.

I sense God's call to better understand, practice, and teach the art of spiritual direction, which I conceive to be a Spirit-guided dialogue where deep *transformation* of the human personality occurs. I want to do whatever I can to see that no one walks alone, that every hungry person who longs to encounter God and enjoy community can find a spiritual director to guide his or her search. Manageable visions are not worthy of an unmanageable God. This one seems worthy of Him.

As never before, this call on my life has put me in touch with my inadequacy and my dependence on divine enabling. But I also recognize my responsibility to move. Convinced that God has provided us with everything we need to encounter Him, to enjoy community, and to experience personal transformation, I want to see a School of Spiritual Friendship begin that will help people more fully tap the life-giving resources available in small groups. (I use *school* not in an institutional sense but in reference to a guided, collective movement of learning and exploration.) I want to see communities develop where people are known, explored, discovered, and touched so their true selves as followers of Jesus can be released.

And I want to see a School of Spiritual Direction established to equip maturing men and women to wisely and graciously enter the interior worlds of other people in order to trace the Spirit's movement as He works to make them more like Christ. I envision people who have given up hope of ever becoming whole experiencing a level of transformation that exceeds their wildest dreams and changing in ways that provoke observers to exclaim "Praise God!" rather than "Glad you found a good therapist."

The first priority—the foundation for community with others and personal transformation—is an encounter with God. The new way makes that possible. It makes a way for us to draw near to God.

However your life is going—whether you're in a season of blessing or a season of pain—I invite you to join me on this journey to joy, to live beyond shattered dreams. The road will take us through some dark nights, but you need not wait for morning to rejoice. Morning will come, but you can welcome your suffering now as an opportunity to meet God, to encounter Him with a passion that will free you to get close to a few people in authentic community and to experience genuine transformation in your personal life, especially in the way you love others.

May we trust God's Spirit to draw on the resources of Christ to lead us into the arms of the Father, even if shattered dreams have made it seem impossible to ever dream again. That's what the new way makes possible.

Let the revolution begin!

The Parable

"What's the world's greatest lie?" the boy asked.
"It's this: that at a certain point in our lives,
we lose control of what's happening to us,
and our lives become controlled by fate.
That's the world's greatest lie."

—Paulo Coelho

The man's life was pleasant. So too was his worship. The two always go together.

God was not pleased. So He allowed the man's life to become unpleasant.

The man responded at once with shock. "How can this be? How could this happen in my life?"

Beneath the shock, the man was smug. But he could not see it. He thought it was trust. "This will soon pass. God is faithful. Life will again be pleasant." His worship remained shallow.

God was not pleased. So He allowed more unpleasant things to happen in the man's life.

The man tried hard to handle his frustrations well, like someone who trusted God. "I will be patient," he resolved.

But he didn't notice that his efforts to be patient grew out of the conviction that a pleasant life was his due. He did not hear his own heart saying, "If I'm patient, God will make things pleasant again. That's His job."

His worship became a way to convince God to restore his pleasant life.

God was not pleased. So He pulled back His hedge of protection around the man a little farther. The man's life became miserable.

The man got angry. God seemed unmoved, indifferent, uncaring. Heaven's door slammed shut. The man knew he could not pry it open.

He could think only of better days—not of better days coming, but of better days before, days that no longer were and that showed no signs of returning.

His highest dreams were a return to those days, to the pleasant life he once knew, when he felt what he had called joy.

He could not imagine a higher dream than going backward to what once was. But he knew life never moved backward. Adults never become children again. Old people never recover the energy of their most productive years.

So he lost hope. God had withdrawn His blessing, and there was no indication He would change His mind.

The man fell into depression. His worship stopped.

God was not pleased. So He released the forces of hell into the man's life.

Temptations that formerly were manageable now became irresistible. The pain of living was so great that the pleasure the temptations afforded, relief really, seemed reasonable and necessary. But after the pleasure came a new kind of pain, a kind of pain that covered his soul with a fog that not even the brightest sun could penetrate.

The man could see only his pain. He could not see God. He thought he could, but the god he saw was one whose job it was to relieve pain. He could imagine this god, but he could not find him.

He addressed the only god he knew. He begged for help. Beneath his words of pleading he could almost hear what his heart was saying: "You *owe* me help. I will never believe I deserved all this to happen. This pain is not my fault. It's yours."

His worship had always taken the form of a demand, but now the demand was so obvious the man could almost recognize it.

God was not pleased. So He let the struggles continue. And God allowed new troubles to come into the man's life.

In the part of the man's heart that dreamed his greatest dreams, he had been certain he would never have to face these new troubles that were now in his life. For years he had said in his heart (without actually hearing it), "*That* could never happen to me. If it did, my life would be over. If *that* happened, I'd have no choice but to conclude that God isn't good. I would have to dismiss God. And no one, not even God, could fault me."

But still the man could not hear his heart speak. What he could hear was a seductive voice that made the worst temptation he had ever faced— to lose hope in God—seem noble, bravely defiant, the only way left for the man to find himself.

The battle waxed hot. But a flicker of hope remained. The man held on to his faith. Even as he did, he could not hear his heart saying, "I have every right to give up on my faith. But I'm choosing the truly noble way. I still believe in You. I still believe You're there and that my highest hopes for joy—whatever hopes are left—lie with you. Does *that* impress you? If not, my God, what does?"

His worship was more desperate than ever. But it was still proud.

God was not pleased. So He allowed the man's trials to continue and his pain to remain unabated. God kept His distance from the man. He provided no comfort, no tangible reason to hope. It was difficult for God not to make everything better in the man's life. It was even more difficult for Him not to appear directly to the man and assure him of His presence.

But He didn't. God had a greater dream for the man than a return to a pleasant life. He wanted the man to find true joy. He longed to restore the man's hope for what mattered most. But still the man did not know what that was.

The fog around the man's soul thickened until he could feel it, like walls closing in. All that was left was mystery; there was fear certainly, even terror, but more acute was the sense of mystery, the mystery of a bad life and a good God.

Where *was* He? When the man became most aware of his need for God, God disappeared. It made no sense. Was God there or not? If He was, did He care? Or didn't He?

The man could not give up on God. He remembered Jacob. So he began to fight. But he fought in the dark, a darkness so deep that he could no longer see his dreams of a pleasant life.

In deep darkness, you cannot see. But you can hear. He could hear for the first time what his heart was saying.

"Bless me!" he cried. From his deepest soul, he could hear words reflecting a resolve that would not let go of God.

"Bless me! Not because I am good, but because You are good. Bless me! Not because I deserve Your blessing, but because it is Your nature to bless. You really can't help Yourself. I appeal not to who I am. You owe me nothing. I appeal only to who You are."

He still saw his pain. But now he saw God. And the cry for blessing was no longer a demand for a pleasant life. It was a cry for whatever God wanted to do, for whoever He was. The man felt something different. It was the beginning of humility. But the very fact of what it was kept him from seeing what it was.

The man had forgotten himself and discovered his desire for God. He did not find God right away, but he had hope, hope that he might experience what his soul most deeply longed for.

Then he saw it. Fresh water bubbled up from a spring in the desert of his soul, and he saw it. It was a new dream. He could see its contours take shape. It was a dream of actually knowing God and representing Him in an unpleasant world. The dream took on a specific focus; he saw how he could know God and represent God to others in a way that was *his* way and not someone else's. It felt like coming home.

He realized immediately that his power to speak on behalf of God to others in the midst of their unpleasant lives depended on his speaking from the midst of his own unpleasantness. He had never before felt grateful for his troubles.

His suffering became to him a doorway into God's heart. He shared God's pain in His great project of redemption. Suffering together for a single cause made him feel closer to God.

A new thought occurred to him. "I will join with whatever forces are opposed to the root of this unpleasantness. I will ally with goodness against evil. I will not wait to see more clearly; what my hand finds to do, I will do. But I will stay close to the spring. My soul is thirsty. A pleasant life is not water for my soul; whatever comes from God—whoever God is—this is the only true water. And it is enough."

The man worshiped God, and God was pleased. So God kept the water bubbling up out of the spring in the man's soul. When the man didn't drink every morning from that spring or return every evening to drink again, his thirst became intolerable.

Some things in his life got better. Some things stayed the same. Some things got worse.

But the man was dreaming new dreams, greater dreams than a pleasant life. And he found the courage to pursue them. He was now a man with hope, and his hope brought joy.

God was very pleased. So was the man.

Chapter One

My Problem
with God

I am one of the fortunate few. I have real friends. I can quickly name a half-dozen people with whom I would say I have a really good relationship. To be certain I'm not kidding myself, I just wrote six names on the outside of the manila folder where I'm filing the early scribblings for this book.

Now, between sips of my single-shot latte at Angel's Coffee Shop, I'm looking at the names I wrote. One impression strikes me at once with near gale force. *The friends who made the list are all friends who do something for me.* It's not what I do for them that got them on the list; it's what they do for me.

My first impulse is to feel selfish.

I can think of several people, a considerable number actually, who would speak warmly of what I do or have done for them. But they're not on the list. It's true that the six people whose names I wrote down would each say that I mean a great deal to them, but that's not why their names are on the list. I thought of them because they mean a great deal to me.

Jesus told us that it is more blessed to give than to receive. If I really believed that, maybe the names on my list would be different. Apparently, the people I'm most happy to be in relationship with are folks who give something to me, not the ones who offer me the chance to give.

The people on my list respond to my concerns. They use their resources on my behalf. When I have a need, they meet it if they can. I like that about them.

Rachael's name is at the top of my list. She knows how tired and frustrated I've felt these past few months. She scheduled me with a special kind of doctor who analyzes blood under a high-powered microscope and has helped lots of people feel better. She also found a week for us to get away and made all the arrangements. I can't imagine her withholding anything I wanted that was within her power to grant.

The same with the other five names. It's an old phrase but true: These people would do anything for me. That's why they're on my list.

LIKE A LITTLE CHILD

So I'm left with an obvious fact. The people I most cherish in all the world are the people I can count on to do for me what I most want. I suspect if you wrote down the names of the six people whose friendship you most value, that same fact might be obvious to you.

As we ponder that fact, our immediate impulse—especially if we're Christians—is to guiltily conclude that we're therefore hopelessly mired in disgusting self-centeredness. It seems that what we most value in friendship reflects our corruption, our depraved natures.

That would be my conclusion about myself if it were not for the words of Jesus. He told his disciples, "Anyone who will not receive the kingdom of God like a little child will never enter it" (Luke 18:17).

Now the most noticeable characteristic of little children (the word Jesus used refers to very little children, to infants) is that they are takers, and often unattractive ones at that. Cornelius Plantinga Jr. points out that when Jesus uttered those words, He was *not* being sentimental. He was not saying, "Look at the little darlings. They're so cute! Here, let me hold each one."

No, when He rebuked His disciples for telling a crowd of parents to stop bothering Jesus with all those sick little kids, He was saying something very different. If we were there, I think we would have understood Him to mean something like this: "Nobody is more needy and has less to give than an infant. Babies never intentionally give anything of value to anyone. Sure, they can be fun to cuddle and fascinating to look at, but never because they want to be. They never look for ways to bless. They're takers through and through, not only because they're *selfish* (though they are) but because they're *helpless*. Be like that! You *are* helpless, so admit it. Learn to receive what you cannot provide for yourself." He was recommending brokenness, something we live to avoid.

Frederick Buechner wrote, "It's not only more blessed to give than to receive, it's also a whole lot easier." I think I know what he means. I find it much easier to counsel than to be counseled, to reach out to a friend in my small group who is feeling insecure than to reveal my own insecurity. The truth is we don't much like being dependent. We don't enjoy admitting how desperately we long for someone's kindness and involvement. It's so humbling.

Which is precisely why Jesus said what He did. He wants us to humble ourselves, to let someone know when we could really use a hug or some quality time, to let the Spirit know we need Him to change our hearts, to confess to our community of close friends the weaknesses we should have resolved by now.

I hear Jesus telling us to stop negotiating with Him, to stop offering something we think we have in exchange for His blessings. "What do you have that I need?" our Lord is saying. "Look, your diapers are full. You've been a colicky nuisance since the day you were born. And you're clumsy to boot. Every time you toddle around the house you break something. All you can do is receive what you need from someone who has what you don't. When you admit your emptiness, I'll see to it you're filled."

When I hear Jesus tell me to be like an infant, I become more aware of how needy I am than of how selfish I am. And then, immediately, I realize how proud I am. I can't get away from the fact of my depravity, and I can see it as my arrogant refusal to trust. I will not let anyone see my true neediness. Oh, I'll grumble about how people treat me and whine about all the pressures I face and how lonely I feel, but I won't simply say, "I really hurt. Would you spend time with me? Would you listen to me as I share my heart?" Suppose no one responds?

Facing that fear helps me realize that selfishness, at its root, is self-protectiveness. Our primary commitment is to make certain no one can hurt us. The best way to do that is never to be fully vulnerable.

That's the first commandment of fallen thinking: *Trust no one and you shall live.* The second is like it: *To make life work, trust only yourself and what you can control.*

The difference between an infant and an adult is this: An infant communicates helplessness without choosing to. Her helplessness is obvious. As adults, we can hide how desperate we are for someone to care. Others will not clearly see our deepest needs unless we choose to make them known. The seed of self-protection is in the infant; in adults, it's a full-grown weed.

My granddaughter was born with a life-threatening infection. Her needs were plain for all to see. Without proper care, she would have died. In the middle of the crisis, there was no evidence she felt even the faintest impulse to relieve her terrified parents with a smile or a wink of her tired little eye. It simply wasn't in her to care how anyone else was feeling. Her tears were always for herself, for *her* pain, never for her mother's or dad's.

But as I watched her receive the care she needed, both from good medical personnel and wonderful new parents, I saw beauty—not just in those giving the care but in the helpless infant receiving it. I wasn't offended by her neediness. Like the sun rising above the plains, it fits the order of things for a puppy with a broken leg to be carried by a child. Both giving and receiving are beautiful.

It is more blessed to give than to receive—that's true. But for needy adults, who in this respect are like sick infants, something of value must be received before anything of value can be given. Receiving always precedes giving. And that never changes. We never outgrow our need to receive. It's a beautiful thing to witness a humility that receives.

Maybe I'm humble. The six people on my list are folks who each give me some of what I need. I'm not wrong for receiving from them or for appreciating them for what I receive. If, however, I do not give out of the abundance I've received, I am wrong. And if I *demand* that I receive, rather than embrace my neediness and plead only mercy, I am wrong. Then I am not humble.

But I'm not wrong for having my most valued friends list consist of people I can count on to give me, if it's in their power to do so, what I legitimately want and need.

Good Dreams

Which brings me to my problem with God. We evangelicals speak about having a personal relationship with Jesus. We hold out the possibility of having a really good relationship with Him. If that relationship hits a snag or develops tension, we know it's always our doing. Since I was a child, I've heard the saying, "If you're not feeling close to God, guess who moved?" The message was clear: Every difficulty in our relationship with God is always our fault. It's never His.

But especially in the years since I turned fifty, that message has not always seemed so obvious. I've gone through some pretty tough times and, in the middle of them, I've positioned myself as a little child (at least I think I have). But on many occasions, including a few really big trials, God didn't do what I thought a good friend would do, especially a friend with the resources to do a lot.

Several friends of mine feel the same way.

Carl told me just this morning that he had begged God for years to make his desire for holiness stronger than his lust for pornography. It hasn't happened. He fights temptation every day. He loses a lot.

Suzanne privately wishes she had stayed with her promising career in marketing. She is fifty-two years old; her husband, Joe, is a workaholic, emotionally numb and rarely there; her three children, on balance, are more a disappointment than a joy. She knows God could have arranged for her never to meet Joe. She would have stayed with the firm that is now doing so well. God could have arranged things differently. He didn't.

Pete never knew his dad. When he came to Christ at age twenty-two, he discovered his longing for a close relationship with an older man. He expected to find one in his new circle of Christian friends. He hasn't.

Peggy is thirty-eight and single. Her job is decent, she likes her dog, and she keeps herself busy. Whenever she watches a movie where a man pursues a woman, she cries. A deep part of her heart remains untouched. She wonders why God doesn't either bring along a good man who would want her or help her to feel more fulfilled in Christ. He's done neither.

Mark always wanted to be a professor. When his dad died, he dropped out of college to support his mother and four younger siblings. He got into sales and made a lot of money. Now, at fifty-seven, he enjoys a good marriage, both his kids are happily married and well off, and Mark is positioned to retire early. His heart still aches when he dreams of a classroom in a small college. His dream will never be. When the pastor preached last Sunday on "The Courage to Dream," he told his wife he wasn't feeling well and left.

It's hard enough to develop a personal relationship with an *invisible* God, one whose voice I never hear the way I hear a friend's voice over the phone; it's even harder to feel close to an *unresponsive* God.

About a year ago I mentioned to my son who lives in Denver that my messy garage was really bugging me every time I drove into it, and I didn't have time to clean it. I asked if he might help. He spent the better part of the next day making my garage look better than it had in years. He's on the list of my six most valued friends. Both my sons are. They respond to my needs.

My wife spent all of last Sunday in her chair in our family room. She had pulled a muscle in her back so badly that any movement generated excruciating pain. When I saw her wince and heard her cry out as she repositioned her blanket, I knelt by her chair and asked God to take away her pain. He didn't do it. He could have, but He didn't. If either of my sons had the power to end her suffering, they would have used it. So would I.

Sometimes God seems like the least responsive friend I have. It never occurred to me to put Him on my list. The name *Jesus* did not appear on the manila folder.

My problem with God extends far beyond a muscular back pain from which I expected my wife to recover in the course of time. (And she did, without any obvious help from heaven.) My real problem with God becomes apparent when long-held and deeply cherished dreams are shattered and He does nothing. And these are *good* dreams, not dreams of riches and fame, but dreams of decent health for those I love and for good relationships among family and friends.

Many of your dreams are good dreams too. You want to enjoy family life. You long for a job you really like, one that gives you opportunity to do what is important to you and to be appreciated for it. You aren't asking for great health or lots of money. But an accident the day after your car insurance lapsed, then your wife coming down with chronic fatigue syndrome—it's just too much. You want to serve God as a missionary, but you can't raise the support you need to get to the field. Your dreams are good. And you're trusting God as best you know how. But nothing is happening.

Depending on an unresponsive God in the middle of crumbling dreams can be tough on faith. Relating personally with a God who is less responsive than friends with far fewer resources is difficult.

Exactly what is God doing with all His power? At some point in your Christian life you'll be forced to admit that Jesus didn't make it on your list of responsive, valued friends. Live long enough, and dreams important to you will shatter. Some will remain shattered. God will not glue together the pieces of every Humpty Dumpty who takes a great fall in your life.

The divorce will go through, the cancer will claim a loved one's life, the Alzheimer's will not be arrested (let alone reversed) by the latest drug. The broken friendship will not be restored despite your best efforts to reconcile. Your marriage will not be satisfying no matter how many counselors you consult or seminars you attend. Your singleness will be an intolerable burden. The budding ministry will never materialize. The lost income will not be replaced by money pouring out of heaven's windows.

You'll feel low for a long time; the dark tunnel will lengthen with no light visible at its end. Your sense of adventure will yield to dutiful drudgery. You will be miserable. Your dream of feeling alive, captivated by beauty and passionately free, will die.

And God won't do a thing. For a long time. Maybe till heaven.

That's my problem with Him. Yet He tells us He is our most responsive friend. He insists that, after giving us His Son, He would never withhold any good thing.

Then why doesn't He cure my mother's Alzheimer's? Why didn't he relieve my wife's back pain? Why doesn't He straighten out your shiftless kid and give him some direction? Wouldn't those be good things for us? Why didn't He arrange for you to get the education you wanted or steer you in a direction you'd really enjoy?

When we see things rightly, we'll write His name in capital letters at the top of our list of friends and, with the angels, bow low before Him in adoration and awe. And hope. I believe that.

But it takes some doing to see things rightly. How can we write His name at the top of our list as the most wonderful, most sensitive, and most responsive friend we've ever had when our fondest dreams shatter and He does nothing? That's the question I'll try to answer in this book.

CHAPTER TWO

WE NEED A GOOD STORY

Pity kills people. Sometimes it is self-pity, sometimes it is pity from other people." This from Kaye O'Bara, a seventy-two-year-old widow who for the last thirty years has cared night and day for her comatose daughter.

On January 3, 1970, Kaye's sixteen-year-old child, Edwarda, lapsed into a diabetic coma. She whispered these last words: "Promise me you won't leave me, will you, Mommy?" Although Kaye herself suffered a heart attack twelve years later and although her younger daughter, Colleen, spent a short time in prison for a drug-related conviction, Kaye has kept her promise. In her words, "Old-fashioned love keeps me going."

It keeps her daughter going as well. According to a study of more than eleven hundred comatose cases, the chances of someone's surviving more than fifteen years in a vegetative state are less than one in fifteen thousand. A member of the task force conducting the study observed that the few who live beyond the fifteen-year mark have most often received "extraordinarily phenomenal" care, almost always from the person's mother. *Extraordinary* is the right word for how Kaye has responded to her life's tragic circumstances as she cares for a daughter who has been unconscious and unaware for thirty years, unable to respond, move, or feel.

Shattered dreams. In one form or another we all go through the experience, if not yesterday then today, if not today then tomorrow.

How do we respond? What happens in us when life throws an unexpected curve our way, when the second shoe drops soon after the first? Most often, a more visible self-concern surfaces as the strongest passion we feel. It takes many forms—often self-pity, sometimes a hardened determination to survive, perhaps a relentless demand that someone see our pain and care. More often it's a decision to hide, to let no one see our real struggles.

A few commit suicide. Many renounce all responsibilities that require them to put someone else's needs above their own. Only a handful, like Kaye, find the spiritual power to make giving a way of life.

Most of us just get on. We stay busy, travel if we can, and become involved with people in ways that do something for us. Those ways range from visiting lonely people in nursing homes (it makes us feel better about who *we* are) to surrounding ourselves with supportive friends. A fair number find a way to stay reasonably happy. We enjoy satisfying small groups, meaningful activities, and fun recreation. Whatever way we can, we live to dull the pain. Who can blame us?

HANDLE THE PAIN!

When dreams shatter, we hurt and the pain won't go away. But it can be numbed. Working hard may do it, perhaps lots of movies and dinners out, sometimes a regime of rigorous self-discipline. Often private pleasures do the job.

Whatever the means, the goal is the same: *Handle pain!* Find some way to keep going in spite of the hurt. Don't think about it. Stay strong, move on to the next chapter, make it. Do whatever helps, whether going on a spiritual retreat, leaning on family, talking to a counselor, or reading books recommended by concerned friends. Relieve the pain if you can. Live through it if you must. Whatever you do, handle the pain!

An elderly widow has written a book, and many have reported great blessings from hearing the story it tells. Yet she can't get a publisher to even look at it. She feels a growing sense of pointlessness. It hurts. She plugs along as best she can, trying to feel a little better.

As long as the goal is to handle pain, relationships suffer. We pull back. And for good reason. We get sick of people looking mournfully at us and asking, "How are you doing?" What are we supposed to say? A glib "Fine, thanks," or an honest "Life sucks"? We'd rather talk about the upcoming Super Bowl or about the decadent dessert tray at the new restaurant in town.

Folks whose lives have gone sour want to be known and treated as normal people, not as the unpublished author or the business executive who just lost his job or the despairing widow living alone or the guy with cancer or the victim of sexual abuse. Yes, those things may be going on in our lives, but *we're* still here. Who we are hasn't changed. We haven't become merely a label, someone who can be adequately identified by whatever trial we've endured. *We are not defined by the things we suffer.*

During my three weeks in the hospital after cancer surgery, I got tired of repeating the story of my disease to every visitor. I liked it when Jeri came in and sang to me for an hour. I liked it when Milt fell asleep in the chair next to my bed. To them, I was still Larry, their friend. I hadn't been reduced to the cancer patient in Room 520.

As Kaye said, pity kills—not just self-pity, but pity from other people as well.

The Question on the Side

In our struggle to handle the pain of shattered dreams, however, one question is rarely talked about with honesty. We wrestle with the demons of self-pity and pitying friends, with the practical consequences of tragedies that change our lives, but one question tends to be pushed to the side, to be placed off-limits as we devote our energies to handling pain and not being defeated by it. The question is this: *What do we do with how we're feeling toward God?* What we want is good; it's not selfish. Why won't God let us have it?

Do we even *like* God, let alone love Him? Is He on our list of cherished friends? Are we resting in His goodness, confidently trusting Him to work all things together for our good?

If we are trusting Him, then we must ask, "For what?" To help us handle our pain? Why not ask Him to relieve it or end it altogether? He could.

A woman told me with a peaceful smile that she knows God will bring her deserting husband back to her. When I asked her the reason for the hope within her, she smiled even more broadly and replied, "He promised me an abundant life." Are we like that? What's our definition of abundance? Does it agree with God's?

In the chaos and heartache of dreams that crumble, God so often seems to pull away. When we cry the loudest, He sometimes turns a deaf ear. Nothing changes. Husbands don't come back. Lesbian daughters stay lesbian. Grudge-holding friends don't forgive. The three-year checkup reveals the cancer is back. Our dull job stays dull.

We pray earnestly for relief from overwhelming job pressures—and new ones pile on. We pray fervently that the Alzheimer's will be arrested—and on the next visit, our mother no longer remembers us; she greets us as she would a stranger.

And nothing improves *inside* us. As we sit in church, we may look content, even joyful. But we're miserable—or at least empty and discouraged. Worship comes hard. Praying seems pointless. Promised spiritual fruit doesn't seem to be growing on our branches. We *pray* for love, joy, and peace and *feel* anger, despair, and fear.

As a close friend recently said, "When I hear of people experiencing God and feeling joy, I have two reactions: one, I'm glad for them; two, I ask, Why not me? I don't feel much of God at all."

It's hard to escape an awful conclusion: Like the nurse who never responds no matter how hard we push that little button next to our hospital bed, God is not coming to help. He is unresponsive to our pain.

And then He confuses us. We throw up a quick prayer for a space in the crowded parking lot, and one opens up right in front of the entrance to the mall. We smile sheepishly and say, "Isn't God kind? He cares even about the little things in our lives." The little things. What about the big ones?

DANGEROUS BUSINESS

Trusting God is dangerous business. Unless we're trusting Him for what He's promised to provide, the step after trust is disillusionment.

In his college days, Ted Turner trusted God. When a loved one contracted cancer and, in spite of his prayers, died a painful death, the young Mr. Turner turned from God. He lost hope when his dreams were shattered. He could no longer depend on God. And he was right. God cannot be trusted to always minimize our suffering in this life.

So what *can* He be trusted for? Exactly what is He doing with His considerable power? What would be different if we experienced that power, if His power were released in us?

These questions are like arrows on the rim of a circle, each pointing to the hub, the central issue of hope. When dreams shatter, we lose hope. We may get on, but the fire is out. There may still be some things worth living for, but the best is gone. The spark has been doused, our passion for life extinguished. At least that's how it seems.

The monitor wired to our soul prints out a flat line. We still play golf and sing in church and do nice things for people, but more out of habit than desire. *We lose the capacity for soul-pleasure.*

And when that happens, when soul-pleasure is unavailable, either we sink into depression and annoy our friends with our negativism, or we decide not to pursue true soul-pleasure to any real depth. This second option helps us pretend we're still okay and helps keep us from imposing intolerable burdens on others.

There is, of course, a price to pay for this adjustment to shallowness. When the capacity for soul-pleasure is lost, we become irresistibly attracted to lesser pleasures—either to counterfeits of soul-pleasure (like power, popularity, and prowess in business or sports or party humor) or to substitutes for soul-pleasure (like addictive eating, drinking, and sexual fun).

Why We're Alive at All

That is my problem with God (and perhaps yours): To people whose souls have been inundated with pain, God seems so unresponsive. We pray and nothing happens. We cannot manage to write His name at the top of our list of most cherished friends. We know we should and we know we would...*if* we could see things as they really are.

How do we find the faith that lets us see what is invisible, to passionately believe that He's always wonderfully and lovingly responsive when

He seems so callous? That's the question: *What does it mean to hope in God as we continue to live in a world where good dreams shatter and God seems to do nothing about it?*

There is an answer, and it is repeated again and again in the Bible. But the answer, the only one that squarely faces the enormous challenge of trusting a seemingly unresponsive God, requires a change in how we naturally look at life. It demands a revolution in our understanding of why we're alive at all, of why God keeps us living in this world for so long before He takes us to heaven.

The problem sincere Christians have with God often comes down to a wrong understanding of what this life is meant to provide. We naturally and wrongly assume we're here to experience something God has never promised. More than perhaps ever before in history, we assume we are here for one fundamental reason: *to have a good time*—if not good circumstances, then at least good feelings. We long to feel alive, to sense passion and romance and freedom. We want the good time of enjoying godly kids, of making a difference in people's lives, of involvement with close friends, of experiencing God's peace. So we invent "biblical" strategies for seeing to it that our dreams come true. We call them models of godly parenting and disciplines of spiritual living and principles of financial stewardship—all designed to give us a legitimately good time. What's wrong with that?

But when we uncover the deepest motives that drive our actions, we discover a determination to feel *now* what no one will feel until heaven. We long to experience a compelling pleasure that eliminates all pain. How we try to satisfy that longing will vary, depending on our ethical philosophy. If we accept the *Playboy* philosophy, we do whatever generates immediate pleasure. We buy nice clothes, attend important functions, and take an occasional cruise. Sometimes we change spouses or cheat on them.

If we're Christians, we invent a paradoxical twist on the ethic of delayed gratification. We give up immediate pleasures in order to later experience a deeper kind of pleasure, but we expect to feel that pleasure soon, certainly before we die. We claim the right to determine the length of the delay. As long as the delay isn't too long, we live by the ethic. If we can't have a really good time today, then we certainly can tomorrow. And if things aren't going as we wish, we still want to feel as if they were. We insist on the internal good time of peace, of self-respect, of feeling at least pretty good if not fully alive.

Sometimes all that separates Christians from non-Christians is our understanding of how to produce those good feelings. The pursuit of soul-pleasure remains primary. It continues to be the aim behind our choices rather than an occasional and welcome by-product of a higher aim: the aim of glorifying God as the object of our deepest, most passionate desire. We continue to want something or someone more than God. We don't think that's our biggest problem, but it is.

As long as our purpose is to have a good time, to have soul-pleasure exceed soul-pain, God becomes merely a means to an end, an object to be used, never a subject rightfully demanding a response, never a lover to be enjoyed. Worship becomes utilitarian, part of a cunning strategy to get what we want rather than a passionate abandonment to someone more worthy than we.

And when He fails—when the One we depend on to give us a good time doesn't do His job—we feel betrayed, let down, thoroughly disillusioned. He neither reverses the tragedy nor fills us with peace and joy. We may jump through spiritual hoops to persuade Him to respond, but He typically remains aloof. Our souls remain unsatisfied. Eventually, we may learn to hate Him.

Going to church doesn't help. The Bible becomes dull. Serving others has no advantage. So we stop living the Christian life. We lose hope. Nothing gives us a good time. Things remain hard and we continue to feel bad. Denial and pretense seem our only options.

FOR A THRIVING HOPE

How then shall we live? What can we do? How are we to find hope when God's kindness hurts, when bad things happen that God could have prevented? How do we trust a fickle God who gives us a convenient place to park the day after we're told our loved one's tumor is malignant?

As we prepare to answer these questions, we must lay down a beginning principle: If we are to discover a hope that continues through shattered dreams, that hope must be available to everyone regardless of their circumstances. We must find a hope available to sick people, poor people, lonely people, unnoticed people. And it must be the same hope we offer to healthy, rich people with lots of friends and talent. We must discover a hope that thrives when dreams shatter, when sickness advances and poverty worsens and loneliness deepens and obscurity continues, the same hope that anchors us to God when dreams do come true.

It's harder to discover our desire for God when things go well. We may think we have, but more often all we've found is our desire to *use* God, not to *enjoy* Him. Shattered dreams are the truest blessings; they help us discover our true hope. But it can take a long, dark time to discover it.

We must identify a hope that has the power to do something truly wonderful when the dark night descends and we see nothing but pain and disappointment in this life, a hope that does exactly the same thing when the sky is sunny.

But what is it? Does such a hope exist? Heaven, of course, is our ultimate hope. Being with Jesus will make all our dreams come true. That's foundational. Without that hope, there is no other. Without heaven as our final hope, Christianity offers nothing, except perhaps a good ethic to follow. The whole thing becomes a sham, and whether we're rich or poor, all efforts to live a Christian life should cease. If we're to die tomorrow, better to eat, drink, and be merry today. Ayn Rand would then be right: Enlightened selfishness makes sense.

But with the hope of heaven as our bedrock, living a Christian life makes sense. Self-protection is both morally wrong and practically foolish. But why? Is the only point to godly living the reward we'll receive in heaven? Is there anything we can hope for now, anything we can count on God to do for us in this life? That's the question. And it's not a selfish one, it's a humble one, a question that admits we're dependent children in need of receiving what we long for but do not have. Our souls need filling.

Difficult questions like this are sometimes best answered with a story. Jesus taught mostly in parables. He answered questions by telling short stories with a point that sincere inquirers could grasp.

After I properly set the stage, I want to tell a story. Actually, I want to retell an old familiar story, one already told in the Old Testament book of Ruth. Recently, through my own experience with shattered dreams, I've come to the conclusion that the story of Naomi was written to answer the question I'm asking. Let me repeat the question one more time: *How do we trust a sometimes disappointing, seemingly fickle God who fails to do for us what good friends, if they could, would do?*

Her story solves my problem with God. The solution hinges on one central lesson that Naomi's story teaches:

Shattered dreams open the door to better dreams, dreams that we do not properly value until the dreams that we improperly value are destroyed. Shattered dreams destroy false expectations, such as the "victorious" Christian life with no real struggle or failure. They help us discover true hope. We need the help of shattered dreams to put us in touch with what we most long for, to create a felt appetite for better dreams. And living for the better dreams generates a new, unfamiliar feeling that we eventually recognize as joy.

Both good hopes and best hopes are guaranteed in heaven. But fulfillment of the best hopes is not yet promised in this life; our hopes for today—the better hopes that follow shattered dreams—do not include the elimination of pain or even an experience of pleasure that exceeds pain.

We will suffer now; what then are those better hopes that make us *welcome* that suffering? From Naomi's story, I learn that dreams for good things may shatter, but our pain will always have a purpose. It will not go away, but it will do its work. It will stir an appetite for a higher purpose—the better hope of knowing God well enough now to love Him above everything else…and trusting Him no matter what happens.

The best hope, our highest dream of being in His presence where nothing ever goes wrong and where we fully enjoy Him more than every other blessing, will not be granted till the next life.

We will not suffer in heaven. Every imaginable dream, everything from good parking spaces to good health, will come true. Pain will have no purpose then, so it will not be allowed. Our appetites will be straightened out. We will not desire the good above the best.

For now, while we still have such a hard time realizing that what's good is not always best, suffering still has a function. As nothing else can, it moves us away from demanding what's good…toward desiring what's better…until heaven provides what's best.

If we learn the lessons taught by Naomi's life, we might be able to live more like Kaye O'Bara. But we must learn those lessons well. And that requires that her story be presented on a well-prepared stage.

Bear with me as I arrange the set a little more before the lead actress and her supporting cast take the spotlight.

CHAPTER THREE

JESUS SPEAKS

What God has in mind when He tells us to keep hoping may not be what we usually mean when we think of hope. We wish for things to get better; we want to feel what we want to feel.

Those are our dreams. But that kind of hope is for later. For now, in this life, the Bible offers a different kind of hope, a kind that at first we don't find attractive or even hopeful.

When her husband and both her sons died, leaving her alone in a foreign country, Naomi lost the kind of hope I prefer to keep. By the end of the story, she discovered a better hope, a kind I sometimes have a hard time liking, a kind she could neither identify nor value so long as she held on to the lesser kind.

(It might be good at this point to put this book down for a brief time and pick up a better one, the Bible. There, in the Old Testament, you can read the short, four-chapter story of Naomi as told in the book of Ruth.)

What God will one day provide in heaven is different from what He provides now. What He provides now, however, can be difficult to appreciate.

DELIVERANCE AND DELAY

One of the most disconcerting passages in the Bible is the eleventh chapter of Hebrews. There the writer produces a long list of Old Testament saints who he claims never lost hope. I understand that claim when he mentions Rahab. She dreamed of not being killed when her city was destroyed. Her dream came true. She longed for safety and she got it. I like that story.

And his claim makes sense to me when he refers to the three good men who abandoned themselves to God and "quenched the fury of the flames." Although they did not make deliverance from the fire a precondition for their obedience, Shadrach, Meshach, and Abednego must have at least silently hoped that the flames would not hurt too much.

Again, their dream came true and then some. Imagine their hilarity when they walked out of the furnace without even their eyebrows singed. Give me an experience like that, and I would be transformed instantly into a model of hope and trust, at least for a while. Let me visit my mother next week and see her mind fully restored from the ravages of Alzheimer's, and I would write a very different book than I'm now writing.

In the Old Testament the idea of salvation almost always means deliverance from tough circumstances. That's the kind of hope I want. Saved from hell later *and* from suffering now. I want to remain cancer free, die healthy, then go to heaven.

But then the writer of Hebrews goes on to talk about others who were not delivered, who suffered the worst kind of trials and died without ever being saved from them. Their gratification was delayed until heaven. He speaks of people who were jeered and whipped and chained, people who trusted God yet were stoned, sawed in two, or run through by a sword.

Even the New Testament figure John the Baptist worried, when he got locked up, that he was following the wrong leader. I wonder if his hope ran thin when Herod's henchmen stretched his neck on the chopping block. Are we seriously expected to keep on hoping when a big man wearing a black hood lifts an ax that he intends to bring down on our neck? Clearly, it would be a flight from reality to hope that the ax would miss. What then are we supposed to hope for? While he was in prison, did John have any hope other than heaven?

As examples of people who never lost hope, the writer of Hebrews presents *both* the mothers whose dead children jumped up at the funeral and cried "Mommy" *and* the believers who were tortured and persecuted. Both trusted God—those whose dreams came true as well as those whose dreams were shattered. That's what the writer is telling us. Did God come through for both groups? From one angle, we must answer a loud no.

And yet we can almost hear the Trinity bursting with pride as the Spirit inspires the writer to say of those who endured the worst horrors, "The world was not worthy of them."

And then this most disconcerting chapter ends on an even more troubling note; the writer insists that these people held on to their faith, they never lost hope, even though "none of them received what had been promised" (Hebrews 11:39).

Apparently God is pleased with people who suffer terribly, whose lives never straighten out, but who keep trusting. We call them fools. Would you go back to a doctor who refused to treat you, who said your pain was a good thing?

When we share answers to prayer, the answers invariably involve a bad circumstance that turned good or a painful feeling that went away. We prayed that the difficult surgery would go well, and it did; we prayed that our depression would lift, and now we feel motivated again to take on life.

When I taught in seminary, the standard testimony we heard from students involved money. "I ran out of cash on Tuesday. On Wednesday, an envelope arrived with a hundred-dollar bill attached to a note that said, 'God loves you. Don't forget it!'"

One gets the impression from reading Hebrews 11 that God would prefer to hear someone share, "My cancer came back, I just lost my job, and my wife filed for divorce; I feel angry, discouraged, and miserable. But I intend to keep trusting God. I believe I can do it. I want Him more than ever. That's my hope. And it brings me deep joy."

WORDS FROM THE PLACE OF HOPE

I've decided I need to rethink my ideas about hope. Maybe what the Bible wants us to hope for in this life is very different from what most of us think.

A good place to begin our rethinking is an occasion when Jesus spoke to His disciples. They were about to face a series of events that, in any rational person, would destroy hope. The occasion was the night that Jesus fell apart in front of them.

It was a Thursday night, two thousand years ago. He knew that He would be tortured and killed the next day, put to death in the most painful manner possible. With that expectation looming, He gathered His disciples and went to pray on the Mount of Olives. Why there? He had already spent the last four nights there, praying alone. Why? This night He took His disciples with Him. Again, why?

Matthew and Mark identify the place as Gethsemane. Gethsemane was apparently a small garden, a wooded area on the lower slope of the hill called the Mount of Olives. John refers to the location simply as an olive grove, then reports nothing more of what happened there. Only Luke makes it clear that the place He went to pray during His hours of deepest distress was the Mount of Olives.

This was the place Jesus chose when He was in most danger of losing hope. When He arrived there with His disciples, He instructed all but three to "sit here while I pray." Peter, James, and John, the same threesome who were invited to watch Jesus raise Jairus's daughter from the dead and to witness Jesus' transfiguration into visible glory, were asked to walk on a bit further.

With these three, Jesus did something no good leader is supposed to do: He broke down. He let them see how intensely troubled and thoroughly overwhelmed He was feeling. He told them, "I am beside myself with anguish."

I cannot imagine Gen. Dwight D. Eisenhower weeping in front of his staff as the invasion of Normandy began. Afterward, perhaps, but not before. When the going gets tough, the tough get going. That's our view of strong leadership.

But when the battle Jesus chose to fight approached its fiercest moment, the Master seemed to collapse. I wonder what His three closest friends felt.

Then, without waiting for a response, He issued a firm order: "Stay here and keep watch." Luke adds that, before He walked off to be by Himself, He also said, "Pray that you don't give in to temptation."

What temptation? Jesus knew that the events yet to transpire that evening and all the next day would be enough to rattle His followers to the core. Their Lord, the One they had given up everything to follow, was about to be led away like a helpless child, beaten by soldiers whose blows He apparently couldn't resist, then crucified as a common thief.

I think Jesus was telling His disciples to not lose hope. Their Messiah, their Leader, their General, the One they had come to believe was their God, was about to become the plaything of a sadistic mob of soldiers. It would be enough to make anyone wonder if He was a real man, let alone the answer to all their problems, let alone God.

Jesus faced His own temptation to quit. His personal battle to persevere was being fought on the Mount of Olives. He had spent every night there since Sunday, every night during the last week before He died.

Why? It was the Place of Hope. It was the place where, after His resurrection and just before His ascension, He would speak to His disciples one last time. On that occasion, with the authority of a man who had just conquered death, Jesus would say, "Soon you will receive power, power to be My witnesses."

He would promise them *not* the power to avoid trouble, but the power to live the only life worth living. He would promise them the same power that was keeping Him on course while His own worst nightmare came true. He knew these words would strike a chord, that they would thrill His disciples and fill them with hope.

"Soon you will have that power," Jesus would say. "You will be able to remain faithful to Me no matter what happens in your life. If your spouse leaves you, you will be empowered to reveal My character. If your son is in jail, you will be able to go on loving him. *That* is your hope till I return. Never lose it!"

And then, like a helium balloon released from a child's hand, He would float up into the sky and disappear in a cloud. Note again: *The place from which a few weeks later He would ascend to heaven was the same place where He now cried.*

And to this same place He will one day return. When He was crying in Gethsemane, He knew that. He had read Zechariah's prophecy. When He comes back, His feet will touch down on the Mount of Olives. The impact will split the ground. That ground where He lay violently weeping before His death will then become command headquarters for the final battle against evil.

General Jesus will not weep then. The Lamb will roar like a lion and with irresistible might lead His troops to claim the victory already won through His chosen weakness.

The outcome is not in doubt. When the dust settles, "The LORD will be king over the whole earth. On that day there will be one LORD, and his name the only name" (Zechariah 14:9).

I read that passage to a small group of friends gathered in our living room the night of January 1, 2000. I felt millennial hope. When I got to the words, "His name the only name," I trembled. I could barely speak.

Earlier that evening, a dear friend sitting in the room had told us that she would be entering the hospital in two days for evaluation of a tumor growing behind her right eye. Earlier tests had indicated the tumor was fast growing and likely malignant.

I felt my chest heave as I remembered what Jesus said. I could hear Him speaking to her: "Pray you won't give in to temptation. Don't lose hope. You may have cancer. It may claim your life. I make no promises about that. But the same power that kept Me nailed to the cross and brought Me out of the grave, the same power I will one day use to forever destroy every cancer cell and to make every dream you can imagine come true, that same power is available to you. It is in you right now. You may use it to experience My love while you suffer and to reveal My love to others no matter what happens. You have the power to be like Me! Don't lose hope!"

It occurs to me, though, that I don't always find that offer of power compelling. When I'm out of touch with my deepest desires, I prefer things going well to becoming more like Jesus. In most of us, our desire for God remains to be fully discovered.

"MY SON IS CRYING"

After I read the passage from Zechariah, our little group turned its attention to Jesus' prayer that dark Thursday night in Gethsemane. In effect, He prayed this:

> "Father, is there a way to reveal how wonderful You are that does not require My death on a cross? Is there another way to give people real life? If so, I want to take it. But if not, I'll do whatever You say."

I learn from this prayer not only that Jesus valued the better above every mere good, but also that God will never allow suffering to come into our lives that is not necessary to achieve His good purpose. He doesn't like to see us suffer. He didn't like to see Jesus suffer either.

With the passion of a father racing across town to be with his son in the emergency room, God sent an angel to Gethsemane.

> "Gabriel, thirty-four years ago I sent you to tell Mary she would give birth to Jesus. I now send you to earth again, this time to the Mount of Olives, to Jesus. Go at once. My son is crying."

The angel (we're not told it was Gabriel, but I think it was) appeared to Jesus and strengthened Him against the loss of hope. I've often wondered what he said.

Perhaps he said nothing but simply stood next to the weeping Son of Man and offered the gift of his presence. Surely he did something other than offer the lame encouragement we so often give each other: "Hang in there. I'm sure things will turn out just fine. I know it's hard, but you can do it." (Maybe the disciples' falling asleep was a mercy. At least they couldn't offer such poor help when they were sleeping.)

We're not told what the angel said. The Bible is silent on that point. However, what we know about the Mount of Olives from Acts 1 and

Zechariah 14 suggests that the angel might have whispered something like this to our distressed Lord:

"From the very ground that now receives Your tears You will soon ascend to Your Father. All heaven is eagerly waiting to welcome You home. You will again hear Your Father say, 'Well done! You are My beloved Son. I am thoroughly pleased with You.'"

And then, as His tears intensified, perhaps He heard the angel add:

"And to this very ground now wet from Your tears You will one day return to destroy all Your Father's enemies and restore all creation to Your Father's design. Then everyone in heaven and earth will sing for joy and every knee will bow before You. Now the pain...then the honor!"

Whatever the angel said to strengthen Jesus, the effect was surprising. I would have expected Him to dry His eyes, smile bravely, and get on with His mission. But instead Jesus cried harder, so hard that His sweat became like drops of blood. That happened *after* He was strengthened. Perhaps we're meant to learn that the richest hope permits the deepest suffering, which releases the strongest power, which then produces the greatest joy. Maybe there is no shortcut to joy. Maybe God sometimes frustrates our desire to experience Him in order to deepen it.

And then, at some point, Jesus did stop crying. The season of anguish yielded to calm resolve. Like a man in charge, Jesus walked back to where He had left His disciples. They were asleep.

And once more He said, "Pray so that you will not give in to temptation."

I titled this chapter "Jesus Speaks." Drawing from all that we have now considered, I hear Him speaking words like these to us. Listen.

"Some of your fondest dreams will shatter, and you will be tempted to lose hope. I will seem to you callous or, worse, weak—

unresponsive to your pain. You will wonder if I cannot do anything or simply will not.

"As you struggle with dashed hopes, you will fail, just as My servant Peter did. You will feel discouraged with yourself to the point of self-hatred. And I will seem to withdraw from you and do nothing.

"When all of this comes to pass, My word to you is this: *Do not lose hope.* A plan is unfolding that you cannot clearly see. If you could see it as I do, you would still hurt, but you would not lose hope. You would gladly remain faithful to me in the middle of the worst suffering. I guarantee you the power to please me, not to have a good time. But pleasing me will bring you great joy.

"In the deepest part of your soul, you long more than anything else to be a part of My plan, to further My kingdom, to know Me and please Me and enjoy Me. I will satisfy that longing. You have the power to represent Me well no matter what happens in your life. That is the hope I give you in this world. Don't lose it."

With the words of Jesus before us, perhaps now we can better understand the story of Naomi.

CHAPTER FOUR

WHEN BOTH SHOES DROP

T*he Lord could have done something. And He did nothing.* How else could she think?

Her husband and both sons, all three dead. And yet God is the God of the impossible. He can do anything.

But He did nothing.

Sometimes He does come through. Naomi knew the stories. I wonder if her mind roamed back through her nation's history, maybe to the story of Abraham, a favorite among her people.

When Abraham was an old man, his dream of becoming a father through Sarah was as dead as her reproductive organs. Then three Agents from Heaven showed up at his tent. (No angel ever visited Naomi.)

Sarah—once a ravishing beauty, now a wrinkled, frumpy old woman—listened as these visitors told Abraham that his wife would bear a child in twelve months. She laughed out loud. Abraham hadn't touched her romantically in years. For both of them, the prospect of making love had all the appeal of taking an unnecessary walk on a hot day to nowhere in particular.

And here these visitors were spouting nonsense: Not only would Abraham approach her for sex and be able to perform, but Sarah would also conceive. She had been infertile for ninety years. And now her womb, as dead as her dream of giving birth, would come alive with a child. That was the prediction.

She laughed. Some dreams come true, but not that kind.

Abraham had earlier heard the same prediction directly from God. He laughed too.

And then, to God, he had said, "Look, we already have a son. And I fathered him, not through Sarah's body but certainly at her initiative. Let him be the Son of Promise. Your plan for Sarah to give birth is frankly absurd. Don't raise hopes now that for so long You've denied. That dream is gone, forever shattered. To even begin putting Your plan into action requires more faith than I have. Let Ishmael be the one!"

God had said no. And now these strange visitors show up saying Sarah will indeed deliver a baby in one year. Abraham and Sarah knew enough about reproduction to scorn the idea.

It happened. Abraham exercised faith. The Lord did something. Sarah gave birth. The hope they had long since abandoned was realized.

Unpredictable God

Why is God so inconsistent, so maddeningly unpredictable? One set of parents raises a child who becomes an honor student, a youth leader. Another set, equally good, maybe even better, places their son in drug rehab. One man's ministry takes off. God's blessing is evident. Another man, just as godly, watches his ministry die. Why? Suffering seems so random; one dream realized, another shattered.

Naomi, with a good husband and two fine sons, was full of hope when together they left Bethlehem. The famine there had prompted a move to Moab. Naomi assumed—it was less a dream and more an assumption— that a short stay in Moab would go well, and then, when the rains came, she would return to Bethlehem *with* her husband, *with* her two sons, perhaps *with* a couple of daughters-in-law.

After all, in a recent battle with Israel, Moab had lost thousands of eligible young men. Pickings for her boys might be good. Had she thought about it, Naomi would have naturally reasoned that bringing her family back home, happy and intact, was easy compared to arranging for a ninety-year-old woman to conceive. But God's surprises aren't always pleasant. Naomi learned that lesson with force.[1]

So have many others. Friends called last night. Their son, a twenty-six-year-old attorney freshly graduated and barred, married to a lovely woman, proud father of an infant daughter, had just tried unsuccessfully to end his life. Six months ago he had been diagnosed with a fatal disease that only a perfect organ match had even a chance of curing. He had been given less than a year to live. The odds of finding a suitable donor were one in one thousand. Overwhelmed by despair, he decided to cheat the disease of another victim.

Now—still alive, still dying—he was depressed. Could I see him? Would I meet with his parents?

What can they hope for? A donor? A cure? An enveloping sense of God's presence that would create peace in them and in their son no matter what happens? Or, like Job, were they doomed to live in fear that their worst nightmare might come true?

An ironic and dreadful twist compounded their problem. The young man's grandfather, a faithful missionary for sixty years, had recently died an agonizing death from lung cancer. He had never smoked a cigarette in his life. His final days were spent screaming, "Where is God? I can't find Him! All I can feel is darkness!"

I heard Billy Graham on television some years ago. He answered a question about his wife's health quite openly. She is in chronic pain, he said, but her faith is strong. She senses God is with her. The Lord, though not relieving Ruth Graham's pain, is providing strength. Why for some and not for others? The young attorney is a committed Christian. He has begged for peace and felt only terror. The elder missionary gave his life to sharing the gospel and died without its assurance.

Naomi's husband, Elimelech, passed away shortly after they reached Moab. One dream shattered. But then her two sons met nice girls and married.

Perhaps she thought, as we all do, that if the other shoe did not drop, she would be able to get on. If enough blessings come along to enjoy, perhaps we can endure the pain. God knows we couldn't handle one more trial. And He gave His word we would never be asked to suffer more than we could endure.

Then *that* becomes our dream—that sufficient blessings would come our way to get us through.

Then the other shoe dropped. Both her sons died. We're not told how. The Lord could have kept them alive; that much we know. But He didn't.

A woman wrote to me recently. I read her letter earlier today. Her daughter is falling in love. "I'm scared to death," she writes. "The young man has a lot in common with my husband. I can't bear to think she'll end up with a marriage like mine."

God could arrange for the girl to meet a wonderful young man. Can her mother count on God to do it?

The first five verses of the book of Ruth tell the story of both shoes dropping in Naomi's life. They tell the story in seventy-one Hebrew words.

Near the end of the book, another paragraph of seventy-one Hebrew words tells a happy story. It presents Naomi as a content older woman, still a widow, still the mother of two unresurrected sons, but now a woman resting joyfully in the fulfillment of a different dream. That's how the story ends.

I confess that when I first began looking hard at the narrative, I was not only disappointed by the ending, I was furious. Clearly the author intends us to rejoice with Naomi as she held her newborn grandson on her lap. It is meant to be a story with a good ending.

My first reaction was frustration. I recalled the many times I've seen Rachael holding our first granddaughter, Josie, on her lap. My wife smiles then as she smiles at no other time. *But what if I were not there?*

When I was in the hospital for cancer surgery, my wife broke down one evening and said, "I don't want to be a grandmother alone." God granted her wish. I lived, our two sons are healthy and doing well, plus Rachael is grandmother to a beautiful little girl. Of course she smiles. I do too.

But Naomi was a grandmother alone. No husband, no sons, a daughter-in-law and a son-in-law and a grandson. Why couldn't God have given her the joy that Rachael knows? It took awhile before the veil lifted and I saw the greater dream that God fulfilled in Naomi's life.

NECESSARY LESSONS

The Lord did nothing to preserve the dreams Naomi once thought essential to her happiness. He did nothing to provide her with the meaningful good time of growing old with a devoted husband, of watching her sons love their wives and mother well, of proudly observing them dotingly father her grandchildren.

He could have provided all those blessings for Naomi. He didn't.

But He did satisfy a dream that most people don't value, a dream that perhaps Naomi had never thought much about. I will tell you a little later what I believe that dream was. If Naomi could speak to us now, I suspect she would report, "Everything worked out for the best. It was hard. But don't let pain cause you to miss the power of shattered dreams to change your life for good, forever."

From the story of Naomi, I learn six lessons—hard ones, wonderful ones, lessons that must be learned if we are to fulfill our destiny. They are necessary lessons if we are to develop into people with peace and power and unspeakable joy no matter what our circumstances may be, if we are to become the community of the joyful broken who reveal by our lives that the gospel is true. Let me simply list the lessons, then tell the story that illustrates them.

Lesson 1—Our fondest dreams for this life, the ones we naturally believe are essential to our happiness, must be fully abandoned if we are to know God well.

But we cannot abandon them without help. The help we need, most often, is suffering, the pain of seeing at least a few of our fondest dreams shattered.

Shattered dreams are necessary for spiritual growth. That's the first lesson.

Lesson 2—Shattered dreams produce excruciating pain, sometimes so extreme that we fear we cannot survive. And that is true. The person we are before the pain cannot survive. We emerge from the experience of shattered dreams as changed people, but not always for the better.

The pain is not evidence of weak faith. It is evidence that we are normal.

It's part of a necessary process. The pain is necessary if we're to discover within us an appetite for better dreams that before we neither noticed nor appreciated.

Something wonderful survives everything terrible, and it surfaces most clearly when we hurt. That's lesson two.

Lesson 3—Some cherished dream will crumble in your life. That's inevitable. It happens to all of us before we're through living down here. No one makes it unscathed to the end.

Whether we believe that God *caused* the trial (as Naomi did) or that God merely *allowed* the trial, one thing is clear: He could have *prevented* the trial. He could have given us a good time, at least a better time than we had. That fact creates within us a tension with God.

Some dreams important to us will shatter, and the realization that God could have fulfilled that dream pushes us into a terrible battle with Him. That's the third lesson.

Lesson 4—A child always given candy never learns to like vegetables. A student never required to read Shakespeare or to listen to Beethoven never develops a taste for more than sensational fiction and noisy music. Similarly, when lesser dreams reliably come true, we have a hard time appreciating greater dreams. We neither envision nor pursue them.

Only an experience of deep pain develops our capacity for recognizing and enjoying true life. That's lesson four.

Lesson 5—Most people never discover true life. Unbelievers don't possess it. Believers, all of them, do possess it, but not many experience it.

Not many Christians drink deeply from the well of living water. As a result, our worship, our community, and our witness are weak. I learn that as the fifth lesson.

Lesson 6—The past is irreparable; the future is always available. In every case, when good dreams shatter, better ones are there to newly value and pursue.

These better dreams are indestructible; they will not be taken away from us either by God (because He is good) or by the forces of hell (because evil has no power to thwart God's highest purposes).

No matter what happens in life, a wonderful dream is available, always, that if pursued will generate an unfamiliar, radically new internal experience. That experience, strange at first, will eventually be recognized as joy. That's the sixth lesson.

Now it's time to tell Naomi's entire story. Not till the story's finish do we discover what the wonderful dream is, the better dream that remains when good dreams shatter.

Don't look for these six lessons as you read. Let them emerge as you immerse yourself in her story. Truths revealed through narrative reach deeper than lessons outlined on a blackboard. You have the outline. Now read the story.

CHAPTER FIVE

THE RHYTHM
OF HOPE

Listen to what people say when their fondest dreams shatter. I heard the first two remarks this past week. The third I heard myself say just last night.

> "It feels like someone kicked me in the stomach. I've gotten my breath back, but now all I can do is cry."
> "If I continue to feel this way, I'd rather be dead. What do I do with the pain?"
> "Right now I feel no hope that I'll ever experience joy again. I have no idea what to do. I can see no way out."

From happiness through despair to joy—that's the cycle. Then, since joy is never fully settled, it repeats itself. Our lives move again from feeling pretty good to hurting terribly to deeper hope, different and richer. The "happiness-to-despair" part at least is familiar to every honest person who sincerely tries to follow this crazy, narrow, pothole-ridden path called the Christian life.

GOD'S GOODNESS AND OUR HAPPINESS

If given the choice, we would prefer to keep whatever happiness we've already found. Like the child who never wants to grow beyond the wide-eyed excitement of Christmas morning, we like to remain naively happy. Keep the blessings coming. Keep the good times rolling. When we signed on to the Christian life, that's what we thought was the deal. We do what we're told, and God stacks presents under the tree.

Our experience of happiness is not entirely wrong; it is, however, naive. It is both innocent and shallow, rooted in a strange blend of a child's optimism and a fool's arrogant spirit of entitlement. Things will go well for us; they're supposed to. *Other* people get cancer and suffer through divorce and lose their jobs and experience a friend's betrayal.

With adolescent maturity we declare that God is good when we ace the physics test or finish law school with honors, when our son is offered an unusually good position or the biopsy comes back negative. "Of course," we say, "God is good!" Without putting it quite this way, we assume God is pleased and grateful that we think so—and maybe just a little relieved.

When blessings come, we should of course enjoy them. It's good when children squeal with delight on Christmas morning; it's sad when they can't. Celebrate the good things of life. Enjoy the juicy steak, the unexpected bonus, the beautiful granddaughter.

Happy people, though they're right to be happy, face a subtle danger. They tend to spiritually gloat, to publicly express gratitude and praise for the good things they enjoy while privately thinking that blessings are their due. They can easily slip into a concern for the less fortunate that carries with it a mood of judgment: *If they were more like me, they would be given the blessings I have.* We don't easily recognize that mood within ourselves.

Unhappy folks face their own unique temptation. Publicly they tell the more fortunate how glad they are for all who are so blessed; privately they wish that the happy person's path would hit a ditch.

Rejoice with those who rejoice and weep with those who weep. No command is more difficult to obey. Beneath the surface, we lament another's joy (that's the sin of jealousy) and feel good when a much blessed friend has reason to cry (that's the sin of smugness, a close cousin of jealousy).

Happy people do not love well. Joyful people do. That's why happiness, the pleasant feelings that pleasant circumstances generate, must be taken away in order to be replaced by joy.

Happy people rarely look for joy. They're quite content with what they have. The foundation of their life consists of the blessings they enjoy. Although they may genuinely care about those less fortunate and do great things to help, their central concern is to keep what they have. They haven't been freed to pursue a greater dream. That's why they cannot love well. In His severe mercy, God takes away the good to create an appetite for the better, and then, eventually, He satisfies the new appetite, liberating them to love.

It comes down to this: God's best is available only to those who sacrifice, or who are willing to sacrifice, the merely good. If we are satisfied with good health, responsible children, enjoyable marriages, close friendships, interesting jobs, and successful ministries, we will never hunger for God's best. We will never worship. I've come to believe that only broken people truly worship. Unbroken people—happy folks who enjoy their blessings more than the Blesser—say thanks to God the way a shopper thanks a clerk.

From the sketchy data we're given in the book of Ruth, we can reasonably assume that Naomi was a happy woman. She had a husband, two sons, an economic difficulty that she expected to be temporary, and the prospect of grandchildren. She enjoyed the same kind of happiness that millions of Western Christians today experience, a kind we often claim as our birthright now that we're in the family of God. Life was going well enough to feel good.

List every blessing you desire. Put them all on the left side of a scale. Now list the blessing that we're told is the very highest, an intimate relationship with God. Put that one, by itself, on the right side of the scale.

Do we believe that what is on the right side immediately and decisively outweighs what is on the left? If we did, we would move more quickly from happiness through the agony of shattered dreams to complete joy.

Only a few in any generation believe that the weight of knowing God is a blessing heavier (and by that I mean more wonderful) than every other. And those who believe it appear to have developed that conviction only through suffering. Happiness must be stripped away, forcibly, before joy can surface, before we will value and pursue dreams whose fulfillment produces true joy.

It's a great tragedy when Christian people make it through life without ever discovering that their happiness is no different from the happiness of circumstantially well-off pagans. I fear that millions of Christians have never made that discovery and therefore blissfully continue to drink watery grape juice when fine wine is available.

I doubt whether anyone makes that discovery without enduring the pain of shattered dreams. The experience of despair is the initial movement in the rhythm of hope. That proved true in Naomi's life.

MOVEMENTS IN THE RHYTHM

Notice three characteristics of Naomi's despair. They're often part of our own journey to hope. First, she believed people would be better off spending time with someone other than herself. Second, she lost all hope of a return to earlier blessings that brought happiness. Third, she believed the tragedies were God's doing.

After her husband and sons died, the famine in Jerusalem ended. "With her two daughters-in-law she left the place where she had been living and set out on the road that would take them back to the land of Judah" (Ruth 1:7). Notice that all three women began the trip together. Only after they had traveled a bit did Naomi tell the girls to return home. What happened?

"Look," she said in effect, "you'll have a much better chance at happiness here in Moab than with me in Judah." She could envision nothing higher for these two young women than circumstance-dependent happiness—marriage, children, a nice house, what every culture rightly calls a good life. And the likelihood of their achieving happiness was better if they left her. That's characteristic number one of people in despair: *You're better off without me.*

"I'm an old woman," Naomi continued. "I have no hope of remarrying and bearing children again. Even if it happened, it would be absurd for you to wait till my sons were old enough to marry you. My dreams for happiness are gone. No, you girls should not come with me. Go home. My hopes are dashed. Yours are still alive."

Characteristic number two: *Happiness is only a memory, never to be experienced again.*

Orpah kissed Naomi and returned to Moab. Like Naomi, she could imagine nothing better than the happiness of a life filled with blessings.

Ruth sensed there was more. Her dreams were tied up with the virtues of relationship, virtues such as loyalty and persevering devotion. She *clung* to Naomi—the word means to stick like glue—and continued with her on the journey to Bethlehem.

When they arrived, Naomi greeted her friends with a request and a statement. "Don't call me Naomi," she requested. The name means pleasant. "Call me Mara." That name means bitter. Naomi quickly let her friends know she was miserable.

Then came the statement, "I went away full, but the LORD has brought me back empty.... The Almighty has brought misfortune upon me" (1:21). Put plainly, Naomi was saying, "It's God's fault. He killed my family."

She called Him *Shaddai*, the Almighty One, the invincible mountain, the force that cannot be resisted. At this point, Naomi sounded like a theistic fatalist. God does what He wants. We can do nothing but endure His choices. Characteristic number three: *Tragedies in our lives are God's doing. Perhaps they come as discipline for our wrong choices or maybe they come for some other reason, but either way, tragedies are God's doing. He could prevent them. He doesn't.*

Naomi's unlikely journey to joy has begun. Happiness has been taken away, replaced by despair. That's the first movement in the rhythm of hope.

The next movement begins unseen. Slowly, sometimes not for years, it becomes visible. When we catch sight of the trickling stream that will eventually develop into a river with enough force to carry us toward joy, a new kind of hope stirs. God is working when we see nothing but darkness. He is moving with rhythmic purpose through our agony and pain to unimaginable joy.

Knowing that He's moving at all sometimes becomes the central piece of faith we need to keep ourselves moving. The courage to not quit, to not settle for immediate pleasure that brings happiness back for only a moment, often depends on our conviction that God is moving, that we are being taken to an experience of ecstasy along a path of suffering, that there is no other way to get there.

God's behind-the-scenes movement in Naomi's life is marked by a series of telling phrases in the narrative, each an expression representing one more point of progress in Naomi's journey to joy.

The first phrase: After more than ten years in Moab, Naomi returned to Bethlehem *"as the barley harvest was beginning"* (1:22). The darkest night precedes the brightest dawn. That is not cliché; it is how God works. In the first phrase, we can see the sun's tip rise above the horizon. Naomi couldn't see it, but it was there. The harvest is coming.

The second phrase: Ruth asked her depressed, inactive mother-in-law for permission to "go to the fields and pick up the leftover grain"; and so, *"as it turned out,* she found herself working in a field belonging to Boaz" (2:2-3). Deliverance from despair always comes through a person. It was no mere stroke of good luck that, "as it turned out," Ruth caught the eye of a rich relative who owned the field where she happened to glean. It was rather one of those sovereign coincidences, a supernatural intrusion into her life.

The third phrase: If Boaz were to marry Ruth, both Ruth's and Naomi's financial problems would be over. But before he could marry her, Boaz had to overcome a legal hurdle stipulated by Jewish law. The obstacle was real. Ruth may well have been anxious. Would it all work out?

Naomi spoke words of wisdom to Ruth: "Wait, my daughter, until you find out what happens. *For the man will not rest* until the matter is settled today"(3:18). It is true that deliverance comes through a person, but it is also true that the person who delivers us must earnestly long to bring us joy. Deliverance always comes through love.

The fourth phrase: After Boaz and Ruth married, "he went to her, and the LORD enabled her to conceive." When Obed their son was born, "Naomi took the child, *laid him in her lap* and cared for him" (4:13,16). Her dream of growing old with her husband and enjoying her sons as adults was gone, but God created within Naomi an appetite for a better dream. The writer intends us to see Naomi at the end of the story as a deeply content old woman, aware of a higher purpose than for things to go well in her life, experiencing a joy that more than replaced the happiness she had lost. We'll see later how the phrase *laid him in her lap* suggests her participation in a much greater dream.

In each of our lives…

…the harvest is beginning; the sun is rising.

…the stage is being set; God is moving.

…the deliverer is eagerly preparing to bless, unable to rest till He does.

…the Spirit is able to conceive whatever fruit we have long been destined to bear.

Hope has its own rhythm. We cannot rush it. The water of life will find its way down the mountain to fill the lake from which we can drink. Let's look more carefully at each point of progress in the story, at each of these four phrases that suggest hope's timeless rhythm.

CHAPTER SIX

BREAKING THE RULES

We Christians are often practicing Buddhists. We kill desire in an effort to to escape pain, then wonder why we don't enjoy God. Naomi didn't make that mistake.

With Ruth in tow, a dejected Naomi returned home after a ten-year absence. She had aged twenty years.

"Could that be Naomi?" her friends asked.

"Don't call me that!" barked Naomi, whose name meant pleasantness. "I'm miserable and you might as well know it. Sorry I can't be cheerful and give you all a hug. I'm even sorrier that I can't share with you stories of God's faithfulness these past ten years, but I just can't. While I was in Moab, God killed my husband and two sons. I'm in no mood for a welcome home party and I don't much feel like getting together to worship."

Imagine a missionary woman coming back from the field talking like that. No church would invite her to speak at *its* missions conference. We prefer stories of hope in sorrow and victory in trial.

Isn't that what Jesus makes available? "Don't let your hearts be troubled," He told His disciples.

What did Jesus mean? Is He telling us to pretend we feel what we should feel when our most deeply experienced emotions are quite the opposite? Are we to admit our troubled feelings only to ourselves and God, while telling others that God's presence and promises are real to us when they're not? Is Jesus agreeing with Buddha in prescribing a form of contentment that requires us to cut off the nerve endings of our souls and to report peace when what we feel is a void? Is He teaching that if we trust Him, we'll feel no pain?

TAKING THE RISK

I recently was one of several speakers at a well-attended Bible conference, the kind where speakers are sometimes regarded more as celebrities than messengers, where to admit you are in a bad mood would, in the minds of many, instantly discredit you as a man or woman of God.

The day after my presentations, a conversation took place that touched a deep wound. I became so distraught that I couldn't bring myself to return to the conference to hear other speakers whom I deeply appreciate and value. For the final day and a half of the conference, I remained in my hotel room.

I didn't keep track, but I must have watched at least six hours of CNN. I finished an Agatha Christie mystery novel when I could not bear to once more hear that booming bass voice announce what I already knew, "*This* is CNN!" CNN is fast-paced and Agatha tells a good story, but I was bored. I decided, however, that boredom was preferable to risk. My isolation provided safety from Christians coming to me and expecting to encounter a spiritual reality that wasn't there.

Naomi took that risk. She openly admitted her bitterness and depression as *present* realities. We're more inclined to report a *past* struggle, a formerly troubled heart that has now been quieted by God's peace.

We Christians are an impatient lot. We insist on gathering grain before it grows. We want to see flowers before spring and fruit before fall. When a brother or sister is going through a tough time, we insist that the Spirit's work be obvious. Unless they speak of their trials from a spiritual perspective, we tend to apply pressure more than we dispense grace. We rarely believe that life is hidden in the barren tree. Let a friend express his exasperation with a four-letter word, and immediately we're more concerned with his language than with his agony.

No farmer goes to the orchard in winter to pick apples. Christians do it all the time. And when the fruit isn't there, we walk off in disgust. The good farmer patiently waits with his basket, knowing he will soon fill it with delicious fruit.

The Christian community is often a dangerous place to be when your dreams shatter. Initially, friends are warmly understanding and supportive. Last week I spent many hours with a friend whose wife was hovering between life and death. At one point I said, "I will walk with you through this experience." Many others surrounded him with love and deeds of kindness.

And that's good. But two unwritten rules eventually surface in our response to one who hurts. First, mourning has a time limit. I once heard a preacher tell his congregation, "We must pray for our dear sister. She lost her husband two months ago and is still battling grief. She should be over it by now."

Only a few heart-dead people would speak such words. But we're not as far removed from that attitude as we think. At some point, we insist on victory.

Second, we think there's a proper way to mourn. Ugly battles should remain out of sight. Acceptable battles may be shared, but only if we season our account with hope. A husband may admit to his small group, "My wife and I sometimes quarrel, but we know the Spirit is working to bring us closer together." I think I would stand up and cheer if just once I heard a man share, "My wife and I right now hate each other's guts. We want a good marriage, but we have no idea what to do and we're scared out of our wits we'll never figure it out." (I should point out that my applause would be for the man's realism, not for the state of his marriage.)

That level of honesty is reserved for the counseling office. Church is too often a place of pretense and therefore a place without hope. When brokenness is disdained, where the real story is never told, the power of God is not felt. Where brokenness is invited and received with grace, the gospel comes alive with hope.

At the Party

Naomi broke both the time-limit rule and the proper-mourning rule. Her husband had died nearly ten years earlier, her sons more recently but still long enough ago that by now she should have gained perspective. But still she was reeling. Where was her faith? Is God good or not? Is He worthy of trust or does He make mistakes? I can see her community pointing fingers while expressing similar admonitions.

And the way she talked about her shattered dreams was unbecoming to a follower of El Shaddai. "Yes, God is an invincible mountain, a force that cannot be resisted. But that is cause for praise, not complaint." Perhaps that's what the elders in Bethlehem told her. It's certainly what many sufferers hear today from their spiritual leaders. No wonder we run off to counselors.

Don't sanitize the story. Naomi did *not* say, "I'm having a hard time. Most nights I cry myself to sleep. But God knows what He's doing. My family died for good reasons that I cannot see but I claim by faith. I know nothing enters my life without passing through His tender hands. My hope is in the Lord."

That may be what we think she should have said, what we wish she had said, but it's not what she did say. She was miserable, and she saw God as the source of her misfortune.

Her misery was compounded by the mood of the townspeople. Naomi arrived in Bethlehem "as the barley harvest was beginning." The famine had ended. The rains had come. Fields that for so long had yielded mostly weeds were now waving with crops just waiting to be harvested. The city was alive with happy activity. It was party time.

Have you ever felt really down but somehow managed to drag yourself to a Bible study? The standard greeting—"How're you doing?"—was met with a chorus of "Great," "Can't complain," "Doin' fine." You could only mutter, "Okay," and quickly shuffle off to the kitchen to pour a cup of coffee.

No one feels lonelier than a depressed person at a party. I suspect half the congregation feels every Sunday morning what Naomi felt when she arrived in Bethlehem. When a friend tells you he is so excited about all that God is doing, it's hard to admit you're irritated over what God is not doing.

The Western church has become a community of either the victorious or the acceptably broken. Either we speak glowingly of our love for Jesus—usually because the blessings are abundant—or we struggle nobly through hard times, convincing others and sometimes ourselves that we're doing better than we are. With each other we're more proper than real, more appropriate than alive.

Naomi broke the rules. She stood broken before her community, admitting who she was rather than pretending to be who she should have been. The result was more pain and, although not right away, more hope. Had she deadened her pain and behaved appropriately, she would have found the contentment of Buddha and missed the joy of Christ. In the next chapter, I explain how that works.

CHAPTER SEVEN

HIDDEN HOPE

When the writer of Naomi's story tells us she returned home "as the barley harvest was beginning," he evidently intends to stir us with excitement. Hope is on the way. The sun is peeking over the horizon. Naomi can't see it—her world is still dark—but soon she will. Her depression will lift, and God will fill her with joy.

I read no hint of rebuke for her depression or bad attitude. Perhaps ugly struggles invariably precede real joy. I think that's true. Buddha thought otherwise.

Gautama Siddhartha one day announced he was Buddha (the awakened one) when he gained the insight that the way to end suffering is to end desire.

"Naomi, don't let your heart be troubled," Buddha would have said to her had he been there. "Get over your discouragement by learning to stop wanting so intensely to have your family with you."

We follow his lead by reminding each other that it's wrong to care so deeply whether we have a job or whether people like us or whether our children are walking with the Lord. Trust God, we insist, and trust Him so fully that all other desires become as nothing. When we hurt, especially when we scream and wail, it's evidence that we're not trusting. Don't feel pain, trust God!

It's a foreign idea to imagine that we might desire God so strongly and passionately that every other desire could still be fully felt and yet not control us. It's a more familiar idea to try hard to fix our eyes on heaven in a way that lets us feel no other desire with passion.

Could we actually love God so much that we could feel all the pain of a teenage daughter's pregnancy and still worship? Could we still love our daughter? Or do we believe that loving God would somehow reduce the pain that a child's rebellion creates?

"Don't let your hearts be troubled. Find some way to feel less pain, to reduce your desire for what you do not have. If you succeed, call it contentment. Call it deep trust."

We think that's what Jesus taught. But it's really advice from Buddha. A Buddhist community would hear the command to not let their hearts be troubled as instruction to feel less, to find some way to deaden the desires that bring pain. When we follow that advice, we experience nirvana and call it victory. And we never discover our desire for God that remains beneath the suffering brought on by unmet desires.

Deaden pain. That's Buddha's way. It eliminates all hope of joy.

Deepen desire. That's the way of Jesus. His way awakens passion within our souls that transcends all other passions, that puts them in their place without weakening them. We still yearn for a friend to be faithful, and we hurt when he isn't. But we long so deeply to know Christ that our hurt has no power to drive us toward revenge.

I wonder if any of Naomi's friends told her to just get over it. I wonder if she ever tried to relieve her suffering by distracting herself with busyness, perhaps hoping to forget what her husband looked like so his face would no longer haunt her in the night.

DIFFERENT PATHS

To help us realize how easy it is for us to follow Buddha but to think we're following Christ, it might be helpful to quickly summarize Buddha's ideas.

Gautama Siddhartha was the son of a wealthy king, a prince whose father prepared him for the throne by shielding him from everything ugly. Against the wishes of his father, the young prince decided to venture outside the castle walls to see what he would find. He came upon "four distressing sights" that unnerved him: a sick man, an old man, a dead man, and a seeking man, one who wanted to unravel the mystery of suffering.

The sights troubled him deeply. He decided to make it his life's mission to understand suffering and to discover its solution.

One day, after much time and thought, he arose from under the sacred tree and announced "I am Buddha." His awakening consisted of the "four noble truths" that make up the core of Buddhist teaching.

Truth 1: *Life is suffering.* There is always, in everyone's life, a gap between desire and reality. The gap is suffering.

Truth 2: *The cause of all suffering is desire.* People suffer because they desire what they do not experience. It is not possible to have everything you desire. Therefore, if you desire, you will suffer.

Truth 3: *The way to end suffering is to end desire.* Want nothing, then nothing can disturb you. A person without dreams will never suffer the pain of seeing them shattered.

Truth 4: *Spend your life learning to eliminate desire.* The "eightfold path," the way of Buddha, shows you how.

Jesus directs us to a different path. When He tells His followers to not let their hearts be troubled, He does not intend for us to deaden desire. Quite the opposite. His teaching might be summarized this way.

Truth 1: *Life includes suffering, but life is good.* In this world, His followers and everyone else will suffer tribulation. But Jesus has made a way for us to satisfy our deepest desire in the midst of unrelieved pain.

Truth 2: *The cause of all suffering is separation.* We are separated from God—and from our own deepest desire, our longing for God—and we're therefore deceived into looking elsewhere for joy. That sets us off on the ultimate wild goose chase. Nothing but God satisfies our most profound desire.

Truth 3: *The way to handle suffering is to discover your desire for God.* Then everything, both good and bad, becomes redemptive. It moves us toward the God we desire. Enter your thirst. Feel your ache, the very worst ache that throbs in your soul. Face how you harm others, your spouse, your children, your friends. And face your disappointment with them. Eventually, you will seek God for…

…forgiveness of your failure to love.

…the love you desire.

…empowerment to love others.

…hope that one day you will revel in love freely given and freely received in a perfect community of lovers.

Truth 4: *The new life provided through Jesus must be accepted as a gift of love.* We then spend the rest of our days discovering our desire to know God better, and we come to realize it's a desire whose satisfaction no shattered dream can thwart.

Don't let your hearts be troubled, even if your husband and both sons die, even when you realize that God could have done something to prevent their deaths but did nothing. The command, however, does not tell us to hurt less.

When you hurt, hurt. Hurt openly in the presence of God. Hurt openly in the presence of the few who provide you with safe community. Feel your pain. Regard brokenness as an opportunity, as the chance to discover a desire that no brokenness can eliminate but that only brokenness reveals.

Remember what brokenness is. It's the awareness that you long to be someone you're not and cannot be without divine help. Never pretend to God, to yourself, or to your safe community that you feel what you don't or that you are what you're not. With everyone else, including Christians attending a Bible conference, choose to be congenial. Not everyone needs to see your brokenness.

KEEPING DESIRE ALIVE

My growing conviction is that no one discovers the fullness of their desire for God without entering the fullness of lesser desires. Sexual abuse victims will not feel how badly they long to know God nor experience the hope that He can be known until they recognize and accept how badly they wanted (and still want) to be cherished by the father who molested them.

We must therefore feel the soul-piercing pain of disappointment, of the imperfect love we've received and the equally imperfect love we have given. But when all we experience is pain, loneliness, and despair, we can know with certainty that we have not yet entered the depths of our souls. Beneath our troubled emotion is a desire for God that in rich measure can be satisfied now.

Bankrupt businessmen can discover that desire. Men whose wives have left them can discover that desire. Widows, cancer patients, and recently fired pastors can discover that desire. So, too, can parents whose children are breaking their hearts. It will take time, agonizing time, characterized more by despair than hope, but the discovery will be made.

Don't let your hearts be troubled. In the middle of shattered dreams, discover a desire that Christ pledges Himself to satisfy. Don't set out to discover that desire. The desire will surface, like bubbling water from a spring that can no longer be held back.

When that desire is discovered, we wake up to a new world of passion, a quiet world where intense desire never disturbs rest. Worship and prayer become our favorite things to do. The world we enter is the world of the Trinity, the passion-filled community of God. We begin to sense a yearning more powerful than all others to join that community, to take our seat in heavenly places where loving community satisfies our souls' deepest desire.

For Buddha, the answer to suffering is to deaden desire, to extinguish passion and to achieve the complete isolation of union with nothingness. It's a heretical stretch to call that peace.

For Jesus, the answer to suffering is to suffer intensely, to risk feeling so bad that you hole up in a small hotel room and watch six hours of CNN, and then to walk through that pain—through prayer, the Word, spiritual disciplines, and community—toward the center of your soul where above all else you desire God.

Naomi was not a practicing Buddhist. She did not deaden her desires. She felt her pain in ways that made her truly ugly and exposed her to the contempt of her community.

By refusing to deaden her pain, she kept alive, even in the midst of her depression, her capacity to desire something more. And that's important. People who insist on happiness never find joy. They allow themselves to feel only those desires that are met. Denied desires they deaden. The effect is to feel happy for a season, perhaps a long season, but it's a selfish happiness. They live for the ongoing satisfaction of desires other than the desire to know God. They become self-absorbed.

God stripped Naomi of happiness to prepare her for joy. What a tragedy when people deaden their souls to the pain that eliminates happiness and, as a result, never discover their desire for God. Desperate people discover that desire. Happy people never do.

If we keenly feel the gap between desire and reality, if we reject the way of Buddha, we will eventually recognize that our harvest is beginning. Hope that was hidden during the long dark night will eventually be revealed. If we enter our dark night and refuse to pretend that we see light when we don't, we will eventually see the plan of God unfold in our lives.

Shattered dreams are the prelude to joy. Always. In the middle of our pain, God is working for our joy. At some point, He works in ways we can see.

That's what happens next in Naomi's story.

CHAPTER EIGHT

EVERYTHING HELPS ME TO GOD

My title for this chapter comes from the writings of the great French spiritual guide Jean-Pierre de Caussade, who died more than two hundred years ago. It's his way of saying what Paul taught two thousand years ago, that all things—a spouse's death, a son's rebellion, a missed career—*all things,* in the hand of God, work together for good for people whose primary agenda is to glorify God, who long to enjoy Him as they enjoy no one else and to reveal Him to others in every relational encounter.

If we're to find hope when everything we've lived for is taken away, if we're to move on with peace and purpose when our hearts are broken by indescribable pain, or when they quietly ache with regret and missed opportunity, we must rescue Paul's teaching and de Caussade's restatement from their usual status as clichés. "All things work together for good" and "Everything helps me to God" are statements that must no longer be regarded as biblical mantras for pious folks to utter when they want to deaden pain.

For men like de Caussade and St. John of the Cross, these words were not clichés, but living and life-sustaining truths.

When he endured the dark nights of undeserved imprisonment and an uncaring community who refused to tend him during a life-ending sickness, St. John found light in his darkness, knowing God was at work in ways he could not see.

In a similar vein, de Caussade once said that "there is nothing safer and less likely to lead us astray than the darkness of faith."[2] De Caussade believed that when dreams shatter and pain is blinding, we're prevented from moving ahead in our own light. We have none. We can move only in the light that faith reveals.

I wonder how Paul or John or de Caussade would direct Naomi to God. I don't think any one of them would throw Bible verses at her and expect instant faith and obedience. And none would say that what happened to her was good. It was not good. It was bad. But in God's hands, it could advance something very good. As wise spiritual directors, they would encourage movement along an unyieldingly narrow path; they would direct Naomi to the next step on a long journey.

Impatient Westerners prefer quick sanctification. Take your car into the shop and drive it again the next day. Bring your soul to a counselor or pastor and get fixed right away.

But wisdom understands that souls are not broken machines that experts fix. Wisdom knows the deep workings of the hungry, hurting, sin-inclined soul and patiently follows as the Spirit moves quietly in those depths, gently nudging people toward God.

There is no Concorde that flies us from immaturity to maturity in a few hours. There is only a narrow, bumpy road where a few people walk together as they journey to God.

What to Tell Her?

Naomi is on that path. She's not doing well. Life has been hard. Ten years ago she was widowed; a few years later she lost both her married sons before either had fathered a child; now she has returned home with a nice young woman, a daughter-in-law from the despised country of Moab.

Naomi is no longer young, her money is gone, her property is sold, she can't manage to shake off feelings of depression, and she is mad at God, convinced that she has been a victim of His ruthless sovereignty. No one wants her in their small group.

Assume she attends the church you pastor. What will you say in next Sunday's sermon that you honestly believe she might hear? What message could you preach that the Spirit might use to draw her along on the path toward God? Do you believe that everything helps a person to God, including a suicidal son, a devastating divorce, a secret moral failure, an unfulfilling job? If so, how do you preach what you believe?

Or assume you're a Christian counselor. Ruth has brought Naomi to your office, then waits outside to let you do whatever you do with depressed clients. What would you say to this slumped-over old lady?

Maybe a better first question is, what would you feel as you listen to Naomi? She tells her story in a flat monotone, until at one point she looks up at you and with fire in her eyes says, "I'm alone. My life is not worth living. I'm utterly miserable, and I have nothing to look forward to. Shaddai could have done something. He did nothing."

It was at a point like this that Ted Turner dismissed God. It's been at points like this that countless others have more quietly dismissed God and learned to live like functional atheists or pragmatic deists. "There is no God I can depend on. The God who exists has left me to make it on my own. He offers no real help." Churches are filled with worshipers who have reached that conclusion. Their worship is not from the heart.

Your session with Naomi is under way. Would you establish rapport with skilled empathy? To what end? So she would feel better knowing at least one person understood her pain?

Would you confront her attitude of distrust and defiance as sinful? But how could you insist she rest in the arms of a God she thinks is cruel or indifferent? Would you simply tell her God is good and demand she believe it?

Perhaps you would probe about in her childhood, looking for experiences of abandonment that make it difficult for Naomi to see God as a loving Father. And then, having identified the roots of her unfaith, you might pinpoint her negative self-talk and suggest more adaptive sentences to use.

Would you urge her to get more involved with her friends, to throw dinner parties and play bridge?

Would you refer her to the physician next door for Prozac?

For years I hid the inadequacy I felt as a counselor behind a professional demeanor, technical jargon, and sound psychological methods of treatment. Recently I've made a truly liberating discovery. I *am* inadequate. My sense of inadequacy is not the effect of deficient intellect or poor training, nor is it a symptom of emotional disorder. It is the painful admission of what is true. On my own, I can make nothing of importance happen. I can help no one.

But if I abide in Christ, if I present myself before God's Spirit for searching and filling, if I study and ponder the Scriptures and live my life in brokenness before a grace-dispensing community, I can transcend my inadequacy. I can find myself as I worship. I can struggle on behalf of others with the energy of Christ powerfully working in me.

THIS GIFT

I have learned that an awareness of inadequacy is neither a curse to lift nor a disorder to cure. It is a gift to be received, a gift that if properly used can make me powerful and strong and clear and wise.

With this attitude, I would work with Naomi differently than I would have earlier in my career. Now, I would want only to follow God's Spirit. I would assume that He is working quietly in her soul, redeeming everything that has happened, everything she is feeling, to direct her to Himself.

If I were her pastor, I would want to preach in the spirit of the New Covenant, inviting Naomi and everyone in the congregation to see the heart of God revealed in the cross of Christ. I would encourage them to interpret all of life's hardships not as problems to fix or struggles to relieve or pain to deaden, but as important elements in a larger story that all God's children long to tell. I would urge them to accept wherever they are on the journey, whether happy or miserable, as the place where God will meet them, where He loves them, where He will continue to work in them. And I would offer my own life as a growing, struggling, sometimes painfully unattractive example of what doing that might mean.

I would beg God to deliver me from Calvary-denying sermons, which leave people feeling scolded and pressured and falsely hopeful because biblical principles are presented as formulas for making life work. I would plead protection from Pentecost-denying church services where we do the Spirit's work for Him with contrived worship and emotional provocation and endless programs that substitute for community. I would ask God to never let me again preach an Eden-denying message where psychological insights replace biblical wisdom in a misguided effort to repair emotional damage when the real problem is a serpent-inspired determination to experience life without God.

If I were Naomi's spiritual director, I would want nothing more than to follow God's Spirit as He slowly works to bring Naomi in touch with her desire for God. I would explore what therapists call psychological dynamics (what I call the subtle workings of her flesh), and I would consider a therapeutic interpretation of what's going on, perhaps offering it to Naomi. But I would count on this: God is always working to make His children aware of a dream that remains alive beneath the rubble of every shattered dream, a new dream that when realized will release a new song, sung with tears, till God wipes them away and we sing with nothing but joy in our hearts.

SOMETHING BIG

God was at work when He brought Naomi home "as the barley harvest was beginning." But His work was not visible. The night was still dark. Naomi was discouraged and depressed. But if we listen carefully as her story unfolds, we can hear God whispering that dawn is on its way. The harvest is beginning. A better dream is about to be revealed—and fulfilled.

Now God begins to work visibly. Ruth asks permission to go to the fields, to take her place as a peasant and pick up whatever grain is left behind by the official workers. Naomi feels the impact of the young woman's humility and love, and with only a little enthusiasm, smiles weakly and says, "Go ahead, my daughter."

That moment is a moment of connecting, where humility and love in one person arouse what little hope remains in another. It is in the community of God's people where God's visible work begins.

Ruth, unfamiliar with both custom and geography, wanders off to find a field. There is no record that she prayed, no indication that she strategized or sought counsel in her decision. It is right, of course, to pray and plan. But those good things can quickly become manipulative techniques that we depend on more than God. Like the seminarian relying more on his knowledge of Hebrew than on the Spirit to hear God's voice in the text, we're more prone to carefully maneuvering our way through life than to abandoning ourselves to divine providence. Discovering our desire for God and finding the path to Him always depend on His merciful and sovereign kindness.

With naive simplicity, Ruth goes off to do good. Listen to the writer as his pen dances across the pages. "*As it turned out,* she found herself working in a field belonging to Boaz, who was from the clan of Elimelech [Naomi's husband]" (2:3).

I picture the writer pausing after recording that sentence, sitting back and quivering with awe and excitement at the realization that something big is unfolding. Aslan is on the move.

Boaz was God's instrument not merely to solve Naomi's financial problem (though he certainly did that), not only to again fill Naomi's house with the sounds of family (though eventually he did that as well), but to arouse in Naomi a new dream.

Consider Naomi's words when she heard where Ruth "happened" to work that day. Immediately she recognized the hand of God. "He has not stopped showing his kindness to the living and the dead" (2:20).

Two things require notice. First, the word she used that we translate *kindness* is the Hebrew *hesed.* It's a word that refers to a strongly bonded relationship where one party continues to be faithfully involved with another because it is the character of the first party to do so. Naomi no longer regards Shaddai as a power who could do something but does nothing. Now she sees His kindness, though her family is still dead. God could resurrect them. He hasn't. She continues to view God as kind.

Second, she views that kindness as actually extending to her dead husband and sons, to "the living *and the dead.*" The dream surfacing in Naomi's heart crosses the borders of this world. The better dream that is emerging out of the debris of her already shattered dreams is not just about her, about her life now and her life here. It reaches higher into another world, an unseen one, and at the same time reaches down into the depths of her soul where she discovers what she really wants.

Naomi was given a glimpse of the movement of God. I can see de Caussade sitting with her, gratefully smiling and worshiping God and saying, "Everything brings us to Him." Naomi would have agreed.

But why? She was stirred by one piece of good fortune to dream a better dream, to begin to move beyond her shattered dreams to hope for something more, something that God was doing. Too often when we receive good news, we stay depressed. ("He'll never marry Ruth. And even if he does, so what? My husband and sons will still be dead.") Or we breathe new life into old dreams. ("If he marries her at least I'll be able to buy a big screen TV, maybe even a vacation house on the beach. He *is* very rich. I guess I shouldn't gripe so much. There are a few blessings I can count.")

When God moved, Naomi began to dream a bigger dream. Why? Lots of people I know never do. It's far more common to remain miserable and grumpy even when a few things go well, or to immerse ourselves in enjoying whatever blessings are still available.

We'll look later at the better dream Naomi dreamed. What captures my attention now is why she was able to dream that dream. That's the question I take up in the next chapter.

CHAPTER NINE

DESIRE OR ADDICTION?

Why was Naomi able to see God's hand when He began to move in her life? Many people can't. Why could she? I think it was because she entered her heart so deeply, feeling all its pain, that she eventually stumbled into the core of her heart, where she wanted God.

People who find some way to deaden their pain never discover their desire for God in all its fullness. They rather live for relief and become addicts to whatever provides it. Think with me about how this works.

Inconsolable pain, the kind that drives away every vestige of happiness and renders us incapable of fully enjoying any pleasure, can be handled only by discovering a capacity for a different kind of joy. That is the function of pain, to carry us into the inner recesses of our being that wants God. We need to let soul-pain do its work by experiencing it fully.

If we deny how badly we hurt, we remain unaware of our desire for God and aware only of lesser desires. When those lesser desires are the only ones we actually feel, they inevitably become compulsive demands. An addiction begins.

We need God. He is all we need. But until we realize that fact, we experience lesser desires as needs and devote our energy to arranging for their satisfaction. That defines addiction.

HEARING THE SONG OF LONGING

Sam and Lori sat in my office, deeply troubled by their teenage son's rebellious depression. At one point, Sam pounded his fist on his knee and declared, "I will fight for my son. I will do whatever it takes to get him better." Sam saw his resolve as godly determination. I saw it as idolatry, as an addiction to a lesser desire. He had not yet discovered the quiet place in the center of his soul where all he wants is God. Legitimate desires had therefore become idolatrous goals. Sam's god was his own power to influence his son. As long as that remained true, nothing he said or did would carry the energy of Christ into his son's heart.

When the deepest desire we feel within our hearts is for something other than God, a spirit of entitlement develops. We see ourselves as needing something we don't have and we believe we *should* have. Justice is on our side. So we think. Prayer becomes demand when desire becomes our tyrant.

Soon we're caught in the addictive cycle. Whatever brings satisfaction relieves pain for the moment, then creates deeper emptiness that, in turn, more rudely clamors for relief. We lose our power to choose. The will becomes a slave to whatever god makes us feel better. We die as persons while Satan chuckles.

Only true worship expresses our deepest freedom. But we do not properly worship until we discover our desire for God. And no experience so powerfully surfaces that desire in our hearts as the horror of shattered dreams.

Naomi's story has a happy ending, not because her husband and sons were resurrected—though God could have arranged for that to happen. He didn't. It ends happily because Naomi is worshiping God, holding her grandson on her lap, aware that through all of her life, both the good times and bad, God is telling His story.

Little Obed grew up to become the father of Jesse who then fathered David, the king of Israel who continued the line to Jesus. Naomi of course did not know how her grandson fit into God's unrevealed scheme. But she felt a quieting, awe-filled sense that more was happening than she could see, and, as we'll explore later, she consciously gave herself over to it. She had discovered her desire for God. From the devastation of shattered dreams to the sure hope of a better dream: That's the story of Naomi.

It's also the unfolding story of a friend of mine named Jim. I just returned from a three-hour breakfast where Jim and I discussed his journey through shattered dreams to hope in God. Six months ago his wife, Gloria, clutched her chest late one evening and before morning was dead.

With a quiet authority that compelled me to seriously listen, Jim said, "I don't know how it works, but in my pain I'm discovering how much I really do love God." Shattered dreams did not harden his heart but rather opened a doorway into the deepest recesses where he discovered a desire for God that was stronger and more alive than any other. He wants Gloria badly, his hurt is excruciating, but he wants God more. I was moved.

Two weeks before Jim lost Gloria, the husband of another close friend died suddenly. She told me, with the same quiet authority, "Everything's different now. What used to matter so much just doesn't matter in the same way. Nothing really matters now but knowing God."

She continued, "Although I'm grateful for all the blessings I still have and although I deeply value the wonderful support of family and friends, nothing has the power to touch me where I most keenly hurt, especially at four in the morning. At those times all I can do is turn to God."

She paused a moment, looked away, then added, "But when I do, when I cry out, 'God, I need You; where *are* You?' I don't always find Him. In fact, I never do, not the way I thought I would."

Jim reported the same thing. At his worst moments of pain, he never hears a happy song coming out of his heart. When he hears a song, it's the music of desire, of longing for what is not now and will never be till heaven. "Tears have become my deepest form of worship." Jim spoke with passion. So did my widowed friend.

When dreams shatter, we long to experience God's nearness in a way that dries our tears. Instead, deeper tears are released.

Perhaps that's why so few make any sustained effort to seek God with all their hearts, to discover how deeply they do in fact desire God. The discovery brings pain. We get in touch with a profound desire that we have no power whatsoever to satisfy. We find ourselves at the mercy of One who could provide satisfaction but may not, a Person we cannot manipulate, an unresponsive God who keeps whispering, "Later." The stark truth is a hard one: Discovering our desire for God introduces us to a whole new world of hurt. When we realize how badly we want Him, He seemingly disappears.

But it's a hopeful hurt. It doesn't feel exactly good, but it does feel clean. Through our tears we actually can sing "Great Is Thy Faithfulness" and "It Is Well with My Soul." We can even sing "I Love You, Lord," not without an ache in our hearts but somehow through the ache.

A profound encounter with pain brings us to make a choice. Either we change or we sink into bitterness, despair, or hedonism. Either we accept the fact that life is *not* all about us and how we feel now and what happens here, or we push back the pain by living for the satisfaction of lesser dreams that might come true.

The decision to live for whatever brings instant pleasure turns us into addicts, sometimes obvious addicts who cruise Internet pornography or drink too much, sometimes subtle addicts, pastors who live to grow their churches, parents who do everything to produce good kids, or businessmen with no higher dream than closing the next deal.

Think how many marriages have ended in divorce because one spouse was addicted to a lesser desire that, in its place, was legitimate. But second-place desires become first-place priorities when we don't discover our core longing for God. Our logic goes like this: God wants me happy. I'm not happy in this marriage. Therefore, God won't mind if I get out. He might actually be leading me to divorce.

The flaw is in the premise. God does want us happy; He's gone to great lengths to ensure our eternal joy. But the happiness He provides now is the strange happiness of longing for what we were designed to experience but must wait to fully enjoy. It's the happiness of serving a God we trust enough to let us cry today, knowing He has promised to wipe our eyes tomorrow.

Our generation has lost the concept of finding joy in unfulfilled desire. We no longer know what it means to hope. We want what we want *now*. Unsatisfied desire has become to us like a bad toothache that justifiably demands quick relief at any cost. It was meant to be a road sign pointing us on to a better place.

C. S. Lewis somewhere said that if we discover a desire within us that nothing in this world can satisfy, we should begin to wonder if perhaps we were created for another world. Jesus told us to lay up treasures for ourselves in heaven. Paul instructs us to fix our eyes on an unseen world, the one Lewis calls "another world," and to set our affections on higher ambitions than will ever be satisfied now.

The message is clear. We are to become aware of better dreams and live for them, not only the better dreams of heaven but also the better dream available now of drawing close to God. When we discover our desire for God, we can live for nothing less.

KEY ELEMENTS OF TRUE SPIRITUALITY

But there's a problem, one I've already mentioned. Becoming aware of our desire for God seems to reliably generate severe frustration.

The night after Gloria died, Jim couldn't sleep. He listened to music that spoke powerfully to his soul. The effect was to intensify the ache to hold her again, to share a hymnbook as they sat in church, to order from the same menu in their favorite restaurant.

But another ache arose from deeper places in his heart. He could literally feel a crushing desire to know God, to feel Him, to experience His presence, to see His face. He did not expect God to satisfy his desire to touch his wife again, not in this life. He did expect to meet God in a new way. And that happened, but not in the way he anticipated.

When Shaddai allows terrible pain to come into our lives, He is removing a satisfaction, often a legitimate one like the enjoyment of one's spouse, that keeps us happy and content whether we know God well or not. He is taking away good food to make us hungry for better fare.

But then He doesn't seem to give it. The table stays bare. Those who claim otherwise most often are feeding on their own resources or on their remaining blessings, mistaking them for God.

Those who, like C. S. Lewis after his wife died, find heaven's door slammed shut, discover their desire for God but not God Himself. It's at that point either we dismiss God and live to satisfy lesser desires or we wait.

Naomi endured ten years of darkness before God's hand became visible. We're forced to draw an unpleasant and disturbing conclusion: When the pain of shattered dreams helps us discover our desire for God, God seems to disappear. Or at least His absence becomes obvious. And then we feel our desire for God as throbbing agony. We discover how badly we long to know Him. *It is the frustration of our desire for God that deepens it.* Only by *not* revealing God to us, at least for a while—sometimes a long while—can the Spirit put us in touch with a desire that eventually displaces every other desire.

That realization brought Jim to understand that tears offered to God were his deepest worship.

Why are you so far from the words of my groaning? I cry out and I hear nothing. How can I sing the songs of the Lord in a foreign land? How long, O Lord, before you deliver me from all my distress? I want to sing a new song, but I can't right now. Darkness is my only friend. *I cannot find you!*

The psalmists were realistic, so much more than we who worship a divine vending machine. Insert the correct spiritual change, punch the right button, and God delivers. What do you want? A new zest for life? No more homosexual desires? Godly kids? Coming right up. Just stick in the right coins—daily devotions, disciplined prayer, determined obedience, faithful church attendance. God will do whatever you ask.

Naomi endured ten years of pain. Ten years with no visible evidence of God's involvement. It would be enough to turn most of us into deists.

But it's in the pain that we discover our desire for God, and it's in the frustration of that desire that we come to realize how sturdy it is. We face the truth that there is no other answer. To whom else shall we go? Moving toward anything else we might desire is idolatry and foolishness. Only God has the life our souls desperately need. We come to really *believe* that.

So we abandon ourselves to Him. And we wait. Any experience of His presence is given as a sovereign mercy. There is no formula for making it happen.

No longer do we live for blessings; no longer do we pray, "God, here is what I need. Give it to me!" Now we rest, an agitated rest that includes the agony of frustration, but still we rest. And we learn to say, "God, whoever You are, whatever You do, that is all I want. I demand nothing. I will wait for You."

If you're seeking God in the middle of shattered dreams, if you've become aware of your desire for Him but are having trouble finding Him, be encouraged that it bothers you. The more you're bothered by not finding Him, the more aware you're becoming of how badly you want Him. Abandon yourself to Him. Let the Cross bring you confidence that He is with you and will reveal Himself to you. Abandonment and confidence—here are two key elements of true spirituality.

When you realize that your desire for God is the most passionate yearning of your heart, you're in the spiritual condition to recognize God's hand when He makes it visible.

Let me paraphrase Naomi's words when she heard that Ruth had caught the eye of Boaz. "The Lord has not discarded me. He has always been there, but now I can see His kind heart at work. My pain is still real. I've felt it keenly for ten years. But now something matters more. I'm beginning to recognize the shape of a dream that is bigger than every dream I have so far valued."

That's the testimony of Naomi, the same woman who earlier had said, "God killed my family, and I'm miserable." She lost what she had been depending on for joy. But she never deadened her pain. In her agony, she discovered a deeper longing, a desire for God. She did not give herself over to lesser pleasures. She refused to settle for inferior joy. She did not become an addict. When God moved, her heart leaped.

But, as is so often the case, when God began to visibly move in Naomi's life, He did not create a smooth path. There was more Naomi needed to learn before she could worship. Through the agony of shattered dreams, her soul was ripped open so she could discover her desire for God. Now she needed to discover God's desire for her. That's what happens next in her story.

CHAPTER TEN

THE ELUSIVE GOD

All of us are trapped by addiction to a desire for something less than God. For many women, that something less is relational control. "I will not be hurt again and I will not let people I love be hurt. I'll see to it that what I fear never happens." They therefore live in terror of vulnerably presenting themselves to anyone and instead become determined managers of people. Their true femininity remains safely tucked away behind the walls of relational control.

More common in men is an addiction to nonrelational control. "I will experience deep and consuming satisfaction without ever having to relate meaningfully with anyone." They keep things shallow and safe with family and friends and feel driven to experience a joy they never feel, a joy that only deep relating can provide. Their commitment is twofold: to never risk revealing inadequacy by drawing close to people and, without breaking that commitment, to feel powerful and alive. Power in business and illicit sex are favorite strategies for reaching that goal.

The only cure for addiction is the gospel. We will not find the power to resist the pull toward lesser desires until we discover a more powerful desire that we long to fulfill, a desire the Spirit creates within our hearts when the Father forgives us. We must discover our desire for God. As we discover that desire, we come to see that we cannot pursue God and a lesser source of pleasure at the same time. The desire for God and the desire for anything else are competitive. Only one can serve as the guiding rule of life.

When we attempt to serve two masters, we end up bowing before the one who is more apparently responsive to our needs and hating the other. An hour of pornography reaps more immediate dividends than an hour of prayer. It's only play money, but it looks real. And it does buy pleasure on demand. Prayer doesn't do that.

We will not win the battle against addiction without discovering our desire for God. Therefore, if you want to know God, welcome shattered dreams. Nothing reveals our desire for Him so effectively.

But we must also discover God's desire for us. A *recognized* desire for God exposes our idolatry and sets us on a better path. But only a *fulfilled* desire for God provides the power to consistently resist the lure of lesser pleasures and to stay anchored in Christ when life's storms rage. The branch must draw life from the vine or it withers and dies.

Will I Find Him?

Many Christians long to experience God in ways that empower them to relate lovingly and live morally, but it never really happens. So they continue in their addictions, privately feeling ashamed, weak, and frustrated. *How do we experience the reality of God?* This is the most important question a Christian can ask.

It isn't easily answered. When we discover our desire for God, we're immediately introduced to a new kind of pain. We experience the terrifying dread that we will not find Him.

It was really much easier when we were satisfied with lesser things. One of my happiest friends is a successful businessman with an attractive wife who stays busy with clubs and shopping trips, three kids who are each athletic, bright, and good-looking, and enough money to take the family to the Bahamas for seven days one month and to hunt for a week in Alaska the next. He wonders why I struggle so much. He goes to church. He loves God. He can't figure out why I make Christianity so difficult.

Until we realize how badly we need God, how empty we are without Him, we can sing "Great Is Thy Faithfulness" without worrying about whether God really shows up. We can enjoy a happy indifference to whether we discover Him.

For many people, things go well. They feel pretty good. The wonderful truth that God is faithful means to them that He will keep their lives moving along pleasantly. When their path hits a bump, they pray and things get better.

They know God can do something, and He does. Why does God seem to provide so well for the pleasantly committed and to withdraw from the seriously committed? It's enough to make us wonder if we've washed our hands of lukewarm Christianity in vain.

In Exodus, every time the Israelites complained, God blessed them. He straightened things out. Bitter water became sweet, meat and bread rained down from heaven when they told Moses they were hungry. But in Numbers, when they were farther along on their trek to Canaan, God changed tactics. Most often He refused to bless them. When they grumbled about manna, God gave them meat that produced serious indigestion. The next time they fussed about His inadequate provisions, He sent deadly snakes to bite and kill them.

Who wants to become mature? Answered prayer seems to be more frequently reported among younger Christians.

God, it appears, accommodates our immaturity not to keep us there, but to give us a confidence in His Presence that will sustain the search for a deeper, more relational expression of His Presence. The farther we travel on our spiritual journey, the less responsive God becomes to our requests for a pleasant life. Things go wrong and God does nothing. He becomes the elusive God. He is inviting us to an experience with Him that is more fulfilling than an experience with anyone else.

Live long enough and important dreams will shatter. Things will go wrong that God will not fix. He could fix them, but He doesn't.

Then, when the pain of unmet desires puts us in touch with how desperately we long to discover the gentle Presence in our lives, we become more aware of His absence. From deep places in our being that we never knew were there when life was pleasant, we cry out, "God, where are You? Do You care? *Let me find You!*"

God used to let people find Him differently than He does today. Moses actually heard Him say, "My Presence will go with you." Paul was stopped in his tracks by an audible voice from heaven. He fell to the ground and was struck blind by a brilliant light. John, on an island called Patmos, saw a vision of heaven as clearly as I can see cars in the parking lot outside the coffee shop where I'm writing. That vision left no room for doubt: John *knew* that the real world is not what we normally see.

Those men had experiences of God I've never had. I've never heard God speak audibly. I've never been blinded by heavenly light and then miraculously healed a few days later. I've never seen seven golden lampstands circling a man with eyes like fire and a sharp sword coming out of his mouth. Have you?

I'm left wondering: What does it mean for you and me, in this day and age, to experience God? It's one thing to discover our desire for God. It's quite another to discover His desire for us, to know with absolute certainty when life is at its worst that His Presence is real, that He is with us, and that He cares.

We're invited to taste the Lord, to somehow catch our elusive God. What does that mean? How do we do it? When we need Him the most, when we scream the loudest for Him to reveal Himself, He seems to pull away. When we most long to sense His presence, we instead feel His absence.

That's the testimony of a great cloud of witnesses. Let me give just one example. As she lay dying a prolonged and miserable death from tuberculosis at age twenty-four, Terese of Lisieux, one of God's choicest and sweetest saints, desired God with all her heart. Out of the agony of her dark night, she cried:

> And now all of a sudden, the mists around me have become denser than ever; they sink deep into my soul and wrap it round…everything has disappeared.
>
> I get tired of the darkness all around me.… I hear the mocking accents: "It's all a dream, this talk of a heavenly country, bathed in light, scented with delicious perfumes, and of a God who made it all, who is to be your possession for eternity! You really believe, do you, that the mist which hangs about you will clear away later on? All right, all right, go on longing for death! But death will make nonsense of your hopes; it will only mean a night darker than ever, the night of mere non-existence."[3]

Terese had discovered her desire for God as few have. Did she also discover God's desire for her? Have you? Have I?

HE IS WHISPERING

We must begin our answer by appealing not to experience but to truth. The Bible is clear. God exists. He exists in heaven. He exists on earth. He exists everywhere. Most important, He exists *in* us. That's where He is most personally and satisfyingly discoverable.

The life of the Trinity flows in our being (Colossians 2:9-10). Christ is in us (Colossians 1:27). The Spirit has entered us and taken up permanent residence (1 Corinthians 3:16). The Father and Son have made Their home in everyone who loves Jesus, and They promise to let us know They're there (John 14:23).

Our search for God is therefore an *inward* search. Silence and solitude are essential to discovering His Presence. We must block out the noise of life and become aware of our interior world if we're to find God. Beneath every heartache, beneath every moral failure, beneath every shattered dream, a divine Presence is waiting to be discovered.

Why then do so few find Him? Because He is hidden.

Like a city after an earthquake, God's Presence is hidden beneath the rubble of the Fall. Look inside. An honest look will first reveal the rubble of our efforts to make life work without God, of our terror that keeps us from naked vulnerability to anyone, of our construction project that has created a false self that we hope will stay together through life.

This is the rubble of dust and stone that hides the Presence. We live in sheer dread of giving up control and abandoning ourselves to God. Only when we discover a desire for Him that is stronger than our desire for relief from pain will we pay the price necessary to find Him.

If we're to encounter the divine Presence, we must enter the interior sanctuary of our heart and, like Jesus in the temple, become indignant over what we find. There is no way to God but through the rubble. We must go through, not around, whatever keeps us from Him. The process is what spiritual people call brokenness and repentance.

That does not mean, of course, that we should dwell every minute on what is difficult in our lives. We would get nothing done and be good to no one if we did. More often, we should lighten up, enjoy what's enjoyable, and seize everyday opportunities to trust God and do good.

But we must let our souls live in a private monastery, in an attitude of contemplation that helps us see that all of life is sacred, where we remain alert to the Spirit's revelation of ourselves and God. When life gets tough and God does nothing, the Spirit is telling us that this world is not our home. He is whispering to us about another world and revealing Someone who is faithfully leading us there along the best path. And He is exposing the rubble that must be cleared away.

If we fail to be quiet enough to hear *all* that the Spirit is saying, we will be in danger of discovering our desire for God and never discovering His desire for us. When that happens, the Christian comes as close as he ever will to hell.

I mentioned a few chapters back a dear friend who was about to enter the hospital to have a tumor evaluated. It is now several months later. Her dreams of a quick and successful resolution have been shattered. The invasive procedure necessary for a clear diagnosis caused complications that should have taken her life. The tumor remains, better understood but entirely untreated. No treatment can begin till her body recovers from the traumatizing measures that kept her alive. So she waits, with a tumor, with little strength, and with the tortures of uncertainty.

It is interesting to notice what is most on her mind. "I wonder if I've ever really worshiped?" she recently asked. "I'm not sure if I've ever actually met God the way I think He wants us to meet Him. But I do know this: I want to meet Him as never before."

She has discovered her desire for God. Shattered dreams have done their work. Now she is struggling to find an elusive God.

She will find Him. She is closer now than ever to a willingness to make no demands, to sacrifice everything she holds dear for the privilege of resting in the Father's Presence. She is moving through the rubble in her soul. Her appetite for God has been aroused. The Spirit is moving. The days of her addiction to relational control are nearly over.

What happens next? How will God appear? How will she know when He does? What more can she do to create space for Him to enter? How will she describe the experience when God shows up?

A Different Person

The episode in Naomi's life we are about to consider is intended, I believe, as a parable of what it means to experience God. It reveals Naomi as a woman who has discovered a passion in someone else that lets her rest.

When we first met Naomi, she was living the pleasant life of the immature, the good life of the untested. Then her world fell apart. Huge dreams were shattered. We met her then as an honest woman, not a visibly good woman, but an emotional realist. She was heartbroken with life and bitter toward God.

God was moving (*the barley harvest was beginning* when she arrived home), but she couldn't see it. His movement made her more miserable.

Then, *as it turned out,* her daughter-in-law, the widowed Ruth, met Boaz, a rich relative who could make new dreams come true. Naomi's capacity to hope returned. Her desire for God to move in her life was reawakened.

And now, in chapter 3 of the book of Ruth, we meet Naomi again. She is a different woman. With the possibility of Ruth's marriage to Boaz in jeopardy because of what must have seemed to Ruth an obscure legal technicality, Naomi tells her, "Wait, my daughter.... *The man will not rest* until the matter is settled today" (3:18).

Naomi has discovered a good man's passion that lets her soul rest and releases her to be powerful in someone else's life.

When we discover our passion for God, He reveals His passion for us. But that revelation is not the experience we expect. It is not the sort of experience that makes us wave our hands in church and shout about His goodness. If that comes at all, it comes later.

First, we're reduced to exhilarating humility, to an interior darkness, a silencing darkness, that lets us see God in the richest way He can be seen in this life. We will see Him in heaven in ways we cannot see Him now. But we can see Him now in ways that release us to worship and love, even when dreams shatter.

Before I return to Naomi's story and consider how its unfolding drama is a parable, let me discuss the reality it pictures. Let me describe the experience of discovering the Presence of God.

CHAPTER ELEVEN

ABANDONMENT AND CONFIDENCE

During his long months of cold imprisonment, St. John of the Cross became acutely conscious of how badly he yearned to feel the Presence of God. He had been betrayed by his peers, his ministry lay in shambles, and he was confined to a barbaric dungeon. From depths in his soul that only pain can reach, he cried out:

> Where have you hidden,
> Beloved, and left me groaning?
> You fled like a stag
> having wounded me;
> I went out in search of you, and you were gone.

But his dark night of unmet longing for God became the occasion for a visit from Christ. He described his encounter with the divine in words that leave us at once bewildered and panting:

Flame, alive, compelling,
yet tender past all telling,
reaching the secret centre of my soul!

Burn that is for my healing!
Wound of delight past feeling!
Ah, gentle hand whose touch is a caress,
Foretaste of heaven conveying
and every debt repaying:
slaying, you give me life for death's distress.

O lamps of fire bright-burning
with splendid brilliance, turning
deep caverns of my soul to pools of light!
Once shadowed, dim, unknowing,
now their strange new-found glowing
gives warmth and radiance for my Love's delight.

Ah! Gentle and so loving
you wake within me, proving
that you are there in secret and alone;
your fragrant breathing stills me,
your grace, your glory fills me
so tenderly your love becomes my own.[4]

It is possible to meet God. He *does* visit people in this life. We *can* experience His Presence. Self-aware people want nothing more.

THE SPACE GOD ENTERS

We hear a lot these days about the "spiritual" life. Contemplative prayer is making a comeback among ordinary Christians. Evangelicals are tiring of a half-hour of contrived worship on Sunday morning and forty minutes of a motivational talk disguised as a sermon. Increasing numbers of hungry people are going away on silent retreats, aware of an unsatisfied longing for God and sincerely wanting to meet Him. Protestants are turning to Catholic priests and nuns to find spiritual direction. Fasting, solitude, and other spiritual disciplines are commonly practiced. Small groups devoted to spiritual formation and to journeying together toward God are entered into by folks who want more spiritual reality in their lives.

Counseling as a technical specialty where professional experts treat diagnosable disorders is yielding to an encounter between two people where soul care is more the focus than psychological treatment. The same problems are addressed—eating disorders, sexual abuse, family dysfunction, anxiety, and depression—but with the view that spiritual emptiness is the root problem and spiritual reality is the cure.

More than ever before in my lifetime, people are self-consciously hungry for God, for spiritual renewal, for deep satisfaction of the soul. And we are more in danger than ever before of managing our search and discovering a spirituality without Christ.

The search to discover God requires that we *abandon* ourselves, that we give up control of what matters most, and that we place our *confidence* in Someone we cannot manage. These requirements are as vital as they are difficult.

As we respond to our desire for God by looking for Him, we make a fundamental assumption, one that is true but one that can easily be taken for granted. It is this: *God can be experienced.* We assume that our job is to put ourselves in line to experience Him, to practice whatever spiritual exercises are necessary, then to wait for Him to make an appearance. And we assume, with more than a touch of arrogance, that He will. As one Carmelite priest put it, "Where God finds space, He enters."[5] We hear that and agree, then set about making it happen.

I've often done all I know to do to create space for God. I've spent time in prayer I thought was contemplative, I've said no to lesser desires to make room for rich fulfillment, I've knelt before God with the bread and wine before me, I've prostrated myself on the floor and agonized before God in tears—and, for all my effort, I've felt only increased emptiness. Frustration. Silence. I created space for God and He didn't fill it.

Or did He, in ways I failed to recognize because I was expecting something else? Or didn't He, because I was arrogantly working hard, thinking He would be impressed and compelled to show up?

Where God finds space, He does enter. He told Israel that if they sought Him with all their heart, He would let them find Him (Jeremiah 29:12-14). In Solomon's romantic song, the groom was filled with desire for his bride and ran toward her. Whether or not the Spirit intended us to see Christ in that story, we aren't wrong for letting our minds drift to the ultimate story of romantic love: Christ passionately loves His church.

Of course God enters space when He finds it. His delight is to be with us and in us, to experience a kind of intimacy that only sexual union can picture.

But there's the rub. Our deepest experience of relational pleasure is often sexual release. We therefore expect union with God to be as physically real as an orgasm. We fail to realize that spiritual pleasure and physical pleasure have both similarities and differences. Too many churches try to re-create the felt intensity of physical pleasure and call it worship. Their efforts properly stir our senses but never reach our spirits.

In our shallow, sensual way of looking at life, we tend to measure God's Presence by the kind of emotion we feel. Happy feelings that make us want to sing, we assume, are evidence that God's Spirit is present. We think a sense of lostness or confusion or struggle indicates His absence.

But the Spirit's invitation to experience God appeals to something deeper than easily produced emotions. It appeals to a capacity of soul that in many modern Christians has dried up through disuse, a capacity that carries us toward a higher dimension than mere emotions can reach.

A SILHOUETTE BECOMING CLEAR

Throughout church history, spiritual guides have been instructing us to *abandon* ourselves to God and to stay alert to a developing *confidence* in His kindness. Our culture has cheapened the meaning of these words.

The idea of abandoning ourselves to God has been reduced to a technique that allows us to retain the illusion that God can be maneuvered by what we do. And the urging to risk confidence in His kindness has been trivialized to mean only that we should feel good. Let me explain.

First, *abandonment has been reduced to technique.* We want to know what we're supposed to do that will get the spiritual results we want. Seminars on centering prayer and books on spiritual disciplines, though often presenting vital truth, can appeal to our desire not to discover God but to control Him. Spiritual activities can become spiritual maneuvers designed to make something happen.

But true abandonment, giving ourselves to God in utter dependence on His willingness to give Himself to us, pleads only mercy. It allows no room for control. It includes no claim on God that obligates Him to do anything. Only suffering has the power to bring us to this point.

When abandonment becomes technique, we assume we have influence that we do not have. A sales technique does more than present someone with the chance to buy something; it intends to persuade someone to make the purchase.

Presenting an opportunity for God to respond is a different matter altogether from persuading Him to respond. Followers of Christ live under His mercy always. We serve at His pleasure, not ours. We have no technique in our arsenal of spiritual disciplines that can persuade God to schedule an appearance. God has no booking agent. There is nothing we can do to *make* Him show up. We merely invite. God chooses whether to respond. We are entirely dependent on what He wants to do, on what kind of Person He is.

The realization of that dependence opens us to discovering His desire for us. As long as we depend on our maneuvering to experience His Presence, we will look more at how we're doing and obsess more over what we can do to win His cooperation other than wait humbly and broken, eager above all else to discover His character as He reveals it to us.

Second, *confidence in God is not best described as a pleasant emotional experience.* Confidence in a chair to bear one's weight can be easily felt. Just sit. Take a load off your feet. You'll feel better.

Confidence in God is not quite the same. It involves an experience that takes us beyond the realm of our five senses. It calls on our capacity to experience spiritual, not material, reality. Spirit-created confidence is a beyond-words awareness of unseen reality, an awareness of a Presence that is not sensually felt, at least not primarily, an awareness that emerges out of deep pain as Warm Truth, and becomes more real as pain grows deeper.

When in the middle of terrible pain we cry out to God, He rarely grants an experience that, with our five senses, we can recognize as God showing up. The Presence of God is not naturally discerned. But as we abandon ourselves more to Him (What else can we do when we discover that He is all we want?), a confidence emerges, a sense of His Presence, that only the awakened spiritual capacities of the soul can identify.

I can't express it better than Iain Matthew. That confidence, he writes,

> is a presence that emerges from within, from behind; as if one entered a room and sat there on one's own; then, after some minutes, yes there is someone there, has always been, a silhouette becoming clear. It is a kind of companionship and inner strength which walks with the soul and gives her strength, a presence that is gentle, imperceptible, dark, which evaporates if one tries to describe it...but which sustains life.[6]

To the degree that pain teaches us that our deepest desire is for God, we will abandon ourselves to Him. We'll do whatever it takes to create an awareness of space in our souls that only He can fill. And in His mercy, we'll find a confidence developing that He *is* there, that He has indeed entered our space. We may not sing, but we will believe. We will rest. Eventually we will sing. That's a guarantee.

The soul's capacity to abandon itself to God and to enjoy confidence in Him is a capacity that the Spirit's companionship inspires. It develops most fully when our capacity for lesser pleasures is frustrated. Shattered dreams give us the chance to discover our desire for God and then to create space for Him (abandonment) and to watch Him enter (confidence). As that process slowly unfolds, we become aware of God's desire for us.

Naomi's story offers a powerful illustration of what it means to abandon ourselves to God with confidence that He is there. It's a parable that may help us to depend more completely on God and to discover His desire for us. As I pick up the narrative in the next chapter, I pray that's what happens. No one can make it happen, but we can ask for it.

CHAPTER TWELVE

HIS PASSION
RESTRAINED

There are times in life when it would be easier to not believe in God at all than to believe in Him and wonder where He is.

A friend's wife tried to take her life. Their older daughter had died two years earlier in a car wreck. Their only son was in a drug rehab unit, fighting his addiction to cocaine. His wife could no longer bear the pain.

As we talked the day after her suicide attempt, he said, "If God lets her die, I don't know how I'll ever be able to trust Him for anything again."

Had he been a womanizer or his wife an alcoholic, I could have more easily dismissed his comment as an irreverent, unwarranted attack on God. If you smoke cigarettes for thirty years, don't blame God when you get lung cancer.

But these folks were sincerely good Christian people who had faithfully served God in ministry for their entire adult lives. Instead of defending God, I wanted to throttle Him. My friend's words seemed eminently reasonable. They made me want to grab God by the shoulders, shake Him till He paid attention, then tell Him to do a better job of caring for His children, to treat these people more fairly, to let up on them a little bit.

I know my reaction is wrong. I know God is God and I'm not. I know He's never promised a rose garden till heaven. I know I'm to believe that behind the scenes a good plan is unfolding. I know I'm called to live for His glory no matter what happens. But sometimes it's hard.

I am discovering that I cannot turn *from* these despairing thoughts that God is uninvolved until I have a better idea of who I'm turning *toward*. If I could see His face, if I could see passionate love coming out of His eyes, perhaps I could rest in the middle of shattered dreams.

Throttling God! The image is as ridiculous as it is insubordinate. But what's the alternative? Are we expected to experience God as unresponsive to our well-being and pretend we like Him anyway? Things that matter deeply to us don't seem to matter to Him. What are we to do with that fact? I find it hard to take comfort in God's commitment to His own glory when it doesn't seem to involve enough interest in me.

My friend with the troubled family put it disturbingly well. "When God does so little about things that matter so much to me, I have no categories for understanding God's statement that He loves me. I know Calvary is God's supreme expression of His love. I'm grateful that my sins are forgiven and I'm going to heaven. And I know all these troubles are somehow useful for good purposes, maybe necessary for making me a more godly person. But I can't get past the thought that real love wouldn't let me suffer like this."

Everyone agrees: Love implies a concern for another's burdens that translates into action. No action? No love! Praying can feel like furiously pressing the "call nurse" button dangling by your hospital bed. Is she drinking coffee? Finishing another chapter in an absorbing novel? I know she may be busy with someone else. But it's hard to think of an absent nurse as caring.

THE CAKE IS CUT

What then are the options to mounting an assault on an unresponsive God? I see only three.

1. *Dismiss Him, turn from bad thoughts about Him to no thoughts at all.* You don't have to reject God, just dismiss Him as irrelevant. Handle life as best you can with your own resources. Do whatever helps you function well and feel better. Define the morality of your choices by their immediate and felt effect. That's the easiest option.

2. *Confess anger at God and frustration with how He handles things as blasphemous irreverence and heinous rebellion.* Grab yourself by the shoulders rather than God. How dare you talk like that to God! Remind yourself what is true, that God is the Almighty Sovereign Lord of the Universe, then kneel before Him.

Of course that's the right thing to do. Why then does it feel like crawling into a small, dark box of uncomplaining submission? Why, when we bow before Him, do we feel more like a chastened criminal crouching in a windowless cell than a liberated slave dancing in the meadow?

What many call the Christian life is lifeless surrender to a system they cannot fight, coupled with an attempt to convince themselves they love the Judge. That seems the hardest option. It requires that I smother my soul, that I kick the life out of myself in order to get along with God.

3. *Scream and holler until the terror of life so weighs you down that you discover solid ground beneath your feet.* The solid ground is not doctrine. It is not merely truth to believe. It is not recommitment and trying harder to believe and do right. It is *Him*. It is our awareness of a Christ whose passion to bless is so strong that His restraint becomes not a cause for complaint, but a sacred and appealing mystery.

Solid ground beneath the pain of shattered dreams is the revelation of a mystery; it is the realization that *it's more difficult for Christ to restrain Himself from making all our dreams come true than for us to watch them shatter.* At our moment of worst pain, Jesus' pain is worse.

He could make everything better. Limited power is not the problem. He is right now holding Himself back from showering us with every conceivable blessing. Imagine what Jesus must feel as He stands next to every bed in every hospital. With a word, He could cure every patient. What must He feel as He observes every divorce proceeding in every court? He could do something. Most often He does nothing. The mystery is why.

Once our feet touch the solid ground of His passion for us, we can neither dismiss Him as uncaring nor cringe before Him as a ruthless despot.

He is not mad at us. He is not indifferent. He is not helpless. And His commitment to His own glory ensures our joy because He glorifies Himself by revealing His character—and His character is love.

Jesus is filled with desire for us. He is right now cutting the cake, eagerly awaiting the Father's signal to clear away the vegetables and bring on the dessert.

If we believed that, we would rest. We would still hurt, sometimes we would scream, occasionally (but never as a lifelong pattern) we would sin to feel the relief of momentary pleasure, but we would rest. Without effort, like a drowning man yielding to his rescuer after receiving a blow to the head, we would abandon ourselves to God and discover a deep confidence in Him forming in our souls.

If we believed it.

To help us believe (Lord, I *do* believe. Help my unbelief!), the Spirit has recorded an episode from Naomi's life that illustrates the point He wants us to believe, that *in the middle of our shattered dreams, Jesus is restraining Himself, for reasons we cannot fully understand, from ending our pain.*

Rather than sorting through His reasons for holding back, we're encouraged to focus on the passion that makes it difficult for Him not to swoop down in power and solve all our problems. A close look at what Naomi told Ruth might help us see that our unresponsive God is really a restrained lover.

HE WILL NOT REST

Picture what happened. Boaz, a middle-aged bachelor, wealthy, a devoted follower of Shaddai, wakes up one night at two in the morning and sees a beautiful foreign girl lying at his feet. Perhaps it was her delicate perfume that aroused him. He rubs his eyes, thinking it's a good dream, then looks again. There she is, dressed in alluring clothing and making a clear statement: "I am available to become your wife."

He recognizes her at once as the peasant woman he'd met earlier. Ruth had caught his eye. Boaz had felt immediately drawn, both by her character (he knew of her loyalty to Naomi) and by her youthful beauty. Apparently his tactful advances to her in the fields had struck a chord. Here she was, cleaned up and pretty, presenting herself to him.

Boaz wanted Ruth. The writer allows no question about that. He wanted to call the rabbi, exchange vows, and take her to bed. If I were writing a steamy novel, I would describe in lurid detail his sexual attraction to Ruth.

The description would be accurate. But his passion, though including physical desire, is deeper, richer, more enduringly passionate than fleeting, easily satisfied lust. The inspired writer tells the story of a man who strongly desires a woman. The picture of Christ is hard to miss.

But there's a problem. The law stands between Boaz and Ruth. Jewish law stipulated that the nearest relative had the first right of refusal to marry his relative's widow and assume responsibility for the bereaved family. Boaz was related to Naomi (and so to Ruth), but there was another man more closely related.

Like an honorable lover refusing to enjoy the pleasures of sex until the covenant of marriage was sealed, Boaz withheld himself from Ruth. He actually moved away from her, giving her the noble gift of his absence until he could be with her without dishonor.

Boaz knew the law of the kinsman-redeemer. To marry a relative's widow and restore her to blessing, the candidate must satisfy three criteria. One, he must be a relative, the closest relative willing to assume the role of kinsman-redeemer. Two, he must have the means to pay the entire debt owed by the widow and her family. Three, he must have the power to remove anyone who wanted to remain on the widow's property after all debts were paid.

Ruth, at best vaguely familiar with Jewish law, was aware only that Boaz was withholding himself from her. She must have worried that he didn't really want her. She had discovered her desire for Boaz but was not yet confident of his desire for her.

I picture Naomi sitting on the floor of their little house, warming herself by the fire on a chilly morning. Ruth returns from her night with Boaz, still wearing her prettiest dress but no longer feeling beautiful.

"Naomi, what shall I do? I love Boaz and I think he loves me. But he said he can't marry me until some legal problem is cleared up. Oh, Naomi, I don't know anything about all those technicalities. All I know is that I want him. I don't want anyone else. I want *him*. Doesn't he want me?"

Naomi sits quietly. She knows. Her heart is at rest, quietly thumping with anticipation.

I've often wondered if it occurred to Naomi to suggest Ruth dress in an old rag, work up a sweat, and present herself the next night to the nearest relative. Maybe that would move them through the legal impasse.

Instead, with the wisdom of a spiritual director, she longs for Ruth to *abandon* herself to the heart of one who loves her, with *confidence*—in spite of his restraint—that his desire will find a way to bring them together.

"Ruth," Naomi says, "Boaz wants you more than you want him. He is withholding himself from you for a time at great personal cost. It is harder for him to keep his distance from you than it is for you to wait for him. Know this, that this man will move heaven and earth to find a lawful way to marry you. And that's what you want, a legal marriage that rests on an unshakable foundation. You want nothing less. Wait, my daughter. *The man will not rest* until the matter is settled today."

Your wife tried to kill herself. Your husband left you. You thought life would get easier once the ugly split with your partner was over. Then the other shoe dropped. You woke up to the realization that your father is disappointed in you, that your friend isn't the friend you thought she was, that your life is not turning out the way you'd hoped.

Perhaps Naomi's words to Ruth can become the Spirit's words to us.

"Wait, my child, your Heavenly Bridegroom is consumed with desire for you.

"For reasons you cannot now understand, He is holding Himself back from filling your life with every imaginable pleasure. He could do what you're asking Him to do.

"When He appears to do nothing, to leave you in your pain and provide no relief, realize this: *The Man will not rest till He makes everything good.*

"In the mystery of suffering, enter the deeper mystery of His restrained passion. As the mother holds her baby still so the doctor can deliver the needed injection, so your Lord is allowing you to suffer for reasons you do not know.

"Don't try to find comfort in explaining the reasons. Don't try to find the spiritual means to trust more. Enter your pain until your feet touch the solid ground beneath you, the solid ground of the restrained passion of Jesus.

"I, the Spirit of Christ, will reveal His passion to you. Create space for Me to fill by waiting, by abandoning yourself to God. When I allow you to discover His desire for you, you will rest with confidence in His love."

We are now in a better position to enter into the meaning of our Lord's words to people whose dreams have shattered: "Don't let your hearts be troubled."

Naomi's words to Ruth are a parable of our Lord's words to us. Both the parable and the reality can be brought into sharper focus by understanding the Jewish customs of marriage in our Lord's day. As I describe them in the next chapter, stay alert to the Spirit's speaking to the secret recesses of your soul, empowering you to believe that Jesus' restraint is a greater mystery than your suffering.

CHAPTER THIRTEEN

A HELL OF MERCY

Gods restraint has a purpose. When He appears to be doing nothing, He is doing something we've not yet learned to value and therefore cannot see. Only in the agony of His absence, both in the real absence of certain blessings and in the felt absence of His Presence, will we relax our determined grasp of our empty selves enough to appreciate His purposes.[7]

He could do something. Yet He does nothing, at least not what we ask Him to do. Why? To deepen our desire for His Presence, to strengthen our passion to pursue Him, to help us see how preoccupied we are with filling our God-shaped souls with something less than God.

Only when we want Him as we want nothing else will there develop in our hearts a space large enough for Him to fill. Because He longs to fill us, He hides His face long enough for us to discover how fervently and exclusively we want Him. When our discovery creates a secret space that nothing else can fill, and when we know that to be true, He enters.

Through the pain of shattered dreams, God is awakening us to the possibility of infinite pleasure. That is the nature of our journey; it's what the Spirit is doing. When we understand that, we'll define "doing well" on this journey very differently than before. We'll come to see that the experience of a woman waiting for her man to come take her away to a better place is a clear picture of true spirituality.

That picture, which the story of Naomi presents, changes most of our expectations for what this life will be like. Let me explain.

SOUL DISTANCE

"I'm tired of doing great." These were the words of a man who had recently suffered an enormous loss. His friends were concerned and supportive.

They sent books on handling grief (I've never liked the term "grief management"; grief can only be embraced, never managed). They spent time with him both in prayer and on the golf course. Several sent letters expressing their love; a few included verses from the Bible they said had been impressed on them by the Lord.

When his friends called or came to visit, the first question after a quick greeting was always "How are you doing?"

He hated the question the first time he heard it and hated it more each time he heard it again. He knew the "right" answer, the one his friends were hoping to hear, the one that had more to do with relieving their concern than with expressing his own heart. The hoped-for answer could be expressed in many ways, but its message was always the same: "It's hard, but I'm okay, or at least getting there."

To the last person who asked, he put the message in these words: "Well, it's still really hard. I miss her so much. Sometimes I worry how I'll manage. But I'm not breaking down as often now. And I'm going out more and getting back to all I need to be doing. Guess I'm moving in the right direction. Thanks for asking."

His words had their intended effect. The questioner smiled with relief and said, "I'm really glad. Not surprised, though. Lots of us have been praying."

I notice three things in this exchange.

> 1. The man's friend assumed prayer has more to do with getting someone to feel better than with pleading for movement along the path into God's Presence.

> 2. He further assumed that if the Spirit were doing His work, the suffering man would indeed feel better. Doing great on the path to God means feeling great—or at least feeling better. That's what most of us think.

> 3. He distanced himself from the sorrowing man's soul. Without consciously intending to, he let the man know that he did not want to be with him in his pain, he wanted rather to be with him only as an agent of improvement.

As the struggling man listened to his friend, he felt a tidal wave of intense loneliness sweep over him. He returned the smile but his soul shriveled behind a familiar wall that left him lifeless, more desperate and alone than before.

We spoke a few hours later. He recounted the conversation and described his reaction to it. That's when he said, "I'm tired of doing great. Just yesterday, I overheard two of my friends talking about me. One asked how I was doing. The other said I was doing great. I wanted to scream."

When life kicks us in the stomach, we want someone to be with us as we are, not as he or she wishes us to be. We don't want someone trying to make us feel better. That effort, no matter how well intended, creates a pressure that adds to our distress.

Why is it so difficult to simply give ourselves to each other when things are hard without yielding to the urge to give relief, to help, to try to make things better?

A Different Journey

Kicks in the stomach come in so many ways. Last night, a close friend gently let me know how I had earlier discouraged her with an insensitive comment. I was again brought close to my capacity for unkindness. The kick was delivered not by my friend, but by that evil capacity staring me in the face.

If you were to ask me right now, the morning after, how I'm doing, I would answer, "I feel empty. I'm discouraged with myself. I feel utterly dependent on God to do something with me, to make me the person I long to be. I hate hurting people, and I seem to do it most to those I love. Sometimes I wonder if I'll ever love well."

After hearing those words, would you report to a mutual friend that "Larry's doing great"? Or, a second option, would you worry about me, perhaps try to cheer me up by reminding me that we all fail, that many folks would say I've encouraged them? Would you think I'm doing poorly?

If your response were the latter, you would not stir me to love and good deeds; you would drive me into a prison of loneliness that I would lock from the inside to prevent you from entering.

The man who suffered loss told me that he was crying far more often than anyone knew. He felt sorely tempted to give up on God. He wished he were dead.

Both he and I, though many would think we're doing poorly, are in fact doing well. The reason is that we're both on the spiritual, not the secular, journey.

It makes no sense to say that someone on the secular journey is feeling terrible but doing great. But on the spiritual journey there are seasons when doing great *requires* that we feel awful.

The secular journey ends in this life. This world is home to secularists. They are not pilgrims passing through; they are citizens settling down.

Those on the spiritual journey, however, believe they were not designed to live as people who do bad things in a world where bad things happen. Unlike secularists, their *primary* purpose is neither to enjoy this life nor the people they meet, nor themselves; it is rather to enjoy God.

The person on the secular journey is doing well when he gets over a tough patch and stops crying so much, when he regains hope that life offers many pleasures and learns to manage its challenges well. A *troubled* heart on the secular journey views this life as disappointing and feels a guilt that shreds self-confidence. A *healthy* secular heart likes living here and feels good about how effectively that life is being lived. Recovery from a troubled to a healthy heart is the goal of secular counseling and secular religion.

The spiritual journey is different. Doing great on the journey to God involves sensing an appetite that is never fully satisfied, an appetite for everything to always go well ("Unrealistic!" the earthbound realist snorts), a relentless desire to be a kind of person no one is ("Perfectionist!" the psychologist declares), a longing to experience God deeply enough to keep moving toward Him no matter what happens ("Opiate addiction!" Marx opines; Freud agrees).

In their anguish, people on the spiritual journey abandon themselves to God. Eventually they discover their desire for Him is stronger than all their other desires, and in their seasons of misery when life disappoints and they fail, they seek Him more earnestly. Making their lives more comfortable and themselves more acceptable is a secondary concern.

For them, a troubled heart is one that has no hope in the middle of shattered dreams. An *un*troubled heart, by Jesus' definition, feels great disappointment with this life and with the way one is relating, but it continues to hope, to wait—eagerly—with confidence in what another is doing. The focus remains on Christ.

Satan's masterpiece is not the prostitute or the skid-row bum. It is the self-sufficient person who has made life comfortable, who is adjusting well to the world and truly likes living here, a person who dreams of no better place to live, who longs only to be a little better—and a little better off—than he already is.

On the secular journey, the one leading to hell, that masterpiece is the person who with an untroubled heart is doing great. For a time.

The Spirit's masterpiece is the man or woman who much prefers to live elsewhere, who finds no deep joy in the good things of this life, who looks closely in the mirror and yearns to see something different, whose highest dream is to be in the Presence of the grace-filled Father. It is the person whose life *here* is consumed with preparing to meet Him *there*.

On the spiritual journey, the one leading to heaven, that masterpiece is the person who with an untroubled heart is doing great. And will forever do far better.

The secular journey is well pictured by the kept woman, the Faustian figure who gives up all hope of soul-pleasure in exchange for intense satisfaction of lesser desires now.

The spiritual journey finds a clear illustration in the Jewish custom of engagement during our Lord's time on earth. When His disciples heard Jesus tell them to not let their hearts be troubled because He would soon go away to prepare a place for them to live together, they would have understood His words against the backdrop of that custom.

LISTEN FOR THE SHOUT

When a first-century Jewish man fell in love with a woman, he would travel from his father's home to hers to seal the engagement.[8] In that culture, an engagement was not what it is today. It wasn't a trial period during which premarital counseling would help the couple decide whether to continue on or break off the relationship. It represented rather a legal contract, complete with a price paid by the groom that set the woman apart exclusively for her man.

They were immediately regarded as husband and wife, irrevocably bound. To symbolize their covenant, each would drink from a cup of wine over which a betrothal benediction had been pronounced. Following that ceremony, the groom would return to his father's home for a period of twelve months. For that entire time, he remained separate from his bride. She would not see him again until it was time to consummate their union.

The bride had one job during his absence—to prepare herself for his coming and for the rest of her life with him. All other activities revolved around that one ruling purpose.

While she waited, she knew what her groom was doing. He was spending the year adding an apartment to his father's home in which they would eventually live together. An honorable man would have an eye for no other woman and would not rest until preparations were made for them to be united. She *would* rest, secure in the knowledge that all the bridegroom's energies were directed toward their being together.

When the engagement year ended, at an exact day and hour that the bride did not know, the groom would gather his wedding party and, in a torch-lit procession, travel to where his bride was living. His arrival would be preceded by a shout from one of his friends, alerting the woman that her groom was arriving.

She was ready. She had no greater dream than his coming and was confident he would arrive to take her to be with him in the home he had prepared. With her attendants, she would travel to that home. When they arrived, she would walk into a party waiting to happen.

Before the celebration began, the bride and groom would be escorted to the bridal chamber where, for the first time, they would express their covenant to each other with physical union. Then the husband would emerge from the room alone, and a seven-day feast would begin. At its conclusion, his wife, unveiled for the first time, would appear and be officially welcomed to her new home as a member of the family.

From then on, the heaven of unhindered intimacy and unrestrained blessing was hers to enjoy.

With that custom in mind, as it was in the minds of the disciples, perhaps we can better hear what our Lord means when He tells us to live now with untroubled hearts.

"I know things are not now as you want them. I know many of your dreams are not coming true. I want you to understand that things are not as I will one day make them. I like neither the distance between us nor the pain you suffer.

"Until I come to bring you to My Father's house, I am devoting Myself to only one thing: I am preparing a place for you. And My Spirit, on My behalf, is devoting Himself to only one thing— preparing you to enjoy Me and all that I will provide.

"I have called you not to the secular journey where you must make everything in your life now as pleasant as possible. I have called you to the spiritual journey, to a process of enlarging your heart to desire Me above everything else.

"Do not be troubled by all the dreams that will shatter while you remain on earth. You will feel deep pain. But every sorrow you experience will be used by My Spirit to deepen your desire for Me. He will speak to you about Me.

"Listen for the voice. You will hear Him most clearly when suffering humbles you enough to want to hear Him, to know you cannot go on without hearing Him.

"This time of distance, when you will feel such disappointment both with your life and with yourself, will awaken your heart to receive Me with great joy when I finally come. I will not delay. I will come at exactly the appointed time.

"My Father will give the signal. Listen for the shout."

And our response is, Come, Lord Jesus; come soon!

Until then, we wait with untroubled hearts. We scream, we cry, we fail, but we wait, abandoned to our Kinsman-Redeemer, to our Boaz, confident that He has paid a price for us that guarantees our eventual intimacy. No one, not even Satan, can prevent us from entering the bridal chamber with Jesus where our *greatest* dream will be realized.

Then, not until, every *good* dream will also come true. The Trinity will pour out every blessing Their infinite imagination can conceive. That will be heaven.

We're not there yet. We sometimes experience now what seems like hell. But it isn't the hell of judgment; it's the hell of mercy, a kind of present purgatory. [9] Shattered dreams subject us to a pain that weakens our stubborn grip on life as we want it and stirs our appetite for the thrill of God's Presence.

Naomi told Ruth to wait because the man who loved her would not rest till all was arranged for them to be together. When we see the heart of Jesus and understand His passion for us, the hell of the spiritual journey becomes the foyer of heaven.

It may be hard, we may hurt and holler, but we're doing great! We can stop pretending we're doing great the way folks on the secular journey understand it. We can rather know that the solid ground of His passion for us is beneath our feet. It's a firm foundation. We need no other, no matter what life may bring, no matter how low we sink in despair or sin.

God will work through it all. Everything helps us to Him.

In the last chapter of Naomi's story, we learn two lessons. First, the work of the Spirit will continue through every bump in the road, through every shattered dream. Second, there is one dream God will fulfill for us now, in this life, before we get to heaven, and its fulfillment will bring us joy. Let me turn our attention to those two lessons.

CHAPTER FOURTEEN

A STRANGE WEDDING TOAST

My first grandson is less than a month away from crying his way into this world. In seven or eight decades, if things go as expected, he will leave this world to enter the next one. Probably with another cry.

What do I wish for him in between?

Soon I will stand over his crib, lift him gently into my arms, and experience the mystery of instant connection. I will sense that unique bond between a grandfather who has lived more years than he has left and a grandson with all of his yet to live.

What prayers will erupt from my heart? What dreams will I beg God to fulfill in the life of that little boy? What requests on behalf of my grandson will I bring to a God who has been unresponsive to so many of mine?

I haven't held him yet; I haven't looked into his eyes. But when I do, I think I know how I'll pray.

"O Lord, cure this child of the fatal moral disease with which he was born. Heal him through the forgiving and cleansing power of Your blood.

"And then, as a beloved child through whom the life of the Trinity will be flowing, guide him through valleys where he will learn to abandon every dream but the dream of knowing You. Grant him dark nights when he feels desperately empty and alone, when he longs to experience a fullness and a joy he cannot provide for himself. In those moments, reveal to him his desire for You and Yours for him. May he abandon his tortured soul to Your seemingly unresponsive care.

"But, please Lord, no more shattered dreams than are absolutely necessary. I do so want his life to be happy and full. Nevertheless, not my will for second things, but Your will for first things be done."

If all goes as expected, my granddaughter, now less than three years along on her journey, will one day marry. If I'm still around to watch my son give this cute little bundle to another man, I wonder what prayers for her will burst from my heart. What dreams will I long to come true as she enters that most mysterious of all human relationships, where both happiness and sorrow run so deep?

I imagine the rehearsal dinner. A younger man will help this crotchety old man to stand. With trembling hand, I'll raise my glass and offer the toast of a doting grandfather. I may not say out loud all that I want to say, but these words will be in my heart:

"O Lord, spare them the pain of divorce. Give them a warm and intimate relationship full of trust and mercy. In Your absence, may they reflect Christ to each other.

"Give them long lives, free of money troubles, free of serious car accidents, free of sickness, especially in their children. Involve them in a good church where friendships are real, where serving Christ is seen as an appealing privilege."

And then, in my vision, I see myself pausing, unsure whether I want to even think the words of the deeper prayer stirring within me.

Of course I want both my granddaughter and grandson to enjoy lives filled with blessings—good relationships, good health, good churches, good incomes. It's just so hard to see all those blessings as second things.

I wonder if I will find the courage to keep my glass raised high and to say:

"May this beautiful young woman, still my treasured little granddaughter, discover that place in her heart where she desires You above everything else. May she discover that place in her heart that only love flowing from Yours can fill.

"*Please*, Lord, shield her from every useless trial, protect her from pointless pain, but—grant me the courage to mean this—allow whatever dreams to shatter that will release her heart to meet Yours, that will empower her to rest in Your ecstatic love, no matter how empty and desperate she may feel.

"Reveal the beauty of Your life to her and through her, whatever it takes. But, Lord, I beg you—be very gentle."

WANTING SOMETHING BETTER

I wonder. Have I found the place in *my* heart that wants something more for my grandson than personal peace (a feeling of interior fullness and comfort) and affluence (at least enough money to live in a nice house and play golf on nice courses)? Do I want something more for him than the good life we Western Christians assume is our due, the good life of not *too* much heartache over aging parents, not *too* much hassle with pain and illness, not *too* much frustration around jobs and money?

Do I want something more for my granddaughter than a satisfying marriage, good-looking and well-behaved children, and sufficient resources for an occasional family trip to Disney World? Do I even believe there is something better?

We so easily pray for ourselves and the people we love that we will all be drawn closer to God. I wonder if we know what we're asking. Are we asking to enjoy His blessings with little interest in enjoying His Person? Not many of us envy Joni Eareckson Tada's special opportunity to know Christ well.

When someone shares his story of shattered dreams, our stomachs tighten with fear lest we should meet a similar fate. We dedicate our strongest efforts to helping that person feel better because we're terrified of ever experiencing deep pain that cannot be relieved.

Why? Why do we undervalue intimacy with Christ? Why does the prospect of becoming like Him and close to Him have less appeal than other good things?

People who spend their lives in the slums, people who have never seen lakes and trees and flowers, suffer from undeveloped imaginations. They wish for nothing better than that their children live in a tenement with uncracked windows and running water and fewer rats. For a hobo, it's really living to ride in a railroad car that doesn't smell.

But God's children are neither slum dwellers nor hobos. We've been empowered to dream bigger dreams than mere earthlings can imagine. In God's eyes, big houses, happy families, and comfortable bank accounts are, in themselves, nothing more than rat-free hovels and disinfected cattle cars.

The finest things this world can offer have no compelling appeal to a reborn spirit. They are as nothing compared to the joy of living in His Presence.

That's how God sees things. It takes some doing for us to see things the same way. It takes shattered dreams.

I think now we can better appreciate the strange toast offered by a religious leader when Boaz and Ruth married. When we understand what he intended, we can see that it's similar to what I expect to pray when I hold my grandson for the first time. And it's not that far off from the toast I may one day propose at my granddaughter's wedding.

WHERE THE BEST DREAMS ARE DREAMED

Before I finish this chapter, let me say just a word about this very strange toast and then, in the next chapter, I'll discuss more fully why I believe the toast was a good one.

Here's what the elder said about Ruth:

> May the LORD make the woman who is coming into your
> home like Rachel and Leah, who together built up the house
> of Israel. (4:11)

Was he hoping that Ruth, like Rachel, would be barren and, in her resentment over the shattered dream of bearing children, insist that Boaz have kids through her servant girl? Did he want Ruth to feel unloved, like Leah, and have all the children she could, thinking that one more child might finally win her husband's love?

Boaz knew Jewish history. He knew the crazy family dynamics that began the nation of Israel. What did he hear when this strange toast was offered?

Before the elder put down his glass, he added:

> Through the offspring the LORD gives you by this young
> woman, may your family be like that of Perez, whom Tamar
> bore to Judah. (4:12)

The first part of the toast was strange enough. This addendum is posi-
tively bizarre. Was he wishing Ruth to disguise herself as a prostitute to
seduce her father-in-law and to bear a child by him? That's what Tamar
did. Perez was one of twin boys born to Tamar after she tricked Judah into
having sex with her.

If at my grandson's dedication I were to pray, "Lord, allow this child's life
to be messed up so You can do the good that can only be done through hard
times," I think the congregation might rise to their feet in unified protest.

If at my granddaughter's wedding I were to propose the toast, "Lord,
may difficulties plague her life so that she discovers a goodness that only
difficulties reveal," I would expect to hear cries of "No! No!" rather than
"Here! Here!"

When the toast was given at the marriage of Boaz and Ruth, I picture
Naomi nodding soberly. She knew the nature of the spiritual journey. She
knew that only the pain of shattered dreams has the power to weaken the
stranglehold of the flesh. She knew that only brokenness provides access to
the depths of the human heart where the best dreams are dreamed.

Perhaps someone approached Naomi after the wedding and said,
"Wasn't that a strange toast? I didn't like it."

I hear Naomi turning to her friend with a look of sad joy and replying:
"In the next life, a different toast will be offered. For this life, the
toast was loving and necessary. I heard the elder wishing that Boaz
and Ruth would develop the wisdom to know that neither human

selfishness nor frailty can thwart God's grand and eternal purposes. He wants them to experience whatever hardships will compel them to abandon themselves to God for good things they can neither see nor provide.

"And I wish the same thing for them. I now know that shattered dreams free us to value what is best; they help us see God's invisible hand moving us toward our deepest joy and moving everything, including our lives, toward Shaddai's greatest glory."

I long for my grandchildren to escape the slums, to climb down from the boxcar and to walk through whatever dark valleys will bring them into God's Presence. I know that no maneuvering, whether through good parenting or spiritual disciplines or psychotherapy or chemical treatment, will enable them to value God's Presence above all other blessings. I realize that only in the experience of emptiness does God's Spirit confront us with the choice either to fill ourselves or to abandon ourselves to a God who leaves us empty for a long time and promises fullness later. I have come to believe that suffering is necessary to awaken our desire for God and to develop confidence in His desire for us.

I therefore pray for myself and the people I love that we will experience the severe mercy of shattered dreams, not because I want any of us to hurt but because I long for every one of us to experience the joy of knowing God's love.

I pray that each of our journeys will carry us into seasons of brokenness.

That prayer requires more explanation. We need more insight into why the very strange toast was very good.

CHAPTER FIFTEEN

BUT LIFE OUGHT TO WORK

Afew days before the Columbine High School shootings, one of the teenagers whose name will be forever associated with that tragedy wrote a poem:

> I'm drowning
> in my own lake of despair.
> I'm choking,
> my hands wrapped around my neck.
> I'm dying.
> Quickly my soul leaves, slowly my
> body withers.
> It isn't suicide,
> I consider it homicide.
> The world you created has led to my death.[10]

Had this poem been found in the diary of one of the shooters, we would have easily and quickly concluded that the sentiments expressed indicated that the writer was abnormally troubled and needed special help.

But it was written by Rachel Joy Scott, a seventeen-year-old girl who, by all reports, was well adjusted and quite normal; troubled perhaps, as all teenagers are, but certainly no threat to grab a gun and kill anyone. A young woman we would all assume was doing just fine.

We tend to hold an unrealistic and twisted view of what is normal, a view challenged by Rachel's poem. Normal people, we think, are untroubled or at least not seriously troubled. They experience no *real* pain, not the kind that tortures the mind to the point where despair seems reasonable. Normal people don't hurt very much. Most of the time, they're doing great.

They come from caring, usually two-parent families; they have learned character and useable knowledge from good schools; they have enjoyed (and still do enjoy) the advantages of special opportunities and the unique talent to make use of them, whether in the classroom or on the athletic field or in the music conservatory.

Normal people, the ones we call healthy, feel good about themselves and about life because they have been enabled by a fortunate mix of blessings to live happily and responsibly. That's what we assume.

Troubled people, on the other hand, the not-so-normal, usually come from broken families, from homes with absent or abusive parents. They have had no scout leader or schoolteacher or youth pastor or caring grandmother who believed in them and helped them make something good out of their lives despite a bad background. They have not been granted the social advantages that help kids turn out well. And their Maker, for no apparent reason, has decided to withhold the blessings of good looks or high IQs or special abilities that could have raised their self-esteem.

That's how we see things. That's why we're surprised that Rachel Scott wrote words of such despair. She was one of the *normal* people, one of the privileged and blessed.

Because this set of ideas is embedded in our collective head, society—especially the government but also the church—has taken on the job of producing more untroubled people and fewer seriously troubled people.

Our method has been remarkably consistent: We work hard to improve people's lives, to help people feel good by seeing to it their dreams come true. We devote our energies to improving circumstances—better homes, better families, better jobs—and when bad circumstances cannot be improved, we work to improve people's ability to cope with hard times. We want people, including ourselves, to feel good.

We focus on second things while God is working on first things.

Politicians use public resources to improve the quality of people's external lives. Religious leaders depend on spiritual resources to improve the quality of our internal lives, to build ethical character and moral habits. Doctors and therapists do all they can to help us recover from damage done to our bodies and souls.

It seems we are devoting our best efforts to one central goal: making this life work better so we can feel better. The unchallenged assumption behind our resolve is a delusion. We assume life is *supposed* to work in ways that make us feel the way we want to feel, the way we intuitively and irresistibly sense we were designed to feel.

We further assume that if there is a God, His job is to do what we cannot do to make life work as we want. We conceive of the spiritual journey as a cooperative enterprise where we pool our resources with God's to see to it that life works well enough to keep us relatively happy till we reach the world where life works perfectly and we always feel great.

According to that thinking, the elder's toast at the wedding of Boaz and Ruth was cruel. The prayers I expect to pray after my grandson is born and when my granddaughter marries are sadistic and mean. And Rachel Scott's poem evidences abnormality that should have received professional attention.

COUNTING ON GOD

Suppose you had been a trusted confidante to Rachel, someone whom she asked to read her poem. What might you have said after reading it? More important, what view of life would have determined your response?

If you believe life is supposed to work well enough for people to feel good, you would have been alarmed by a struggle you could not explain. You might have encouraged her to trust in the God who loved her to make her dreams come true. If she couldn't respond to that encouragement, you might have referred her for counseling.

But suppose you were convinced of a very different understanding of life. Suppose you believe God is *not* committed to making our lives work well enough for us to feel good. What would you say then? Perhaps something like this:

"Rachel, your pain is legitimate. You've discovered the part of your soul that longs for what this world will never provide. Your integrity has burdened you with the severe mercy of realizing that nothing in this world provides true joy.

"You've come to a fork in the road. One path beckons you with the promise that life can work well, and God exists to see to it that things go well enough for you to feel pretty good.

"The other path, the narrow one that not many choose, invites you to live in a disappointing world where good dreams will shatter and you will sometimes feel empty and alone, sometimes so empty and alone that it will seem like death. But this path prom-ises the eventual discovery of a consuming desire within you for God and, far better, the thrilling discovery of His consuming desire to be intimate with you.

"After many dark nights, you will taste the joy of that inti-macy. You will not be able to describe it, but you will feel alive, hopeful, solid, even in the middle of continued anguish over hard circumstances.

"Abandon yourself to God. He will seem at times cruelly unre-sponsive, callously indifferent. You will be tempted to manage life on your own, to do whatever you can to feel better.

"But if you're quiet, you will hear both His voice and yours leading you to the narrow path."

In our deceived culture, we must grasp the truth of what God is now doing in our lives or we will miss the joy of Christianity. God is *not* coop-erating with us to make life work so we can feel now all that He has created us to feel. But many people think He is. They think that's His job.

There are two problems with that view: *One,* better circumstances, whether winning the lottery or saving your marriage, can never produce the joy we were designed to experience. Only an intimate relationship with Perfect Love can provide that joy. *Two,* in this life, we can never feel what God intended us to feel, at least not in full measure. To be completely happy, we must experience perfect intimacy with Perfect Love *and* every "second-thing" blessing that Perfect Love can provide. In this life, we have neither. God will provide both, but not till heaven.

It's hard to hear, but it is important to know that God is *not* commit-ted to supporting our ministries, to preventing our divorces, to preserving our health, to straightening out our kids, to providing a livable income, to ending famine, to protecting us from agonizing problems that generate in our souls an experience that feels like death.

We *cannot* count on God to arrange what happens in our lives in ways that will make us feel good.

We *can* count on God to patiently remove all the obstacles to our enjoyment of Him. He is committed to our joy, and we can depend on Him to give us enough of a taste of that joy and enough hope that the best is still ahead to keep us going in spite of how much pain continues to plague our hearts.

God's intense desire is to intimately relate with us. For His desire to be realized, He must remove the obstacle within us that, more than any other, stands in the way of intimacy with Him. That obstacle is this:

When we feel bad, when our internal experience as we live in this world is different from and less than what we know we were created to feel, we assume there is no higher value than to change that experience. We therefore devote our central energies to feeling better and to justifying whatever does the job.

"Rachel, your pain is legitimate. You've discovered the part of your soul that longs for what this world will never provide. Your integrity has burdened you with the severe mercy of realizing that nothing in this world provides true joy.

"You've come to a fork in the road. One path beckons you with the promise that life can work well, and God exists to see to it that things go well enough for you to feel pretty good.

"The other path, the narrow one that not many choose, invites you to live in a disappointing world where good dreams will shatter and you will sometimes feel empty and alone, sometimes so empty and alone that it will seem like death. But this path promises the eventual discovery of a consuming desire within you for God and, far better, the thrilling discovery of His consuming desire to be intimate with you.

"After many dark nights, you will taste the joy of that intimacy. You will not be able to describe it, but you will feel alive, hopeful, solid, even in the middle of continued anguish over hard circumstances.

"Abandon yourself to God. He will seem at times cruelly unresponsive, callously indifferent. You will be tempted to manage life on your own, to do whatever you can to feel better.

"But if you're quiet, you will hear both His voice and yours leading you to the narrow path."

In our deceived culture, we must grasp the truth of what God is now doing in our lives or we will miss the joy of Christianity. God is *not* cooperating with us to make life work so we can feel now all that He has created us to feel. But many people think He is. They think that's His job.

There are two problems with that view: *One,* better circumstances, whether winning the lottery or saving your marriage, can never produce the joy we were designed to experience. Only an intimate relationship with Perfect Love can provide that joy. *Two,* in this life, we can never feel what God intended us to feel, at least not in full measure. To be completely happy, we must experience perfect intimacy with Perfect Love *and* every "second-thing" blessing that Perfect Love can provide. In this life, we have neither. God will provide both, but not till heaven.

It's hard to hear, but it is important to know that God is *not* committed to supporting our ministries, to preventing our divorces, to preserving our health, to straightening out our kids, to providing a livable income, to ending famine, to protecting us from agonizing problems that generate in our souls an experience that feels like death.

We *cannot* count on God to arrange what happens in our lives in ways that will make us feel good.

We *can* count on God to patiently remove all the obstacles to our enjoyment of Him. He is committed to our joy, and we can depend on Him to give us enough of a taste of that joy and enough hope that the best is still ahead to keep us going in spite of how much pain continues to plague our hearts.

God's intense desire is to intimately relate with us. For His desire to be realized, He must remove the obstacle within us that, more than any other, stands in the way of intimacy with Him. That obstacle is this:

> *When we feel bad, when our internal experience as we live in this world is different from and less than what we know we were created to feel, we assume there is no higher value than to change that experience. We therefore devote our central energies to feeling better and to justifying whatever does the job.*

The *belief* that there's no higher good than feeling better now, and the top priority *urge* to feel better now—these represent the single biggest obstacle to our enjoying God's Presence. The Bible calls it *the flesh.*

THE SPIRIT'S PULL

When life is hard and we feel bad, we turn to God to change things—if not our circumstances then at least our emotions. When He proves unresponsive, we turn from Him to ourselves to find some method of easing the pain.

That's why frustrated men masturbate and men incapable of intimacy have affairs. That's why Christian business folks cut an occasional corner to close the deal. That's why wives demand their husbands be more attentive to them and handle their difficult children with more strength. That's why husbands require their wives to be more sensitive to their struggles and retreat from them when they fail.

That's why sincere Christians lose the energy to worship when dreams shatter and they feel bad.

Life is *not* an opportunity for things to go well so we can feel good. Life *is* an opportunity for us to be forgiven for requiring God to make us feel good and for turning from Him when He doesn't.

And life is an opportunity to live through shattered dreams and discover that we really long to abandon ourselves to the Perfect Love of God, the love revealed when Jesus died. It is an opportunity to trust Him with our experience of emptiness and fear, to trust Him to forgive our resentment over bad things that happen and our determination to feel good with or without Him.

Life is an opportunity to feel the pain that Rachel Scott felt, to realize that what we most deeply want is simply not available in this life, and then to trust God as He purges us of depending on the pleasures that blessings bring.

So far I've lived a reasonably "successful" life. My wife loves me as I love her; my sons are both responsible, godly men of whom I am enormously and gratefully proud; only a few people intensely dislike me, many appreciate my life and ministry, and a treasured handful believe in me despite my failings.

I know what it is to feel good when life works. For that I make no apology. We should enjoy God's blessings; the good things of life should generate good feelings. But I am coming to see something wrong that before I thought was spiritual gratitude: Those good feelings have become my basis for joy. I claim them as my right. I pray they will continue. It's praying from that mind-set that makes God seem so unresponsive.

I can now feel the powerful undertow within me that has long been pulling me out to sea, into cold waters and uncaring waves. That undertow is an attitude insisting that life continue well enough for me to feel pretty good. When dreams shatter, I then feel alone, unloved, and desperate. And I resolve, more than anything else, to feel better. That resolve is the flesh.

But I can also feel gentle arms around me pulling me toward shore, inviting me to abandon myself to their strength, to believe with confidence that, despite what goes wrong and how bad I feel, they are guiding me toward deep joy. That pull is the Spirit.

In this world, the dream of feeling as good as we want to feel *will* shatter. If we have the courage, we all will write Rachel's poem. Shattered dreams will create the opportunity for God to work more deeply than ever before, to further weaken our grasp on our empty selves.

They will also create the opportunity for bitterness and its children, defeat and immorality, to develop. Bitterness carries us farther from shore, into dark nights that never had to be.

Brokenness, on the other hand, allows us to relax in the arms that will bring us to shore, where a warm fire is burning and food has been prepared.

The elder's toast is a prayer for brokenness, for the power to trust God no matter what life brings. I pray the same for my grandchildren, that they may experience the brokenness that brings them to shore. I pray the same for myself and for you.

A further understanding of brokenness seems in order. It hurts, but it's a *good* thing. It's the difficult blessing the elder wished for Boaz and Ruth.

CHAPTER SIXTEEN

IT ISN'T ALWAYS
GOOD TO FEEL GOOD

The soul has a difficult time opening to its own possibilities. Imagine hearing that your unmarried daughter is pregnant and, with tender concern for her, saying, "I'm not about to throw up my hands and walk off the job."

Imagine learning one day that a necessary source of income has dried up, finding out the next day that your car has been stolen, then discovering the next that you have diabetes, and after all that responding, "I'm surrounded and bothered by troubles, but I'm not demoralized; I've been spiritually terrorized, but God hasn't left my side."

Imagine after years of financial comfort being forced to sell your large house because you can't make the payments, then moving into a duplex and saying, "Cramped conditions don't get me down; they only remind me of the spacious living conditions ahead."

Imagine finding out from your trusted wife of thirty years that she's had multiple affairs and now plans to divorce you, yet saying, "It's what I trust in but don't see that keeps me going. Do you suppose a few ruts in the road or rocks in the path are going to stop me?"

Imagine facing another twenty or thirty years at an unfulfilling, tedious job, having a husband you constantly argue with or just ignore, and watching your three kids all apparently head in bad directions, and saying, "When the time comes, I'll be plenty ready to exchange exile for homecoming. But neither exile nor homecoming is the main thing. Cheerfully pleasing God is the main thing, and that's what I want to do, regardless of circumstances."[11]

That's exactly what the apostle Paul said when he faced big troubles. Each of those sentences consists of his words.

I could say similar things when a phone call delivers a punch to my stomach that takes my breath away. *I* could respond with faith like Paul's when I wake up to a day filled with heartbreaking circumstances I can't change.

I am capable of living like that. *I* could become a spiritual person. *I* could be happy, not because things always go well in my life (though I like it when they do) but because I could learn to fly with wings the Spirit provides. *I* could be like Paul. Even better, I could be like *Jesus*.

A friend lives in a difficult marriage. It's been rocky since day one. He recently told me, "I love her and I believe she loves me. We'll never divorce but I think things will always be pretty tough."

I long for my friend to catch a vision of the lover he could become. His wife may never change, though she could. Whether she changes or not, he could be transformed into a gentle, patient, solid, caring, sacrificing husband; he could experience the joy of the Lord, even when he walks into his home and is greeted by a disparaging attack.

We could all learn to fly.

But there's a problem. A weight has been strapped to our ankles. We walk about with a chain attached to our legs, a chain hooked to a lead ball that we drag with us wherever we go. The weight of that ball makes flight impossible.

The chain can be broken. In fact, it already has been broken. Now we need to walk through an experience of brokenness that will make us shake our leg and see the ball roll away.

THE GREATEST CRIME

It helps in all this to know what the ball is.

"May your wife be like Rachel and Leah." I read that as a toast to brokenness, a wish that things might happen in Boaz's life that would help him to recognize the ball chained to his leg and to shake his leg vigorously until the already cut chain drops to the ground.

Boaz, a son of Adam like you and me, was dragging the same ball we drag. Let me describe it.

When something goes wrong in our lives, when dreams shatter, big ones or little ones, we hurt. We feel bad. Perhaps we feel terror, often self-hatred or guilt, more often shame, sometimes rage. Whatever it is, it's a feeling we do not like because it gets in the way of joy.

We know we were designed to feel better than we do. We recognize that the experience of pain, though realistic in this world, is somehow abnormal. We were created to be happy. But we're miserable. Like physical pain in our chests that tells us something's wrong in our bodies, the emotional pain in our hearts tells us something's wrong in our lives.

We have a penchant to explain things. We hate mystery. When we don't know what's causing a problem, we have less hope of fixing it, of making things better. So we scramble to discover the cause of our pain.

It seems obvious. We hurt because something has gone wrong. Our daughter got pregnant, our car was stolen, we lost our job—some dream in our lives has been shattered and that's the reason we're unhappy.

So we pray, "Dear God, I know You love me. I know You designed me to be happy. But right now I'm miserable. I know nothing of the joy You promised, nothing of the fruit Your Spirit can produce in my life. Please make things better so I can feel good again."

He doesn't. The shattered dream He could have prevented from happening in the first place stays shattered. He doesn't glue the pieces back together and put Humpty Dumpty back on the wall.

Our pregnant daughter doesn't repent or miscarry; she hardens and gives birth. The police don't find our stolen car, and the insurance company sends us a check for half its value. Our adulterous wife carries through on the divorce and marries her lover.

God could do something. He does nothing.

At some point, our prayer shifts. We give up asking God to make *things* better. Fatalism creeps into our attitude. What's the point of praying? Nothing will change. My handicapped child will stay handicapped. My dead husband will stay dead.

Now we ask God to make us *feel* better. "Dear God, fill me with hope. I know You never promised me a rose garden, but I want to sense Your Presence with me as I walk through the weeds. Send Your Spirit to fill me with that unspeakable joy the Bible talks about. Grow the fruit of the Spirit in my soul. Please. I can't go on unless you do!"

We wait. Our circumstances remain unchanged and we stay miserable—scared, angry, untrusting, troubled.

Without knowing exactly when it happens, we give up on God—not on His getting us to heaven, but on His making us whole, or at least a little more whole, in this life. We realize there is no guarantee He will change either what's happening in our lives or how we feel inside.

We still believe Jesus died for us, and we know that's our ticket to heaven. God's love is good for that, but what's it good for now? We're not sure. God is good, we still profess, but we're not sure what He's good for now, in this life. We begin to wonder if we have misread all the promises He made, promises about a peace that passes understanding, promises to anchor our souls with hope and lavish us with joy.

If God didn't withhold heaven's best, if He gave us His Son, then why would He hold back any other good thing? The Bible says He wouldn't, that He doesn't.

But we can draw up lists, long ones, of good things He has not put into our lives. It's hard to count our blessings when our trials seem to outnumber them.

So we take matters into our own hands. We work hard to improve our marriage, to straighten out our kid, to make enough money to pay for the bare necessities. We want things to improve, and now it's clear *why* we want things to improve—we want to feel better. That's our bottom line.

We love our spouses and children and friends, but it isn't love for them or for God that drives us. Our misery drives us not to seek God, but to seek to feel better; not to please Him, but to use Him.

We come to a point where there is no more important fact in the world than that we feel bad and there is no deeper desire in our hearts than to feel good. It seems that someone ought to cooperate in helping us feel better.

We turn to God and all we hear are more instructions: Don't be so lazy. Don't eat so much. Don't complain. Do go to church. Do worship Me. Do keep tithing.

It makes us mad. "Fat lot of help He is," we mutter under our breath.

We can now begin to see that we're living to do whatever it takes to feel better. And since no one (including God) seems to be helping much, we feel justified in our efforts. Watching hours of television feels legitimate. At least it dulls the pain and keeps us from fighting with our spouse and kids.

That's the ball chained to our legs. What I have written is a description of what the Bible calls our *flesh*. It's the way we think; it's the energy that pushes us to do what we do, the energy that drives us to evaluate everything that happens in our lives according to how it makes us feel.

When we feel unhappy, we view that experience as the greatest crime ever committed. We are victims of a fickle world, an unresponsive God, a variety of insensitive people. Our chief aim is to feel better. It seems a righteous cause, a noble crusade. If we can make a few dreams come true that will help us feel better, we go to work. If we can engage in activities that directly create better feelings or, failing that, numb the troubling emotions, we do it.

Look into your heart, study your interior world, and you will find that attitude. It's there in all of us. It was there in Boaz. It's the heavy ball we drag around. As long as we define our problem as something else, we will never fly.

"Because I Wish You Joy"

Only shattered dreams reveal the problem clearly, and only shattered dreams create a brokenness that helps us hate that attitude enough to give it up. Only shattered dreams help us feel appropriately impotent.

I hear the elder telling Boaz something like this:

"Boaz, you've married a lovely woman. I want the best for you. But even if the unimaginable happens and Ruth turns out to be as conniving as Rachel or as insecure as Leah, God will still be at work to bring about the good He intends.

"No matter how bad life may one day make you feel, remember something good is happening that you may not be able to see.

Give yourself over to the God who is working out a good plan. Do not settle for rearranging your world merely to feel better. Remember the twelve sons of Israel were born through the likes of Rachel and Leah."

And when the elder added the words, "May your offspring be like Perez whom Tamar bore to Judah," I hear him saying:

"Your life might turn into a mess. Trust God to bring good out of whatever happens. Boaz, things will go wrong in your life. Since Eden and until the Second Coming, things have gone wrong and will go wrong in everyone's life. You are immune from no evil. Your failure may trigger even worse failure that will cycle into worse failure still. Look at Judah and Tamar. But their offspring became an ancestor of the Messiah.

"Give up your demand for blessing that will always help you feel good. When life falls apart, lose all confidence in yourself to put things back together. Yes, I know you're wealthy and powerful. But only God is the author of the truly good. And only the pain of shattered dreams can strip you of confidence in yourself to do anything truly good. Boaz, I wish you brokenness because I wish you joy."

Something bad happens. I hurt. I feel unhappy. I long to feel good. I ask God for help. I am resolved to feel better. I do whatever I can to make at least a few dreams come true. *That is the way of the flesh.*

Something bad happens. I hurt. I feel unhappy. I long to feel good. But I trust God. His pleasure matters more than mine. But His pleasure includes mine. I believe that. So I abandon myself to His pleasure. I live to please Him. I work hard and live responsibly and strive to put balance in my life because that pleases Him. Making Him feel good is a higher priority than making me feel good. And somehow, inevitably, at some point, I discover joy. *That is the way of the Spirit.*

I shift from walking in the way of the flesh to walking in the way of the Spirit when the pain of life destroys my confidence in my ability to make life work and when it exposes as intolerable, insubordinate arrogance my demand to feel good. That is the experience of brokenness. It is then that the chain falls off my leg and the heavy ball rolls away. It is then that I fly.

I want my grandson and granddaughter to experience whatever shattered dreams will help them learn the lessons of the elder's toast, the lessons of brokenness. There are three.

CHAPTER SEVENTEEN

THE THREE LESSONS OF BROKENNESS

As God's inscrutable actions drew Boaz and Ruth together in marriage, the elder's strange words at their wedding encompassed three lessons for us all. Here are the three:

MAKING HIM LOOK GOOD

> Lesson 1—*The good news of the gospel is not that God will provide a way to make life easier. The good news of the gospel, for this life, is that He will make our lives better. We will be empowered to draw close to God and to love others well and to do both for one central purpose, to glorify God, to make Him look good to any who watch us live.*

That's it! That's the promise for now. God thinks it's a good one.

We have a hard time understanding the nature of our journey through this life. We still think that things should go well and that we should feel good. The commitment arising from this belief is what makes it so difficult, so unreasonable, to forgive people who have hurt us (we think they have violated our purpose for living). That same commitment ruins prayer, spoils worship, and makes true recovery from painful backgrounds impossible.

When Jesus lived here, His closest friends had the same problem. They assumed He would free their nation from Roman oppression. It made no sense to them to think that Jesus was not committed to feeding them well, keeping them healthy, and restoring their status as special people. With only a few sandwiches He could spread a picnic for five thousand people. He could make blind people see. He could raise the dead. And He was a compelling speaker who could draw huge crowds.

Jesus had the power and charisma to build a financially prosperous and spiritually exciting ministry and to let His followers share in the fun. Why wouldn't He do it?

His disciples couldn't understand when Jesus said that people wouldn't like them, that they would make a lot of mistakes, and that their lives would be filled with painful troubles till they died.

We can't understand either. Sure, Christians in China suffer and believers in Africa may go hungry. But not us, not in America, not in Western culture. We expect things to go well, at least not *too* badly. We're looking for a way to feel good now—it's what *should* happen—and God has the power to make it happen. Why wouldn't He use it? He does love us, doesn't He?

Then, when dreams shatter, when God does nothing, we move in one of two directions. Either we rebel in some form—perhaps in outright sin, more often through indifference to spiritual things—or we try to become spiritual enough to experience spiritual fruit, especially the peace and joy Paul mentions. Either we enjoy the pleasures of sin or we strive to arrange for the pleasures of His Presence. The first is doable but stupid; the second is impossible.

What needs breaking remains unbroken. We continue to think life should work well and we should feel good. The nature of our spiritual journey, we assume, is that God's glory will be revealed in our prosperity, whether financial, relational, physical, or emotional. As long as we believe that, we walk in the flesh.

It's so natural to think the Presence of Jesus has no greater purpose than to improve the quality of our journey through life—with *quality* defined as a pleasurable, satisfying, self-affirming existence—a journey where certain things don't go wrong or, if they do, they correct themselves. Marriages should work, biopsies should come back benign, ministry efforts should succeed, and we should feel pretty good about the way most things go.

If dreams never shattered, we would continue to believe that lie and value only what God can do for us now; we would value neither His Presence nor all that He intends to do later. And we would not be willing to pay the devastating price required to experience His Presence now. Without trials, only spoiled brats would enter heaven. And that would turn heaven into hell.

That's the first lesson broken people learn.

His Most Important Work

Lesson 2—*When God seems most absent from us, He is doing His most important work in us.*

I spoke recently with the woman I mentioned earlier who lost her husband to a heart attack. She told me that her biggest surprise was how distant God could seem when she needed Him most.

When He said, "I will never leave you nor forsake you," apparently He didn't mean, "and you'll always sense that I'm there."

Perhaps we should encourage pastors and others to publicly admit when they don't feel God's Presence and to describe the agony and confusion and sense of deep letdown that strangles their souls during those dark nights. It is a normal experience. It is part of a good journey.

Counselors and spiritual directors must not diagnose depression too quickly and prescribe medication or therapy. Seasons of personal suffering are opportunities for God to do His deepest work.

When the dark night comes and it seems nothing good is happening because of it, we tend to numb our desires, to shift into autopilot, to manage what we can, to seek relief where available, to feel nothing deeply, and to lose interest in difficult questions about God.

If we get mad at God, we eat too much or spend too much or enjoy what is not ours to enjoy.

If we feel afraid of God, we busy ourselves with doing good things. We exercise too much or examine ourselves too much or read our Bibles too much.

Or, if we love God from a distance and have little idea of the intense and passionate communion He longs for us to enjoy as His bride, if we have a rigid, no-nonsense approach to Christian living, we compulsively obey whatever law we can think of and commend ourselves on our dutiful lifestyle. We live as we should in order to make ourselves proud, not with longing to enter His Presence. Suffering becomes an obstacle to overcome, a chance to prove we're committed. It loses its power to generate a brokenness that creates a space only God can fill.

When dreams shatter and God disappears, we don't need to get mad at Him, to be afraid of Him, or to obey Him from a distance. And we must not resolve to feel nothing deeply. We need rather to realize that He vanishes from our sight to do what He could not do if we could see Him. In the spiritual journey, I know of nothing so difficult to believe. But it's true.

Think of those three hours of darkness on the cross. Jesus screamed in agony, "God, where are You?" God said nothing. But it was during that exact time that God was in the Son reconciling the world to Himself.[12]

Imagine the comfort we would experience and the hope we would feel if we realized that during His felt absence, Jesus is working to cut the chain from our ankles, to remove the weight that keeps us from flying. That's the second lesson of brokenness.

OUR BEST OPPORTUNITY

Lesson 3—*It isn't always good to be blessed with the good things of life. Bad times provide an opportunity to know God that blessings can never provide.*

Before we ate dinner last night, my older son prayed that the little boy about to enter this world as his son would arrive healthy. My heart echoed a fervent amen. No one wants it otherwise. We long for legitimate blessings, knowing their power to fill us with the happiness of gratitude.

Only a demented masochist denies that the good things of life make us feel legitimately good. Only a dour legalist cut off from his own heart behind a wall of rigid moralism claims not to care whether blessings come or not.

Healthy, normal people feel wonderful when good things happen. They should. My friend with the tumor behind her eye just received a far more favorable prognosis. She feels relieved. "Now I can relax a little more." Of course she can. And all her friends rejoice with her. It's an answer to prayer. We praise God.

But when things go badly, do we therefore *curse* God? Or can we understand that the mix of fulfilled dreams and shattered dreams in our lives is necessary if we're to grow?

We fight against three enemies: the world, the flesh, and the devil. Each does terrible damage, often in subtle ways.

Suffering is required if we're to discover a desire for God strong enough to help us decline the world's invitation to an immediately good time, to resist the devil's suggestion that all goodness may not reside within God, and to see through the false reasoning of the flesh.

Only the maturing Christian feels the full soul-wrenching distress that bad news generates, because only the maturing Christian senses, in still moments, a desire for God lodged in the center of his or her redeemed heart that is more real than the terror-riddled longing for good news.

Remember the flesh's argument: God made us to feel happy. We don't feel happy. Therefore, nothing matters more than to find some way to feel happy.

Blessings can actually strengthen that argument. When things go well, we may think happiness is our birthright. How often have I said when prayers are answered, "Of course! My life should run smoothly." I may not have heard myself, but I said it nonetheless.

Only trials have the power to break that argument. Only pain exposes our commitment to happiness for what it is, an arrogance that displaces God from His rightful place. Only in brokenness over our refusal to abandon ourselves to God for His glory will we discover our desire to do precisely that.

TRUE FAITH

Three lessons:

> 1. The journey to God will always, at some point, take us through darkness where life makes no sense. Life isn't easy; it's hard, sometimes very hard.

2. The felt absence of God is a gift to gratefully receive. During those seasons of darkness He is doing His deepest work in us.

3. Feeling good is not the goal. When we feel bad, we have the opportunity to do battle against the enemy within that keeps us from entering the Presence of God with no greater passion than to glorify Him.

My friend David Shepherd is right in the middle of learning these lessons. I have his permission to quote from a recent letter he wrote. After several years of following what he sensed was God's clear leading into a new ministry and meeting mostly with discouragement, he said this:

> Faith, as I am growing to understand it more, is about looking beyond my circumstances to a person. To have faith in better circumstances, even in God creating better circumstances, is not true faith. I want to be the kind of man who can watch every dream go down in flames and still yearn to be intimately involved in kingdom living, intimately involved with my friend the King, and still be willing to take another risk just because it delights Him for me to do so. And my flesh shivers to think about it.

I'm persuaded that David is on his way to truly *living* in the middle of shattered dreams. He's catching a glimpse of a better dream.

It's the same one that was supernaturally fulfilled in Naomi's life. It's time now to see what it was.

CHAPTER EIGHTEEN

OUR HIGHEST DREAM—IF WE ONLY KNEW IT

Is there really a way to write Jesus' name at the top of our list of best friends?

And if there is, can we keep from erasing it when bad things continue to happen and He does nothing, at least nothing we can see? How are we supposed to think about Christ when we feel terrible, when dreams shatter and He disappears? Are we really expected to feel good about Him, to enjoy Him, to like Him as we would a really close friend?

The answers to these questions must not be issued as a command. No one can choose to feel genuine affection when they feel mad or indifferent. True obedience to Christ springs from a deep passion for Christ.

But where does the passion come from? How do we get it?

Naomi's story ends with her feeling passion for God. She's no longer resentful, depressed, and empty, but quiet, joyful, and aware of more than she can see. This last episode of her life is recorded by the Spirit, I believe, to help us see the path to joy and to draw us to join Naomi on the journey.

MY FEARS

The book of Ruth ends with a simple scene. Picture yourself in the theater. The curtain rises for the last act.

The stage is barren except for a rocking chair. A wrinkled but peaceful-looking old woman sits on that chair, holding a month-old boy on her lap. We watch as she looks down into the innocent eyes of the child with her eyes of love. Then, slowly, she lifts her gaze to heaven.

She says nothing. It's as if we aren't there. No one is there. Naomi is in the Presence of God. We hear a chorus of women's voices sing, "Naomi has a son." She continues holding him on her lap, looking up. The curtain drops. And we sit.

What have we just seen?

Before I look at the significance of this final scene, may I suggest that you set this book aside for a few minutes and pray. If your heart feels chilly and uninvolved, ask the Spirit to make you aware of a hunger for Christ that is stronger than your hunger for anything else. Ask God's Spirit to press the meaning of this final scene into the deepest part of your mind and into the center of your heart.

With that prayer offered to God, ponder with me the impact of the way Naomi's story ends. As I reflect on what I've just seen before the curtain dropped, I'm strangely aware of a dream rising from somewhere within me.

I long to experience the Presence of God moving through every detail of my life, both good details and bad ones, carrying me into a richer *encounter* with God, into a closer experience of *community* with others, and into an experience of personal *transformation* that makes me more like Christ.

Where does that come from? How does a scene of an old grandmother holding her newborn grandson on her lap stir that dream?

I must pause here for a minute.

I am about to share what I believe is possible for us to experience in this life, what can go on deep within us even when everything around us is going badly.

And I am afraid. I'm afraid of two things. One, I'm afraid that, like me, you'll frantically ask, "What can I do to experience all that?" There's an answer to this question, but it can be heard only when we first admit we have no right to that experience but still humbly long for it.

Two, I'm afraid that you'll dismiss what I'm about to describe as a lovely fairy tale. Either you'll have little interest in deeper joy because your life is going well, or your inward experience is so far removed from what I believe is possible that you'll shrug your shoulders and continue to think you'll never have a real experience of God.

Both fears—that you'll insist right away on a formula for joy, or that you'll regard what the Spirit could do in your life as an impossible dream—come from forces hidden within me as I pursue God. Let me describe them.

Nothing makes me feel more alone than personal pain. When I'm in the middle of shattered dreams, I often hear myself saying, "If you knew the anguish I feel, if you knew how desperate I am despite how together I look, you would not taunt me with the promise of joy. You would come to me in my pain and just be with me, saying by your silent presence that my pain is justified and so too is my loss of hope. An invitation to dream higher dreams is as cruel as talking to a pilgrim lost in the burning desert about water that does not exist."

We won't catch the excitement of Naomi's dreams unless we set it squarely against the backdrop of human misery. Bear with me as I arrange the set where Naomi is sitting.

NOW WE SEE

There are two kinds of misery, the kind that people without God feel but live to deny and the kind that people with God assume they should never feel. I am speaking now only of the second kind.

In our day of feel-good Christianity, we have come up with a wrong view of our spiritual journey. We think of suffering as something abnormal, as evidence that we lack faith. We work so hard to escape suffering that we fail to realize what good things might be happening in us as we suffer. But that's wrong. That's more Buddhist than Christian.

Life can be tough. It can be tough for sincere Christians who have walked faithfully with Christ for many years.

It can be so tough that the best you can do is just hold on.

Nights can be darker than you feared. Your soul can feel so alone, so filled with agony, so untouched by love, that the most honest thing you can do is cry. The only alternative is rage, a powerful, destructive rage that in a moment of expression can give you the comforting sense that someone is finally administering justice. That's what fuels our spirit of revenge.

It's a testimony to how desperately we're committed to finding ourselves apart from God that the choice to abandon ourselves to Him is often most powerfully made when life has dragged us to the brink of blasphemy. Until we know how close we come to giving up on God ("Look what He allowed to happen in my life!"), we'll know little of what it means to give ourselves fully to God.

That deplorable condition of our hearts gives shattered dreams their unique power. Let me explain.

The pain created by trouble carries us into the depths of our being where everything revolves around us, where there's no love for anyone else, where we feel only pity for ourselves and sullen disappointment in others. It's a place where we actually believe God has failed us, that He has given us a raw deal. We think we have an airtight case against Him that requires true justice to be our advocate.

The pain of shattered dreams helps us admit what we really think, that our demand for a better friend than Jesus (or for Him to be a better friend) is legitimate.

It's here that we must not become Buddhists. We must not confess all these ugly thoughts too soon in an effort to find peace. We must rather trace them to their deepest roots.

If we do, we'll feel like the cancer that the surgeon with his sharp scalpel is determined to cut out. That surgeon is no friend of ours. When we're only in touch with our ugliness, the Spirit cannot be seen as friendly. He is here to destroy, to kill.

Then terror sets in, the sheer terror of absolute aloneness with ourselves. We realize that we're done for, that we've set ourselves up as god and that we sit alone on the throne we've made, wearing a crown of fool's gold.

If we weren't so terrified, we would feel silly. No one bows before us. No one carries out our orders. No one worships us. No one even likes us. We have become an impotent deity, an Ebenezer Scrooge counting his money in an empty room.

We're separated from God—no encounter. We're distant from others—no community. And we're grotesquely ugly—no transformation.

Involuntarily, we cover our head with our hands. We cower in the corner before a holy God who, with passionate fury, hates everything evil.

What will He do? Our guilt and shame overwhelm us. We can see nothing else. We can feel the blazing wrath of God directed at us.

We expect the lightning to strike, to sizzle us until we're burned up. It never comes.

We look up. We see Jesus. He is screaming, hanging on a cross. The lightning has just struck Him.

We keep looking, and we listen. We hear God declare, "It is enough!" We hear Jesus cry, "It is finished!" We hear the Spirit whisper to us, "Look now into the face of God. The veil covering His glory is removed. See Him and live!"

We see a smile. We hear a song. We realize, as if for the first time (though we've been Christians for years), that our deepest need, our deepest desire, is *not* for relief from current troubles. We don't even deserve relief.

Our deepest desire is for a kind of life only mercy makes possible, a life only grace provides. It is for life from God, life with God, life for God.

And we have it. We've had it since the day we trusted Christ to forgive our sins. But it took shattered dreams to put us more deeply in touch with what we already have. The pain carried us into depths of our heart that are still ugly, but the Spirit took us deeper, into the very core of our being, where Christ lives, where we are alive.

Now we pray, not because we're told to, but because we want to. In the middle of a dark night that has revealed the Son within us, we say:

"Lord, I can feel within me the demand that You be a better friend.

"I can sense my almost irresistible urge to turn to sources of pleasure that provide the relief You withhold. There are many. Some are people—my spouse, my kids, my counselor, my golf buddies. Others are activities like sex and busyness, or things like money and competence.

"But none provides life. Only You, on Your terms, can satisfy my soul.

"At this moment, though, I don't feel satisfied. I feel empty, desperate, alone. If I believed that there was a better friend than You, I would turn from You.

"But I see the cross. I see Your holy wrath and my blaspheming arrogance and I know I deserve not relief but eternal misery. I deserve the emptiness of eternity without love or meaning. And I see Jesus bearing Your wrath so I can receive Your eternal kindness. I have no other friend like that.

"How can I turn to anyone else? It would be insanity, foolishness. You are God. I am not. I abandon myself to You.

"Like Jabez, I ask that you bless me. I ask that you satisfy the highest dream my heart can envision—an encounter with You."

That's the backdrop. That's the set in which Naomi's final scene takes place. She is contentedly holding a child on her lap in a world full of misery.

As I look on this ending to Naomi's story, the dream to experience God rises from deep within me. I see the possibility of living beyond shattered dreams. Why?

The key is in the phrase "on her lap."

CHAPTER NINETEEN

A DREAM COME TRUE

Here is what I conclude as I read the end of Naomi's story. The name of Jesus does not belong at the top of my list of most cherished friends. It belongs on a page by itself.

No name compares with His. He is never a best friend among others. In all things, He stands apart, high and lifted up above every other friend and above every other source of pleasure. When He said, "I will never stop doing you good," He meant it. He delights in doing His people good (Jeremiah 32:40-41).

I believe that's true. If you're a Christian, so do you. The Spirit has placed that conviction in our hearts. But still we cry, "Lord, help my unbelief!"

Naomi's story might provide that help.

HERE AND MOVING

She's now an old lady. Her first grandson has just been born. She remains a widow. Elimelech is not with her to share her joy. Her son is absent. The child's father should be Mahlon. Instead it is Boaz, a kind relative but not Naomi's son.

So many of her dreams are still shattered. God has done nothing to restore them. But He has surfaced a higher dream and is right now fulfilling that dream as Naomi holds Obed on her lap.

The specific phrase "on her lap" occurs three times elsewhere in the Bible, all in Genesis. A brief look at those instances will reveal the climax to Naomi's story hidden in this final scene.

First, Rachel, Jacob's wife, is barren and none too happy about it. She demands that Jacob sleep with her servant girl so that when a baby is born, Rachel can hold it on her lap. "Sleep with her," she instructs Jacob, "so that she can bear children *for me*"—literally, "on my lap" (Genesis 30:3).

Second, Jacob, now an old man, can barely see. Just before he dies, he holds his two grandsons Ephraim and Manasseh (Joseph's sons) on his lap. He turns to Joseph and says, "I never expected to see your face again, and now God has allowed me to see your children too" (48:11). In the next verse, the boys are lifted from Jacob's *knees*—literally, from his lap.

Third, Joseph is in Egypt, years later. He longs to be in the Promised Land, but faces death in Egypt. We're told that by now he has seen "the third generation of Ephraim's children. Also the children of Makir son of Manasseh are placed at birth on Joseph's knees," literally, on his lap (50:23). With the children on his lap, he speaks his final words to his family: "I am about to die. But God will surely come to your aid and take you up out of the land to the land he promised." Then he adds, "And then you must carry my bones up from this place" (50:24-25). Joseph doesn't want to miss the party he knows is coming, a party that death would not prevent him from enjoying.

Rachel longed to be part of God's story but wouldn't trust God to make it happen. In the pain of her shattered dreams, she took control.

Jacob saw his highest dream realized in watching God move through his life and on through others to continue the journey to joy. When he saw not only his long absent son but also his son's children, he rested in the joy of knowing God was continuing to do him good.

Joseph realized that his death was not an ending but rather another chapter in a story that would end well.

And now Naomi, as her life nears its end, is holding her grandson *on her lap*.

After her journey through shattered dreams, I hear this prayer flowing from her heart:

"O God, the path has been rough. I miss my husband. I miss my sons. The pain is still real.

"But you have given me a sense of Your Presence and the certainty that You have called me to be part of Your sovereign plan.

"And I am tasting community as never before. Ruth is a wonderful young woman, Boaz is a good man, and this baby—well, I've never seen anything so beautiful. This is spiritual community, a community of people through whom You are working toward a higher purpose.

"God, I am not now who I used to be. I was depressed, angry, and afraid of the future. Now I am content, grateful, and full of joy knowing You are here and You are moving. I am a transformed woman. My pain continues, but I'm anchored in hope."

Encounter, community, transformation: There is no higher dream.

Can you feel it? Can you sense the Presence and movement of God leading His children through pain on a journey to joy?

First-Order Hope

I have now held my grandson on my lap. I held him when he was just thirty minutes old. He is wonderful, handsome, clearly brilliant beyond his days, a talented little boy with a perfectly shaped head, three or four chins depending on his posture, and agile limbs that will one day hit a golf ball four hundred yards and write answers on exams that will put him at the top of his class.

Now, seven weeks later, he looks up at my giant face with eyes that wordlessly ask,

"Could someone explain to me what's going on? I was quite comfortable in another world, a much smaller but a much safer one. Then some masked monster dragged me into this world and I'm not at all sure I like it. Now I have to make lots of noise before someone will fill my stomach.

"Look, I know what I want. I want a full stomach, but now, in this world, I have to take charge of arranging for that pleasurable experience to happen. I'm working on a plan, but it's obvious I need you, or someone, to cooperate. Will you? Am I in a safe place where my strategic efforts to fill my stomach will ensure your help in making me feel good?"

I look down into his bewildered, anxious, sometimes angry eyes, and I feel old. Not a tired oldness, not the oldness of impatience, but a humbling sense that I've learned something this little boy needs to know.

I know that his empty soul is the real problem, not his empty stomach. He wants a full stomach. That is important and it does feel good, but filling his soul is a far deeper passion. He just doesn't know it yet.

I know, too, that many people die having never discovered the food that could fill their souls. They never even discover their desire for that food. They live all their lives the way Jakob Lawrence Crabb is beginning his, aware only of an empty stomach and determined to seize whatever pleasure fills the void. They live their entire lives trying hard to be satisfied with shallow pleasures while their souls silently scream for delights they were designed to enjoy.

With tears the Spirit looks over the earth and says, "Dead men walking."

I want Jake to change his plan. If he doesn't, his soul will be empty forever.

That thought terrifies me. I realize the very best thing I can do for my newborn grandson is to be a grandfather who delights in the pleasures of God. Maybe the passion coming out of my soul for God will give him the courage to face his own deepest yearnings with hope that more than his stomach can be filled.

My eyes turn away from his. I look up. Tears blur my vision enough to see the face of God.

My heart swells with worship. I discover again how deeply my soul pants for God. Encounter with God, not holding my grandson, defines life. And because I know that, I long for God to reveal Himself to Jake, even if it requires shattered dreams to make it happen.

I still hope Jake stays healthy, does well in school, has lots of friends, meets a nice girl, marries, fathers beautiful kids, and leads his family into meaningful involvement with a local church. But those are all second-order hopes. My first-order hope for Jake is that he encounter God.

PASSION RESTORED

The patriarch Jacob held his grandsons on his lap. Naomi held Obed on hers. I now hold Jakob Lawrence on mine.

And I discover what my predecessors discovered. My grandson holds a special place in my heart. So does my granddaughter and so do my sons and my daughter-in-law and my parents and my friends and (tears now fill my eyes) my wife.

I love the blessing of wonderful people in my life. I love the blessing of restored but precarious health. I love the blessing of a nice home, two cars that work, and a set of golf clubs that on occasion perform as they should. And I love the blessing of ministry. I love to write, speak, and spiritually direct.

But with Jake on my lap, I am aware that the center of my heart belongs to God. I long to know Him, to encounter Him, no matter the cost, to let His glory fill my life as it once filled Solomon's temple.

It's interesting that when someone (like Jake lying on my lap) pulls out of me such strong affections and stirs such deep yearnings, I can feel my even deeper desire for God. Perhaps it is the unforced rhythm of grace that carries me from the pain of shattered dreams through the yearnings I feel for those I love into a profound desire for the only One who can end all our pain and satisfy all our souls.

There's no higher dream than experiencing God as He moves through every circumstance of life to an eternal encounter with Himself where transformed people will enjoy perfectly loving community around Jesus Christ, the source of Perfect Love.

If that really is the highest dream of the human soul, why do so many of us dream only of lesser things and then despair when those dreams are shattered?

To ask the same question another way, why is our experience of spiritual reality so limited?

There will be no revolution in the church without personal revival. And there will be no revival without restored passion, without an encounter with God that captures our hearts and liberates us to enter into community with one another and to experience profound transformation in the way we think and live our lives.

In the next chapter I suggest that an encounter with God is possible—now, in this life, in the midst of still-shattered dreams—and that we can actually experience a pleasure in knowing God that exceeds all other pleasures.

Then, in the final chapter, I present a way of approaching God, a new way that, though it has no power to make God reveal Himself to us, puts us in a position to experience the encounter He longs to provide—on His terms.

CHAPTER TWENTY

THERE'S A NEW WAY TO LIVE—AND IT'S POSSIBLE

Even Martin Luther struggled with seeing Christ as his best friend. He once wrote, "I expect more from Kate my wife, from Philip Melancthon, and from other friends than from my sweet and blessed Savior Christ Jesus; and yet I know for certain that neither she nor any other person on earth will or can suffer that for me which He has suffered; why then should I be afraid of Him! This my foolish weakness grieves me very much."

In his unmistakable style, Luther went on to say, "Fie on our unbelieving hearts, that we should be afraid of this Man, who is more loving, friendly, gentle, and compassionate towards us than are our kindred, our brethren and sisters; yea, than parents themselves are toward their children."

Then he added a thought that to modern ears sounds wrongheaded: "Oh! His grace and goodness toward us is so immeasurably great, that *without great assaults and trials it cannot be understood*"[13] (emphasis mine).

That's not how we naturally think. It makes sense to assume that we would more easily appreciate God's immeasurable goodness if we could measure it by fewer trials and more blessings. Good friends make our lives easier, not harder. So we think.

With pain-killing drugs, more accessible counseling, and support groups in churches that focus on the healing power of Jesus (usually interpreted as His power to make our lives more comfortable), we've grown increasingly impatient with suffering. Suffering is a bad thing that should be minimized or eliminated. We're more willing than ever before to admit we're hurting, but we're more insistent that someone make things better. A good friend would do just that.

But God insists that in our suffering He is doing us good, a greater good than relieving our suffering. He never stops doing us good (Jeremiah 32:40). The problem is with our blessing-based, happiness-centered understanding of goodness. It is too small. And with our small idea of goodness, we dream small dreams, and small dreams lead to small prayers.

Luther's idea of God's goodness was different. It was big, so big that "without great assaults and trials" it could not be understood.

I think the revered reformer is making the same point I'm trying to make in this book, that our conception of goodness is entirely too small until we dream no greater dream than to experience the pleasure of God's company. And Luther's apparently wrongheaded notion that trials are necessary to dream that dream is thoroughly rightheaded. Here's how I would put it.

> We will not encounter Christ as our best friend, as the source of all true goodness, as the One who provides the sweetest pleasure to our souls, until we abandon ourselves to Him. And full abandonment, real trust, rarely happens until we meet God in the midst of shattered dreams,

until in our brokenness we see in Him the only and overflowingly sufficient answer to our soul's deepest cry.

Let me make this point clearly.

THE EXACT CENTER

We will encounter Christ as our best friend when shattered dreams help us become aware of…

…the strength of our desire to know Him.

…how unworthy we are to receive even the smallest expression of kindness from Him.

…the intensity of His longing to draw us into satisfying, soul-thrilling intimacy with Him and His Father (which, in His mind, is the greatest blessing He can give and worth whatever it takes for Him to give it and for us to receive it).

…the unparalleled value of intimacy with Him.

The evangelical church has made a serious mistake. For years we've presented Christianity as little more than a means of escaping hell. Knowing Jesus has been reduced to a one-time decision that guarantees the chance to live in a perfect, pain-free world forever.

Christianity is about going to heaven, but that's not the center of Jesus' kindness to us.

Nor is it the opportunity to lead fulfilled, meaningful lives now. Returning to our Maker's manual and following biblical principles to make our marriages work and our kids turn out well and our bank accounts comfortably bulge is not God's plan for our lives.

We've shrunk Christianity into a neat little package full of blessings that, if opened, will empower us to feel good now and feel even better in the next life.

Jesus revealed His highest dream for all His followers when in prayer He defined the true abundant life in these words: "that they may know you, the only true God, and Jesus Christ, whom you have sent" (John 17:3).

The exact center of Christianity is the opportunity it provides to enjoy God, to be more satisfied with Him than with anyone or anything else.

It is not primarily about getting saved out of hell and into heaven. It is not primarily about living a certain way that creates fewer problems and makes us feel better about ourselves and our lives. It is about knowing Jesus as the most wonderful person there is, the very best friend anyone could ever have. It is about glorifying God by enjoying Him more than any other source of pleasure.

Now, if all that is true, then the church is in bad shape. We're missing the point of our faith. We enjoy a lot of people and a lot of things more than we enjoy God.

If Luther is right—that only in suffering do we learn to fully delight in God's goodness—then it becomes immediately clear why our enjoyment of God is so shallow. We don't like to suffer. We see no value in suffering. We arrange our lives to minimize suffering. And we believe Christianity offers a God who will cooperate with that plan.

As a church, we've lowered our sights; we ask for too little. We dream only of escaping the pain of life by entering the bliss of heaven. And until then, we dream only of surviving this life with less heartache and more blessing. We have given up the dream of knowing God now.

J. I. Packer looked over the modern church and observed, "While my fellow believers are constantly seeking to advance themselves in godliness, they show little direct interest in God himself.... There is something narcissistic and, to tell the truth, nutty in being more concerned about godliness than about God."14

Our nuttiness grows out of our unbelief. We do not believe that knowing God could ever provide the joy we're looking for or the fullness our empty souls crave. So we settle for lesser joys, for more manageable pleasures that come with a smaller price tag, at least for now.

I struggle to believe that God is my greatest pleasure. I'm right now considering the purchase of a new car. Sitting in the showroom model brought me pleasure. Driving one home will bring even more. Do I really believe that knowing God could create a deeper, more satisfying pleasure than pulling a new car into my garage? Am I willing not to buy the car if doing so would bring me closer to God?

Friends of mine are troubled by their teenage daughter. She's using drugs and sleeping with her boyfriend. Do they really believe that knowing God could bring more pleasure to their souls than seeing their daughter straighten out?

Another friend is addicted to pornography. He recently told me, "I have never experienced more immediately satisfying pleasure than when I look at the magazines I've hidden in my closet." Does he believe that knowing God could bring pleasure to deeper places in his soul than pornography will ever reach?

If we believe there's more pleasure in something other than God, then our obedience will never rise above required duty, our prayers will never aim higher than using God, and our joy will always leave an emptiness that drives us to further self-centered efforts to find the fullness we demand.

So the question we must squarely face is this: Does knowing God really provide the pleasure our souls were designed to enjoy? Can we enjoy God more than anyone or anything else?

Is it possible?

The Encounter That Frees

Listen to the testimony of Augustine, arguably the church's greatest theologian after Paul. As a young man, Augustine struggled with what counselors today would call a sexual addiction. Despite his best efforts, he could not control his lust. Nothing he had experienced provided greater pleasure. The commandment to confine sexual activity within marriage was not a light burden or an easy yoke. It was a maddening demand that only made his problem worse and stirred his sinful passions.

In an unusually candid account of his struggle, he reports that he came to a point where he was most bothered not by his immoral acts but by his powerlessness to change. He knew what was right, but he couldn't do it. It was that reality that tortured him most.

We must note this carefully. Augustine was not looking for help to overcome his sexual addiction so he could have better relationships with others or like himself better or enjoy a more pleasant, socially acceptable life. He was crushed by his inability to do what God required. God's holiness and his sinfulness were the chief sources of his torment.

Here's how he put it:

> I found myself driven by the tumult in my breast to take
> refuge in the garden where no one could interrupt that fierce
> struggle in which I was my own contestant. I was frantic,
> overcome by violent anger with myself for not accepting
> your will.

(In his *Confessions,* the book that details his life, Augustine was speaking directly to God.)

I tore my hair and hammered my forehead with my fists; I locked my fingers and hugged my knees.[15]

Augustine identified the exact center of his battle as his inability, not to control his sexual passions, but to enjoy God more than sex. He reports his search "for a means of gaining the strength I needed to *enjoy you*" (emphasis mine).

Freedom came for Augustine when he encountered God, when he met God in a way few Christians in our generation have ever experienced. "I shall now tell and confess to the glory of your name how you released me from the fetters of lust which held me so tightly shackled and from my slavery to the things of this world."

Notice carefully what it was that transformed Augustine's life and empowered him to involve himself productively in Christian community. It was not teaching, exhortation, an untangling of internal dynamics, or a healing of emotional wounds. It was an encounter with God that provided more pleasure than sex.

> How sweet all at once it was for me to be rid of those fruit-
> less joys which I had once feared to lose!... You drove them
> from me, you who are the true, the sovereign joy. You drove
> them from me and took their place, you who are sweeter
> than all pleasure.

What can we learn from Augustine's account of his transformation from sexual addict to spiritual leader? The central lesson is this: The cure for sexual addiction and for every form of slavery to something other than God is worship. Not the dull worship of rote routine or the shallow worship of contrived excitement, but worship that creates deep pleasure in the One who receives it and the one who gives it.

> *Only a thrilling, soul-pleasuring encounter with God that generates more pleasure than sin will free us from our addiction to sin.*[16]

That is not the teaching we hear from most pulpits today. Most of what we hear remains stuck in the old way, the way in which God used to deal with His people when He spoke from Mount Sinai to tell folks what to do.

Today's version of old-way preaching emphasizes two approaches to living the Christian life: *One,* do what you should, and here are godly principles to follow. *Two,* if you cannot do what you should, something's wrong with you that perhaps counseling can fix, or something's missing in you that the Spirit must still provide.

PRAYING FOR A REVOLUTION

I am praying for a revolution in the church of Jesus Christ, a revolution that takes full advantage of the new way of the Spirit. We're now forgiven and can draw near to God. We're new creations whose core identity is no longer sinner but saint. We have a new appetite within us, a desire for God that is stronger than every other desire, waiting to be discovered and nourished.

And we have a new power. The Spirit of God exists literally within us. His central passion is to awaken our appetite for Christ and to reveal Him to us.

I envision a revolution that creates a community of broken people united not by their problems or diagnoses but by their hunger for God. I envision a revolution that frees people to fully participate in that community because they feel the safety of the gospel that embraces people rather than judges them, that joins hurting folks more than advises them on how to feel better, that supernaturally equips people to pour life into one another.

I envision a revolution that creates true community and transforms lives, a revolution that centers on an encounter with God that fills the soul with sheer delight.

That's my vision, an *encounter* with God that creates *community* and *transforms* lives. The vision begins with encounter, an encounter with God that the new way makes possible.

God longs to give us an encounter with Himself. We want it. It requires that we enter the pain of living in a world where good dreams shatter. But it's worth it.

What then must we do, not to produce an encounter with God (we can't do that), but to put ourselves in a position to receive His sovereign joy, to experience the pleasure of His company?

I answer that question in my final chapter.

CHAPTER TWENTY-ONE

THE JOURNEY TO JOY

Perhaps you're aware of how badly you long to experience God. Many dreams have shattered in your life, important ones, but you don't want to dishonor God. You don't want to dismiss Him. You desire to know Christ as your best friend.

You want to enjoy Him and know His power to relate well with others, to be a better friend, to parent your children more wisely, to touch hurting people more deeply.

And you want to change, to find the strength to resist sinful urges, to persevere in your difficult marriage, to replace self-hatred and despair with an awareness of your unique value in the kingdom of Christ.

You long for an encounter with God, community with others, and real transformation within your self.

You're reading your Bible some; should you read it more? You're praying as best you can; should you attend a seminar on prayer and discipline yourself to start a prayer journal? You attend church most Sundays; should you go more often and get more involved?

You know you're not terribly disciplined. You hear a lot these days about spiritual disciplines, activities like silent retreats and fasting and contemplative prayer. Should you seek out a spiritual director or buy a book that might get you started with a few of these spiritual disciplines?

Or maybe you need counseling. There are some hard memories you've never really faced, a few losses you've never fully grieved. Perhaps the emotional damage you've suffered from earlier abuse needs to be worked through. Would it be wise to ask your pastor to refer you to a qualified Christian counselor?

To all these questions, yes, of course. More time in the Bible, more time on your knees, more time in church—they're all good things, activities that can contribute to spiritual formation.

And spiritual disciplines guided by a wise spiritual director have immense value. You will not grow as you desire without some involvement with such disciplines.

Counseling, too, has a place. Open discussion about your life with a person trained to understand what may be happening in you can do great good.

But you want to encounter *God,* to find in your relationship with Him a pleasure that exceeds all other pleasures, a joy that sustains you in every sorrow.

Let me show you a new way. It involves asking yourself two questions:

The first: *How do I think about God?*

The second: *How do I think about myself?*

Let's take them in order.

How Do You Think About God?

The Bible reveals God as absolutely holy. The angels who continually surround Him cry out, "Holy, holy, holy is the Lord God Almighty."

Paul introduces God to us in Romans as a holy God who is passionately furious at all that is unholy. His presentation of the good news of the gospel starts with bad news for us. God is a God of vengeance, of wrath, of retribution. He will not allow the guilty to remain unpunished. The picture is not one of a nice man; He is not presented as a warm and loving father who likes His children and who sees to it they all have a good time.

Our Christian culture has weakened our understanding of the holiness of God by introducing too soon the idea of grace. We now talk about grace in a way that changes our view of God from holy to paternal, from justifiably enraged to strict but understanding.

Very few Christians today see God as an irate judge who violently hates our sin. He is now a bit more flexible, more tolerant, still insistent that we measure up to at least some of His standards, but gracious when we don't.

I remember talking to a young married man who said, "I know I'm wrong to continue my affair, but you're wrong to insist I end it. God doesn't want me to continue it, but I know He'll forgive me. I sense only judgment from you. God is a God of grace."

God means for us to obey His rules, we say, but if we don't (and no one does, of course, not completely), He's really quite understanding. That's our view of grace. It's what Dietrich Bonhoeffer calls cheap grace. It develops when we talk about grace before we tremble at God's holiness.

That's our first mistake in answering the first question. We reduce the holy God of passionate wrath to a fatherly God with strict standards. And we do it in the name of grace.

But we're still uncomfortable with the idea of standards. It restricts our freedom; it denies us the chance to be ourselves, to express who we really are. So we dismiss God's standards by attacking them as holdovers from legalism. God is the God of liberty. We're told to stand fast in the freedom Christ provides.

That freedom, we say, consists in our opportunity to find ourselves and become whole persons by following God's wise counsel, by listening to our inner voice. In His kindness, God has given us a lot of ideas about how to live. If we listen to them and practice them, we'll enjoy life as it was meant to be enjoyed. Things will go well for us. We'll feel good about ourselves and how our lives are turning out.

God has now become the helpful God of useful principles.

Let me sketch what I've just presented.

Question 1: Who Is God, the God We Desire to Know?

He is…

the Holy God of Passionate Wrath.

But we've weakened this view of Him by introducing grace too soon.

God has now become…

a Fatherly God of Strict Standards.

But we've dismissed His standards in our misguided campaign against legalism.

So we've reduced God further to…

a Helpful God of Useful Principles.

And now we spend our religious energy seeking to know the principles a helpful God provides for handling our lives, principles that will make our lives better. The result is that we never encounter God.

Now, ask the second question.

How Do You Think About Yourself?

It takes two people for an encounter to happen. God has become useful, full of good suggestions about how we should live. Who have we become?

If you're looking for a quick boost to your self-esteem, the Bible is not a good book to read. You might especially want to skip the first three chapters of Romans. They reveal us as hopelessly arrogant, foolish enough to think that we're the point of things, that our happiness, our sense of well-being, matters more than anything else.

We hear that assessment and agree with it, wondering exactly what the problem is. Is the Bible saying we're wrong to look out for ourselves? Why would God get upset with us for making it a priority to have a good life?

We believe self-interest is a virtue, a reasonable commitment useful for guiding our lives. God tells us it's the essence of evil. It utterly contradicts and opposes reality. God is the point. We are not. He gets the glory. We don't.

Our evil demand—that our sense of well-being be honored above God's glory—deserves punishment. It arouses God's wrath. He declares us guilty, worthy of eternal separation from the source of everything good.

We want our own way. In His justice, God lets us have it. As Dorothy Sayers put it, hell is the enjoyment of our own way forever.

What we thought would bring us joy does exactly the opposite. Hell is an existence of eternal misery. And the Bible declares that's exactly what we deserve.

In the modern evangelical church, I wonder if anyone really believes that. Do I believe that apart from Jesus' blood shed for me it would be fair if God sent me to a place where I would be miserable forever?

A few days ago, a policeman pulled me over. He clocked me at twenty-seven miles per hour in a twenty-mile-per-hour zone. Do you know what it feels like to drive twenty-seven miles per hour? I thought I was crawling. Certainly I was endangering no one.

He checked my record, which is pretty good, handed me back my license, smiled, and said, "Slow down."

I thought that was reasonable. Had he given me a ticket, I would have felt irritated. What I did wasn't *that* bad.

Had he cuffed me and thrown me in jail for twenty years, at the top of my lungs I would have screamed, "Unfair!"

That's how we see ourselves, as minor offenders who perhaps deserve a scolding, maybe even a ticket. But our reasons for breaking the law seem reasonable. I wanted to get to the bathroom I knew was around the next corner, so I drove a little too fast.

In our Christian culture, we've weakened our understanding of personal sin by talking too soon and too much about our longings and our needs. We want to feel good about ourselves, we long for enjoyable relationships, we desire effective and recognized ministries. *We* become the point and see nothing really wrong with it.

Because we focus more on our longings than our evil, we see ourselves not as hopelessly arrogant, worthy of eternal misery, but as scoldably selfish, deserving of perhaps a slap on the wrist.

Listen to how we talk. "Yes, you're right, pastor. I yelled at my wife. That was wrong. Sure, go ahead, confront me. I made a mistake. What? You want to discipline me in front of the elders? That's ridiculous!"

No longer do we see ourselves as hopelessly arrogant. We've weakened our view of sin by centering on what we long for to the point where, at worst, we see ourselves as deserving only a scolding.

We take it one step further. We may admit that our minor offenses warrant a reprimand, but we really believe that if someone knew what we've been through and the pain we feel, the scolding would give way to a sympathetic hug. We struggle and we make mistakes, but given our hurt, given how poorly the people in our lives have responded to our longings, our struggles are quite understandable. If God loves us, He really ought to help.

Let me complete the sketch.

WHY OUR ENCOUNTER WITH GOD IS WEAK

Question 1: **Who Is God, the God We Desire to Know?**

The Holy God of Passionate Wrath

has been weakened, by introducing grace too soon, into…

The Fatherly God of Strict Standards,

whose standards we've dismissed by rejecting them as impositionally legalistic, so that God now becomes…

The Helpful God of Useful Principles.

Question 2: **Who Are We, As People Longing to Enjoy God?**

We are…

Arrogant People Who Deserve Eternal Misery,

whose awareness of that arrogance is weakened by our talking too soon and too much about our longings, until we become merely…

Scoldably Selfish People Who Really Ought to Do Better,

a view of ourselves we then dismiss as insensitive to our deep hurt, so we come to see ourselves as…

Understandable Strugglers Who Deserve to be Understood and Helped.

Several points can be made from this sketch.

1. When understandable strugglers meet a helpful God of useful principles, they use Him to make their lives more comfortable. They never encounter God as their greatest pleasure, they never enter into an other-centered community of broken people, and they never experience a deep change in their interior being. Their experience of God is shallow.

They become spiritual narcissists, nutty people who live only to feel better.

2. When scoldably selfish people meet a fatherly God of strict standards, their encounter with God is never intimate. It breeds resentment and distance. They, too, never encounter God as their greatest pleasure. Their approach to community becomes appropriate and well-mannered, and they turn into self-righteous Pharisees who congratulate themselves on being better than others.

They become spiritual hypocrites, nutty people who think of themselves as quite mature.

3. But when arrogant people who know they deserve eternal misery tremble before a holy God of passionate wrath, they discover grace. They encounter the depths of God's kindness and love, a kindness and love they find nowhere else. They fall to their knees and worship Christ as their Lord and Savior and as their truest friend, really their only true friend. They know they don't *deserve* a hug, no matter how badly they're hurting; but they get an eternal one anyway. That's the grace that takes their breath away.

They enter into the community of broken, forgiven people who are hungry for all of God they can get. Nothing stands in their way—not shame, not the fear of revealing too much, not a desire to be well thought of. With abandon they seek God, alone and in the company of like-minded others.

They're startled when they discover that their interior worlds are changing. They discover that they actually *want* to obey God. They find themselves caring less about their own reputation than about God's.

They become spiritual people, not nutty but wise as they dream the dream of knowing Christ even better.

And they welcome shattered dreams as friends. They enter their pain and discover an arrogant spirit that says, "I don't deserve this." They tremble in their unholiness before a holy God and discover how passionately they want to have a good relationship with Him. Then He reveals the new way of grace, the gospel that lets them draw near to God and discover how wonderful He is.

But they learn slowly. More dreams must shatter before they experience their deepest joy in Christ.

The journey continues, a journey through shattered dreams to the exquisite joy of encountering Christ.

ON THE RIGHT TRACK

If Paul were writing this chapter, I think he might conclude with the words he wrote to the Philippians two thousand years ago:

> I'm not saying that I have all this together, that I have it
> made. But I am well on my way, reaching out for Christ,
> who has so wondrously reached out for me. Friends, don't

get me wrong: By no means do I count myself an expert in all of this, but I've got my eye on the goal, where God is beckoning us onward—to Jesus. I'm off and running, and I'm not turning back.

So let's keep focused on that goal, those of us who want everything God has for us. If any of you have something else in mind, something less than total commitment, God will clear your blurred vision—you'll see it yet! Now that we're on the right track, let's stay on it.

Stick with me, friends. Keep track of those you see running this same course, headed for this same goal. There are many out there taking other paths, choosing other goals, and trying to get you to go along with them.... All they want is easy street. They hate Christ's Cross. But easy street is a dead-end street. Those who live there make their bellies their gods; belches are their praise; all they can think of is their appetites.

But there's far more to life for us.

(from Philippians 3, THE MESSAGE)

The journey to joy takes us through shattered dreams. That's the lesson of Naomi's story.

A new way to live is available to us, a way that leads to a joy-filled encounter with Christ, to a life-arousing community with others, and to a powerful transformation of our interior worlds that makes us more like Jesus.

Pray with me that many will walk together in the new way, that the revolution will begin. We can live beyond shattered dreams.

WORKBOOK

QUESTIONS YOU MAY HAVE
ABOUT THIS WORKBOOK

What will the *Shattered Dreams Workbook* do for me?

The message in this workbook is about discovering God when life isn't "working." It's also about discovering sacred opportunities to experience joy.

This workbook will help you—in a practical and carefully reflective way—to look *through* life's disappointments and tragedies and to see, as never before, just how lavishly God is blessing you, for *His* pleasure as well as for your own.

It will help you understand and release your truest and deepest desires in life and to realize God's surprising ways of putting you in touch with these desires. You'll see how God moves His children from shattered dreams to better dreams—to the highest dream and the joy that comes from dreaming it.

Should I read *Shattered Dreams* before I do the workbook?

Your best approach is to read *Shattered Dreams* as you go through this workbook. However, many key portions from the text of *Shattered Dreams* are included here to give you a sufficiently broad and accurate indication of the book's content. You also will find the appropriate chapters to read listed at the beginning of each lesson.

The lessons look long. Do I need to work through all of each one?

This eight-lesson workbook is designed to promote your thorough exploration of each week's material, but you may find it best to focus your time and discussion on some sections and questions more than others.

Also, you may decide to follow a slower pace than one lesson per week. This could be true whether you're going through the workbook individually or in a group. In a group that meets weekly, for example, you may decide to spend two weeks of discussion time on each lesson. (In your first meeting, decide together on what you believe to be the best pacing and schedule.) If you're going through the workbook on your own, you may simply want to try completing two or three questions each day.

Above all, keep in mind that the purpose of the workbook is to help guide you in specific life-application of the biblical truths taught in *Shattered Dreams*. The wide assortment of questions included in each weekly lesson is meant to help you approach this practical application from different angles and with expansive reflection and self-examination.

Allowing adequate time to prayerfully reflect on each question will be much more valuable for you than rushing through this workbook.

OUR PROBLEM
WITH GOD

THIS WEEK'S LESSON IS BASED ON

THE INTRODUCTORY MATERIAL

("A NEW WAY" AND "THE PARABLE")

PLUS CHAPTER 1, "MY PROBLEM WITH GOD"

A s you begin, ask the Holy Spirit for help in hearing and obeying His words for you. Keep a Bible and a notebook within reach, so you can write down your responses, questions, prayers, and action steps. (Included in each study you'll find a number of excerpts from *Shattered Dreams,* each one marked at the beginning and end by this symbol: 📖. These excerpts serve not only to convey Dr. Crabb's message, but also to stimulate your reflection and discussion and to guide your exploration of Scripture.)

God's Longing and Ours

In his introduction, Dr. Crabb tells of three ideas that filled his mind as he wrote *Shattered Dreams.* Think about these ideas as presented in the following quotations, then respond to the questions below each one.

1. The first idea:

> 📖 *God wants to bless you.* He gets a kick out of making His children happy. He feels much the same way parents feel on Christmas morning as they anticipate watching their kids unwrap presents amid squeals of delight....
>
> There's never a moment in all our lives, from the day we trusted Christ till the day we see Him, when God is not longing to bless us. At every moment, in every circumstance, God is doing us good. He never stops. It gives Him too much pleasure. God is not waiting to bless us after our troubles end. He is blessing us right now, in and through those troubles. At this exact moment, He is giving us what He thinks is good. 📖

What is your response to the basic idea expressed in the preceding quotation? How fully do you accept and believe it? What doubts or questions, if any, does it raise in your mind?

2. The second idea:

> 📖 *The deepest pleasure we're capable of experiencing is a direct encounter with God.* In God's new way of dealing with people, He does us the most good by making Himself available to be enjoyed and by seeing to it that we seek an encounter with Him with more energy than we seek anything else....
>
> The highest dream we could ever dream, the wish that if granted would make us happier than any other blessing, is to know God, to actually experience Him. 📖

How do you respond to this idea? How fully do you accept and believe it? Does it raise any doubts or questions in your mind?

3. The third idea:

> 📖 The problem is that we don't believe this idea [that encountering God is our deepest pleasure].… We assent to it in our heads. But we don't feel it in our hearts.…
>
> So the Holy Spirit awakens that appetite. *He uses the pain of shattered dreams to help us discover our desire for God,* to help us begin dreaming the highest dream.…
>
> Our shattered dreams are never random. They are always a piece in a larger puzzle, a chapter in a larger story. 📖

Once more, what is your response to this idea? How fully do you accept and believe it? What doubts or questions does it raise in your mind?

4. Following the introduction in *Shattered Dreams* is a section titled "The Parable." Read this short section now.

How would you summarize what happens to the man in "The Parable"?

In your own words, how would you express the message or point of this parable?

Your Best Friend?

5. Dr. Crabb tells about jotting down a list of his best friends.

> 📖 I'm looking at the names I wrote. One impression strikes
> me at once with near gale force. *The friends who made the list
> are all friends who do something for me.* It's not what I do for
> them that got them on the list; it's what they do for me....
>
> The people on my list respond to my concerns. They use
> their resources on my behalf. When I have a need, they meet
> it if they can. I like that about them....
>
> So I'm left with an obvious fact. The people I most cher-
> ish in all the world are the people I can count on to do for
> me what I most want. I suspect if you wrote down the
> names of the six people whose friendship you most value,
> that same fact might be obvious to you. 📖

After questioning whether this fact proves that we're all "hopelessly
mired in disgusting self-centeredness," Dr. Crabb then realizes that it
never occurred to him to put God's name on his best-friends list.

> 📖 Sometimes God seems like the least responsive friend I
> have.... Depending on an unresponsive God in the middle
> of crumbling dreams can be tough on faith. Relating per-
> sonally with a God who is less responsive than friends with
> far fewer resources is difficult. 📖

In what ways, if any, have your impressions and concerns been similar
to what is expressed above?

Like a Little Child

6. Dr. Crabb's words in the following quotation reflect his thoughts on
   Luke 18:17, where Jesus speaks of receiving the kingdom of God "like
   a little child."

> 📖 [Jesus] wants us to humble ourselves, to let someone
> know when we could really use a hug or some quality time,
> to let the Spirit know we need Him to change our hearts, to
> confess to our community of close friends the weaknesses we
> should have resolved by now.
>
> I hear Jesus telling us to stop negotiating with Him, to
> stop offering something we think we have in exchange for
> His blessings.... "All you can do is receive what you need
> from someone who has what you don't. When you admit
> your emptiness, I'll see to it you're filled." 📖

In keeping with this childlike openness and dependence, how would
you express some of your own personal needs or emptiness that you
can honestly bring to Jesus today?

7. Keep these perspectives on childlikeness in mind as you choose to
   explore any of the following familiar passages. Reflect on them in a
   fresh way, then feel free to express in your own words (a) the message
   they give us and (b) your response to that message.

Psalm 145:18-19
Matthew 11:28
Hebrews 4:16

Hebrews 10:22

James 4:8-10

8. Dr. Crabb points to our self-protective tendencies as he mentions "the first commandment of fallen thinking," stated in these words: "Trust no one and you shall live." In what ways, if any, have you adopted and followed such a "commandment" in your life?

9. Now consider the "second commandment of fallen thinking," which Dr. Crabb expresses in these words: "To make life work, trust only yourself and what you can control." To what extent have you ever followed this approach to life?

Taste and See

> 📖 We evangelicals speak about having a personal relationship with Jesus. We hold out the possibility of having a really good relationship with Him. If that relationship hits a snag or develops tension, we know it's always our doing. Since I was a child, I've heard the saying, "If you're not feeling close to God, guess who moved?" The message was clear: Every difficulty in our relationship with God is always our fault. It's never His.
>
> But especially in the years since I turned fifty, that message has not always seemed so obvious. 📖

10. What has been your own belief regarding the issue addressed in the preceding quotation? If there's tension or distance in your relationship

with God, have you viewed this as being always your own "fault"? Why or why not?

> 📖 When we see things rightly, we'll write His name in capital letters at the top of our list of friends and, with the angels, bow low before Him in adoration and awe. And hope. I believe that.
>
> But it takes some doing to see things rightly. 📖

11. What do you think we may need most in order to "see things rightly," so that God's name is at the top of our list of friends?

12. In the early pages of *Shattered Dreams,* Dr. Crabb writes this:

> 📖 This book is an invitation to taste and see that the Lord is good even when the bottom falls out of your life....
>
> How can we write His name at the top of our list as the most wonderful, most sensitive, and most responsive friend we've ever had when our fondest dreams shatter and He does nothing? That's the question I'll try to answer in this book. 📖

With those words in mind, how would you express your personal goals or expectations for the time you'll spend going through this workbook?

13. In quietness, review what you have written and learned in this week's lesson. If further thoughts or prayer requests come to your mind and heart, you may want to write them down.

14. What for you was the most meaningful concept or truth in this week's lesson?

How would you talk this over with God? Write a response as a prayer to Him.

What do you believe God wants you to do in response to this week's study?

TRUSTING GOD IS DANGEROUS BUSINESS

THIS WEEK'S LESSON IS BASED ON

CHAPTER 2, "WE NEED A GOOD STORY,"

CHAPTER 3, "JESUS SPEAKS,"

AND CHAPTER 4, "WHEN BOTH SHOES DROP"

In this lesson we begin seeking what Dr. Crabb calls "a hope that has the power to do something truly wonderful when the dark night descends and we see nothing but pain and disappointment in this life, a hope that does exactly the same thing when the sky is sunny."

As you begin, remember to ask for the Holy Spirit's help in hearing and obeying His words for you at this time.

Handle the Pain

Dr. Crabb reminds us that we all go through the experience of shattered dreams in one form or another—"if not yesterday then today, if not today then tomorrow. How do we respond? What happens in us when life throws an unexpected curve our way, when the second shoe drops soon after the first?"

This is the central question we want to ask ourselves in this week's study.

1. For many of us, the response is captured in these words:

> 📖 *Handle pain!* Find some way to keep going in spite of
> the hurt. Don't think about it. Stay strong, move on to the
> next chapter, make it. Do whatever helps, whether going on
> a spiritual retreat, leaning on family, talking to a counselor,
> or reading books recommended by concerned friends.
> Relieve the pain if you can. Live through it if you must.
> Whatever you do, handle the pain! 📖

In what ways has this ever been your own response to shattered
dreams? And how would you evaluate that response, as best you can,
from God's perspective?

> 📖 In our struggle to handle the pain of shattered dreams,
> however, one question is rarely talked about with honesty....
> The question is this: *What do we do with how we're feeling
> toward God?* What we want is good; it's not selfish. Why
> won't God let us have it?...
>
> Why is God so inconsistent, so maddeningly unpre-
> dictable?... Why? Suffering seems so random; one dream
> realized, another shattered. 📖

2. Think back to times when you've squarely faced the shattering of your
dreams. In those moments, what were your feelings toward God?

3. Look up some of the verses listed below from the Psalms (or similar passages you know). In what ways and to what extent do these inspired words of Scripture mirror feelings that you have experienced?

10:1
13:1-2
22:1
43:2
69:2-3
88:14

A Story of Shattered Dreams

In chapter 2 of *Shattered Dreams,* Dr. Crabb writes this:

> 📖 After I properly set the stage, I want to tell a story. Actually, I want to retell an old familiar story, one already told in the Old Testament book of Ruth. Recently, through my own experience with shattered dreams, I've come to the conclusion that the story of Naomi was written to answer the question I'm asking.... *How do we trust a sometimes disappointing, seemingly fickle God who fails to do for us what good friends, if they could, would do?* 📖

Naomi's story, says Dr. Crabb, "solves my problem with God." We'll be exploring that story as presented in the short book of Ruth.

4. Begin your fresh encounter with Naomi's story by reading through the first chapter of Ruth. As a helpful exercise for deepening your grasp of the story, write out a concise outline of the events in Naomi's life as told in Ruth 1.

5. In the first chapter of the book of Ruth, how do you see Naomi responding to shattered dreams?

6. Below are comments from Dr. Crabb about the way Naomi's story begins in Ruth 1. After reading each comment, reflect on how it relates to your own observations of this passage. List also any relevant questions that come to your mind.

📖 The Lord could have done something. And He did nothing. How else could she think?

Her husband and both sons, all three dead. And yet God is the God of the impossible. He can do anything.

But He did nothing.

Sometimes He does come through. Naomi knew the stories. I wonder if her mind roamed back through her nation's history, maybe to the story of Abraham, a favorite among her people. 📖

📖 Naomi, with a good husband and two fine sons, was full of hope when together they left Bethlehem. The famine there had prompted a move to Moab. Naomi assumed—it was less a dream and more an assumption—that a short stay in Moab would go well, and then, when the rains came, she would return to Bethlehem *with* her husband, *with* her two sons, perhaps *with* a couple of daughters-in-law.

After all, in a recent battle with Israel, Moab had lost thousands of eligible young men. Pickings for her boys might be good. Had she thought about it, Naomi would have naturally reasoned that bringing her family back home, happy and intact, was easy compared to arranging for a ninety-year-old woman to conceive. But God's surprises aren't always pleasant. Naomi learned that lesson with force. 📖

📖 Naomi's husband, Elimelech, passed away shortly after they reached Moab. One dream shattered. But then her two sons met nice girls and married. Perhaps she thought, as we all do, that if the other shoe did not drop, she would be able to get on. If enough blessings come along to enjoy, perhaps we can endure the pain. God knows we couldn't handle one more trial. And He gave His word we would never be asked to suffer more than we could endure. Then *that* becomes our dream—that sufficient blessings would come our way to get us through.

Then the other shoe dropped. Both her sons died. We're not told how. The Lord could have kept them alive; that much we know. But He didn't. 📖

When the Fire Goes Out

📖 When dreams shatter, we lose hope. We may get on, but the fire is out. There may still be some things worth living for, but the best is gone. The spark has been doused, our passion for life extinguished. At least that's how it seems....

How do we find the faith that lets us see what is invisible, to passionately believe that He's always wonderfully and lovingly responsive when He seems so callous? That's the question: *What does it mean to hope in God as we continue to live in a world where good dreams shatter and God seems to do nothing about it?* 📖

7. At this season in your life, how would you answer the final question posed in the preceding quotation?

> 📖 Trusting God is dangerous business. Unless we're trusting Him for what He's promised to provide, the step after trust is disillusionment....
>
> So what *can* He be trusted for? Exactly what is He doing with His considerable power? What would be different if we experienced that power, if His power were released in us? 📖

8. Again, how would you answer the questions in the preceding quotation, to the best of your understanding today?

> 📖 There is an answer, and it is repeated again and again in the Bible. But the answer, the only one that squarely faces the enormous challenge of trusting a seemingly unresponsive God, requires a change in how we naturally look at life. It demands a revolution in our understanding of why we're alive at all, of why God keeps us living in this world for so long before He takes us to heaven. 📖

9. How would you evaluate your present ability to take on a "revolution" in your thinking about God, as called for above? How open are you to thinking in ways drastically different from your accustomed thought patterns? On what basis and by what criteria can you gauge this openness within yourself?

    📖 Is the only point to godly living the reward we'll receive in heaven? Is there anything we can hope for now, anything we can count on God to do for us in this life? That's the question. And it's not a selfish one, it's a humble one, a question that admits we're dependent children in need of receiving what we long for but do not have. Our souls need filling. 📖

10. The second sentence in the above quotation pinpoints another crucial question in our relationship with God. How would you answer it, according to your current understanding of Scripture?

A Different Kind of Hope

11. From Hebrews 11, Dr. Crabb draws the following conclusion: "Apparently God is pleased with people who suffer terribly, whose lives never straighten out, but who keep trusting." As you look over Hebrews 11 for yourself, what portions of it lead you to the same conclusion? What other significant conclusions can you draw from this passage that may pertain to this week's topic?

12. In the following quotation, we find a much different approach to life than the one taught in Hebrews 11.

📖 More than perhaps ever before in history, we assume we are here for one fundamental reason: *to have a good time—* if not good circumstances, then at least good feelings. We long to feel alive, to sense passion and romance and freedom. We want the good time of enjoying godly kids, of making a difference in people's lives, of involvement with close friends, of experiencing God's peace. So we invent "biblical" strategies for seeing to it that our dreams come true. We call them models of godly parenting and disciplines of spiritual living and principles of financial stewardship—all designed to give us a legitimately good time. What's wrong with that?

But when we uncover the deepest motives that drive our actions, we discover a determination to feel *now* what no one will feel until heaven. 📖

In what ways—and how strongly—can you identify with the feelings and motives described in the words above?

📖 What God has in mind when He tells us to keep hoping may not be what we usually mean when we think of hope. We wish for things to get better; we want to feel what we want to feel.

Those are our dreams. But that kind of hope is for later. For now, in this life, the Bible offers a different kind of hope, a kind that at first we don't find attractive or even hopeful....

The best hope, our highest dream of being in His presence where nothing ever goes wrong and where we fully

enjoy Him more than every other blessing, will not be
granted till the next life. 📖

13. To what degree, if any, might you be seeking fulfillment in this life for
hopes that won't be granted until eternity? What are these hopes?

14. When our life's purpose "is to have a good time, to have soul-pleasure
exceed soul-pain," Dr. Crabb writes, "God becomes merely a means
to an end, an object to be used, never a subject rightfully demanding a
response, never a lover to be enjoyed." To what extent might this have
been true in your life in the past, or even in the present?

> 📖 It's harder to discover our desire for God when things go
> well. We may think we have, but more often all we've found
> is our desire to *use* God, not to *enjoy* Him. Shattered dreams
> are the truest blessings; they help us discover our true hope.
> But it can take a long, dark time to discover it.... Shattered
> dreams open the door to better dreams, dreams that we do
> not properly value until the dreams that we improperly
> value are destroyed. Shattered dreams destroy false expecta-
> tions, such as the "victorious" Christian life with no real
> struggle or failure. They help us discover true hope. We need
> the help of shattered dreams to put us in touch with what
> we most long for, to create a felt appetite for better dreams.
> And living for the better dreams generates a new, unfamiliar
> feeling that we eventually recognize as joy. 📖

15. How fully do you agree with the statements about shattered dreams
in the preceding quotation? To what extent have you come to any of
these same conclusions on your own?

Jesus Speaks

16. Dr. Crabb portrays the Mount of Olives as a "Place of Hope" for Jesus, despite the agony of His prayers there on the night before He was crucified. Explore Luke 22:39-53 and Acts 1:6-12 (you may also want to refer to Zechariah 14:3-5 and Matthew 24) to find the verses that speak most directly to what Jesus wanted His followers to learn from their experience with Him in this place.

    How would you summarize those lessons? And how do they relate to the topic of this week's study?

17. In a chapter of *Shattered Dreams* titled "Jesus Speaks," Dr. Crabb writes: "Drawing from all that we have now considered, I hear Him speaking words like these to us. Listen."

    These words are listed below. Read them reflectively, accepting each paragraph, as you're able, as the Lord's personal communication to you. Then choose one or more of the paragraphs and record your prayerful response.

    📖 Some of your fondest dreams will shatter, and you will be tempted to lose hope. I will seem to you callous or, worse, weak—unresponsive to your pain. You will wonder if I cannot do anything or simply will not. 📖

    📖 As you struggle with dashed hopes, you will fail, just as My servant Peter did. You will feel discouraged with yourself to the point of self-hatred. And I will seem to withdraw from you and do nothing. 📖

📖 When all of this comes to pass, My word to you is this: *Do not lose hope.* A plan is unfolding that you cannot clearly see. If you could see it as I do, you would still hurt, but you would not lose hope. You would gladly remain faithful to me in the middle of the worst suffering. I guarantee you the power to please me, not to have a good time. But pleasing me will bring you great joy. 📖

📖 In the deepest part of your soul, you long more than anything else to be a part of My plan, to further My kingdom, to know Me and please Me and enjoy Me. I will satisfy that longing. You have the power to represent Me well no matter what happens in your life. That is the hope I give you in this world. Don't lose it. 📖

18. In quietness, review what you've written and learned in this week's lesson. If further thoughts or prayer requests come to mind, you may want to write them down.

19. What for you was the most meaningful concept or truth in this week's lesson?

How would you talk this over with God? Write out your response as a prayer to Him.

What do you believe God wants you to do in response to this week's study?

THE PATH OF HOPE

THIS WEEK'S LESSON IS BASED ON
CHAPTER 5, "THE RHYTHM OF HOPE,"
CHAPTER 6, "BREAKING THE RULES,"
AND CHAPTER 7, "HIDDEN HOPE"

Hope has its own rhythm," writes Dr. Crabb. "We cannot rush it. The water of life will find its way down the mountain to fill the lake from which we can drink." In this lesson we'll explore this rhythm as well as some other surprising aspects of true hope.

As you begin, remember again to ask for the Holy Spirit's help in hearing and obeying His words for you at this time.

God's Goodness and Our Happiness

Think about your personal definitions for "happiness" and "joy" as you read carefully through the following extended excerpt from *Shattered Dreams*.

📖 If given the choice, we would prefer to keep whatever
happiness we've already found. Like the child who never
wants to grow beyond the wide-eyed excitement of Christmas
morning, we like to remain naively happy. Keep the blessings

coming. Keep the good times rolling. When we signed on to the Christian life, that's what we thought was the deal. We do what we're told, and God stacks presents under the tree.

Our experience of happiness is not entirely wrong; it is, however, naive. It is both innocent and shallow, rooted in a strange blend of a child's optimism and a fool's arrogant spirit of entitlement. Things will go well for us; they're supposed to. *Other* people get cancer and suffer through divorce and lose their jobs and experience a friend's betrayal.

With adolescent maturity we declare that God is good when we ace the physics test or finish law school with honors, when our son is offered an unusually good position or the biopsy comes back negative. "Of course," we say, "God is good!" Without putting it quite this way, we assume God is pleased and grateful that we think so—and maybe just a little relieved.

When blessings come, we should of course enjoy them. It's good when children squeal with delight on Christmas morning; it's sad when they can't. Celebrate the good things of life. Enjoy the juicy steak, the unexpected bonus, the beautiful grand-daughter.

Happy people, though they're right to be happy, face a subtle danger. They tend to spiritually gloat, to publicly express grati-tude and praise for the good things they enjoy while privately thinking that blessings are their due. They can easily slip into a concern for the less fortunate that carries with it a mood of judg-ment: *If they were more like me, they would be given the blessings I have.* We don't easily recognize that mood within ourselves.

Unhappy folks face their own unique temptation. Publicly they tell the more fortunate how glad they are for all who are

so blessed; privately they wish that the happy person's path
would hit a ditch.

Rejoice with those who rejoice and weep with those who
weep. No command is more difficult to obey. Beneath the
surface, we lament another's joy (that's the sin of jealousy)
and feel good when a much blessed friend has reason to cry
(that's the sin of smugness, a close cousin of jealousy).

Happy people do not love well. Joyful people do. That's why
happiness, the pleasant feelings that pleasant circumstances
generate, must be taken away in order to be replaced by joy.

Happy people rarely look for joy. They're quite content
with what they have. The foundation of their life consists of
the blessings they enjoy. Although they may genuinely care
about those less fortunate and do great things to help, their
central concern is to keep what they have. They haven't been
freed to pursue a greater dream. That's why they cannot love
well. In His severe mercy, God takes away the good to create
an appetite for the better, and then, eventually, He satisfies
the new appetite, liberating them to love. 📖

1. What statements or descriptions in the above selection can you most
identify with, and why?

How would you describe, as fully as possible, your own view of
happiness?

How would you describe your understanding of true joy?

2. "It comes down to this," Dr. Crabb says:

📖 God's best is available only to those who sacrifice, or
who are willing to sacrifice, the merely good. If we are satisfied with good health, responsible children, enjoyable marriages, close friendships, interesting jobs, and successful
ministries, we will never hunger for God's best. We will
never worship. I've come to believe that only broken people
truly worship. Unbroken people—happy folks who enjoy
their blessings more than the Blesser—say thanks to God
the way a shopper thanks a clerk. 📖

What thoughts come to mind as you read these conclusions? In what
ways is it easy for you to agree with them? In what ways do you find it
difficult to agree?

Heavy Blessing

📖 List every blessing you desire. Put them all on the left
side of a scale. Now list the blessing that we're told is the
very highest, an intimate relationship with God. Put that
one, by itself, on the right side of the scale.

Do we believe that what is on the right side immediately
and decisively outweighs what is on the left? If we did, we
would move more quickly from happiness through the
agony of shattered dreams to complete joy.

Only a few in any generation believe that the weight of
knowing God is a blessing heavier (and by that I mean more
wonderful) than every other. And those who believe it appear
to have developed that conviction only through suffering.

Happiness must be stripped away, forcibly, before joy can surface, before we will value and pursue dreams whose fulfillment produces true joy. 📖

3. What do you think it takes for someone to be convinced that knowing God is a greater blessing by far than all other blessings? And how important is it to have this conviction?

4. In what ways and to what extent do you see this conviction reflected in any of the following passages?

Psalm 16:2
Psalm 42:1-2
Psalm 73:25-26
Habakkuk 3:17-18
Matthew 10:37
Philippians 3:8

The Rhythm of Hope

5. Take a few moments to review the first chapter of the book of Ruth.

Dr. Crabb points out "three characteristics of Naomi's despair" that emerge in Ruth 1, characteristics which are "often part of our own journey to hope."

His summaries of these characteristics are shown below. For each one, list the verse or verses in Ruth 1 where you see this characteristic in

Naomi. Feel free to mention also your own impressions of Naomi's despair and to tell about times when you have had similar thoughts.

  📖 First, she believed people would be better off spending time with someone other than herself.... *You're better off without me.* 📖

  📖 Second, she lost all hope of a return to earlier blessings that brought happiness.... *Happiness is only a memory, never to be experienced again.* 📖

  📖 Third, she believed the tragedies were God's doing.... *Tragedies in our lives are God's doing.* Perhaps they come as discipline for our wrong choices or maybe they come for some other reason, but either way, tragedies are God's doing. He could prevent them. He doesn't. 📖

6. At this time in your life, what gives you the most help in patiently following God's "rhythm of hope," as Dr. Crabb expresses it in the following quotation?

  📖 God is working when we see nothing but darkness. He is moving with rhythmic purpose through our agony and pain to unimaginable joy.
   Knowing that He's moving at all sometimes becomes the central piece of faith we need to keep ourselves moving. The courage to not quit, to not settle for immediate pleasure that brings happiness back for only a moment, often depends on

our conviction that God is moving, that we are being taken to an experience of ecstasy along a path of suffering, that there is no other way to get there. 📖

7. With honesty, describe the degree of confidence you now have that God indeed is working and moving in your life and in your circumstances.

The Desire Beneath the Pain

📖 The Western church has become a community of either the victorious or the acceptably broken. Either we speak glowingly of our love for Jesus—usually because the blessings are abundant—or we struggle nobly through hard times, convincing others and sometimes ourselves that we're doing better than we are. With each other we're more proper than real, more appropriate than alive....

Could we actually love God so much that we could feel all the pain of a teenage daughter's pregnancy and still worship? Could we still love our daughter? Or do we believe that loving God would somehow reduce the pain that a child's rebellion creates? 📖

8. How would you answer the questions raised in the second paragraph of the preceding quotation?

📖 When you hurt, hurt. Hurt openly in the presence of God. Hurt openly in the presence of the few who provide

you with safe community. Feel your pain. Regard brokenness
as an opportunity, as the chance to discover a desire that no
brokenness can eliminate but that only brokenness reveals.

Remember what brokenness is. It's the awareness that you
long to be someone you're not and cannot be without divine
help. Never pretend to God, to yourself, or to your safe
community that you feel what you don't or that you are
what you're not. With everyone else, including Christians
attending a Bible conference, choose to be congenial. Not
everyone needs to see your brokenness. 📖

9. How do you respond to the advice given in the preceding quotation?
   How possible would it be for you to fully follow this advice?

10. Revisit some of the familiar biblical passages listed below that relate to
    handling your own hurts or the hurts of others. In what ways, if any,
    do you view them differently as a result of this study? In what ways
    might they communicate more strongly to you than before? Write
    down your thoughts about these passages.

Romans 12:12-15
1 Corinthians 12:26
2 Corinthians 1:3-5
Galatians 6:2
Ephesians 4:2
Philippians 1:29
Hebrews 13:3
James 1:2-3
1 Peter 1:6-7

Keeping Desire Alive

📖 My growing conviction is that no one discovers the fullness of their desire for God without entering the fullness of lesser desires....

We must therefore feel the soul-piercing pain of disappointment, of the imperfect love we've received and the equally imperfect love we have given. But when all we experience is pain, loneliness, and despair, we can know with certainty that we have not yet entered the depths of our souls. Beneath our troubled emotion is a desire for God that in rich measure can be satisfied now....

Don't let your hearts be troubled. In the middle of shattered dreams, discover a desire that Christ pledges Himself to satisfy. Don't set out to discover that desire. The desire will surface, like bubbling water from a spring that can no longer be held back. 📖

11. What do you think it means to "enter the fullness of lesser desires," as this term is used in the above quotation?

Is it easy for you to agree with the author on this? Why or why not?

Breaking the Rules

12. Think about how you generally respond to others who are experiencing pain or loss. Dr. Crabb notes that "two unwritten rules eventually surface in our response to one who hurts."

📖 First, mourning has a time limit.... Second, we think there's a proper way to mourn. Ugly battles should remain out of sight. Acceptable battles may be shared, but only if we season our account with hope. 📖

Then he notes that "Naomi broke both the time-limit rule and the proper-mourning rule." In your own reading of Ruth 1, where do you see Naomi breaking these "rules"?

13. Below is an excerpt of Dr. Crabb's further comments on Naomi's "rule-breaking." Once more, record your own response to his analysis plus any other reflections or questions you have. (You may also want to look once more at Ruth 1 with these fresh thoughts in mind.)

📖 Her husband had died nearly ten years earlier, her sons more recently but still long enough ago that by now she should have gained perspective. But still she was reeling. Where was her faith? Is God good or not? Is He worthy of trust or does He make mistakes? I can see her community pointing fingers while expressing similar admonitions.

And the way she talked about her shattered dreams was unbecoming to a follower of El Shaddai. "Yes, God is an invincible mountain, a force that cannot be resisted. But that is cause for praise, not complaint." Perhaps that's what the elders in Bethlehem told her. It's certainly what many sufferers hear today from their spiritual leaders. No wonder we run off to counselors.

Don't sanitize the story. Naomi did *not* say, "I'm having a hard time. Most nights I cry myself to sleep. But God knows what He's doing. My family died for good reasons that I cannot see but I claim by faith. I know nothing enters my life without passing through His tender hands. My hope is in the Lord."

That may be what we think she should have said, what we wished she had said, but it's not what she did say. She was miserable, and she saw God as the source of her misfortune. 📖

14. At the end of chapter 1 in the book of Ruth, we read that Naomi returned to Bethlehem "as the barley harvest was beginning."

Dr. Crabb notes that this is the first of four "telling phrases" that point to "God's behind-the scenes movement in Naomi's life." He highlights this first "telling phrase" in these words:

📖 After more than ten years in Moab, Naomi returned to Bethlehem *"as the barley harvest was beginning"* (1:22). The darkest night precedes the brightest dawn. That is not cliché, it is how God works. 📖

In this phrase, he says, "we can see the sun's tip rise above the horizon. Naomi couldn't see it, but it was there. The harvest is coming." Dr. Crabb then adds, "In each of our lives...the harvest is beginning; the sun is rising." What evidence do you see that this process may be happening in your own life at this time—that the harvest is beginning, and the sun is rising? If you don't see that evidence now, can you tell of some time in the past when you were able to see it?

Different Paths

📖 "Don't let your hearts be troubled," He told His disciples. What did Jesus mean? Is He telling us to pretend we feel what we should feel when our most deeply experienced emotions are quite the opposite? Are we to admit our troubled feelings only to ourselves and God, while telling others that God's presence and promises are real to us when they're not? Is Jesus agreeing with Buddha in prescribing a form of contentment that requires us to cut off the nerve endings of our souls and to report peace when what we feel is a void? Is He teaching that if we trust Him, we'll feel no pain? 📖

15. In the past, what has been your own deepest understanding of the command from Jesus to "let not your heart be troubled"?
16. Dr. Crabb mentions "the 'four noble truths' that make up the core of Buddhist teaching":

📖 Truth 1: *Life is suffering.* There is always, in everyone's life, a gap between desire and reality. The gap is suffering.

Truth 2: *The cause of all suffering is desire.* People suffer because they desire what they do not experience. It is not possible to have everything you desire. Therefore, if you desire, you will suffer.

Truth 3: *The way to end suffering is to end desire.* Want nothing, then nothing can disturb you. A person without dreams will never suffer the pain of seeing them shattered.

Truth 4: *Spend your life learning to eliminate desire.* The "eightfold path," the way of Buddha, shows you how. 📖

In what ways have you adopted one or more of these perspectives?

17. Dr. Crabb then compares those "four noble truths" of Buddhism with the fundamentally different path of following Jesus.

Showing the contrast, he summarizes the teachings of Christ in the following four statements. For each one, think about how fully you recognize and believe it. Record your responses and reflective thoughts:

📖 Truth 1: *Life includes suffering, but life is good.* In this world, His followers and everyone else will suffer tribulation. But Jesus has made a way for us to satisfy our deepest desire in the midst of unrelieved pain. 📖

📖 Truth 2: *The cause of all suffering is separation.* We are separated from God—and from our own deepest desire, our longing for God—and we're therefore deceived into looking elsewhere for joy. That sets us off on the ultimate wild goose chase. Nothing but God satisfies our most profound desire. 📖

📖 Truth 3: *The way to handle suffering is to discover your desire for God.* Then everything, both good and bad, becomes redemptive. It moves us toward the God we desire. Enter your thirst. Feel your ache, the very worst ache that throbs in your soul. Face how you harm others, your spouse, your children, your friends. And face your disappointment with them. Eventually, you will seek God for…

…forgiveness of your failure to love.

…the love you desire.

…empowerment to love others.

…hope that one day you will revel in love freely given and freely received in a perfect community of lovers. 📖

📖 Truth 4: *The new life provided through Jesus must be accepted as a gift of love.* We then spend the rest of our days discovering our desire to know God better, and we come to realize it's a desire whose satisfaction no shattered dream can thwart. 📖

18. In quietness, review what you've written and learned in this week's lesson. If further thoughts or prayer requests come to mind, you may want to jot them down.

19. What for you was the most meaningful concept or truth in this week's lesson?

How would you talk this over with God? Write down your response as a prayer to Him.

What do you believe God wants you to do in response to this week's study?

GOD IS MOVING

THIS WEEK'S LESSON IS BASED ON
CHAPTER 8, "EVERYTHING HELPS ME TO GOD,"
CHAPTER 9, "DESIRE OR ADDICTION?"
AND CHAPTER 10, "THE ELUSIVE GOD"

As you begin, remember again to ask for the Holy Spirit's help in hearing and obeying His words for you at this time.

📖 If you're seeking God in the middle of shattered dreams, if you've become aware of your desire for Him but are having trouble finding Him, be encouraged that it bothers you. The more you're bothered by not finding Him, the more aware you're becoming of how badly you want Him. Abandon yourself to Him. Let the Cross bring you confidence that He is with you and will reveal Himself to you. Abandonment and confidence—here are two key elements of true spirituality. 📖

Everything Helps Me to God

1. Chapter 8 in *Shattered Dreams* is titled "Everything Helps Me to God," a quote from the French spiritual guide Jean-Pierre de Caussade.

📖 It's his way of saying what Paul taught two thousand
years ago, that all things—a spouse's death, a son's rebellion,
a missed career—*all things,* in the hand of God, work
together for good for people whose primary agenda is to glorify God, who long to enjoy Him as they enjoy no one else
and to reveal Him to others in every relational encounter....

Do you believe that everything helps a person to God,
including a suicidal son, a devastating divorce, a secret moral
failure, an unfulfilling job? If so, how do you preach what
you believe? 📖

How would you answer the questions in the last paragraph of the
quotation above?

Counseling Naomi

2. Dr. Crabb summarizes Naomi's situation at the end of Ruth 1 in these
words:

📖 She's not doing well. Life has been hard. Ten years ago
she was widowed; a few years later she lost both her married
sons before either had fathered a child; now she has returned
home with a nice young woman, a daughter-in-law from the
despised country of Moab. Naomi is no longer young, her
money is gone, her property is sold, she can't manage to
shake off feelings of depression, and she is mad at God, convinced that she has been a victim of His ruthless
sovereignty. 📖

He then asks you to assume that Naomi attends a church of which you are the pastor.

> 📖 What will you say in next Sunday's sermon that you
> honestly believe she might hear? What message could you
> preach that the Spirit might use to draw her along on the
> path toward God?… Or assume you're a Christian coun-
> selor. Ruth has brought Naomi to your office, then waits
> outside to let you do whatever you do with depressed
> clients. What would you say to this slumped-over old
> lady? 📖

Think back to where you were in your spiritual understanding and experience two or three years ago. If you were Naomi's pastor or coun- selor at that time, what would you most likely have said to her?

What might you say differently to Naomi *today*, as her pastor or counselor?

> 📖 Our generation has lost the concept of finding joy in
> unfulfilled desire. We no longer know what it means to
> hope. We want what we want *now*.…
>
> Impatient Westerners prefer quick sanctification. Take
> your car into the shop and drive it again the next day. Bring
> your soul to a counselor or pastor and get fixed right away.
>
> But wisdom understands that souls are not broken
> machines that experts fix. Wisdom knows the deep workings
> of the hungry, hurting, sin-inclined soul and patiently follows

as the Spirit moves quietly in those depths, gently nudging people toward God.

There is no Concorde that flies us from immaturity to maturity in a few hours. There is only a narrow, bumpy road where a few people walk together as they journey to God. 📖

3. In your own life, how much do you think impatience and an inability to hope might be factors in slowing your progress in knowing God?
4. If impatience and a shortage of hope are indeed obstacles in your spiritual life, how can they be removed? Consider the possibility that they cannot be removed but only overcome. If that's true, *how* can they be overcome?

The Gift of Inadequacy

📖 For years I hid the inadequacy I felt as a counselor behind a professional demeanor, technical jargon, and sound psychological methods of treatment. Recently I've made a truly liberating discovery. I *am* inadequate. My sense of inadequacy is not the effect of deficient intellect or poor training, nor is it a symptom of emotional disorder. It is the painful admission of what is true. On my own, I can make nothing of importance happen. I can help no one.

But if I abide in Christ, if I present myself before God's Spirit for searching and filling, if I study and ponder the Scriptures and live my life in brokenness before a grace-dispensing community, I can transcend my inadequacy.

I can find myself as I worship. I can struggle on behalf of others with the energy of Christ powerfully working in me.

I have learned that an awareness of inadequacy is neither a curse to lift nor a disorder to cure. It is a gift to be received, a gift that if properly used can make me powerful and strong and clear and wise. 📖

5. In what significant ways have you recognized your own inadequacy, particularly in relating effectively in another person's life?

6. In practical, everyday terms, what do you think it might mean to properly accept and use your inadequacy as a gift? Think about this question especially in the context of significant relationships, not tasks.

Naomi's Story Continues

📖 God was at work when He brought Naomi home "as the barley harvest was beginning." But His work was not visible. The night was still dark. Naomi was discouraged and depressed. But if we listen carefully as her story unfolds, we can hear God whispering that dawn is on its way. The harvest is beginning. A better dream is about to be revealed— and fulfilled. 📖

7. Read carefully the second chapter of Ruth, and write out a concise outline of the events narrated there.

8. In the second chapter of Ruth, Dr. Crabb finds another "telling phrase" to indicate God's behind-the-scenes movement in Naomi's journey to joy:

Ruth asked her depressed, inactive mother-in-law for permission to "go to the fields and pick up the leftover grain"; and so, *as it turned out, she found herself working in a field belonging to Boaz*" (2:2-3). Deliverance from despair always comes through a person. It was no mere stroke of good luck that, "as it turned out," Ruth caught the eye of a rich relative who owned the field where she happened to glean. It was rather one of those sovereign coincidences, a supernatural intrusion into her life.

Dr. Crabb further explains:

Now God begins to work visibly.... Naomi feels the impact of the young woman's humility and love, and with only a little enthusiasm, smiles weakly and says, "Go ahead, my daughter." That moment is a moment of connecting, where humility and love in one person arouse what little hope remains in another. It is in the community of God's people where God's visible work begins....

Listen to the writer as his pen dances across the pages. "*As it turned out, she found herself working in a field belonging to Boaz, who was from the clan of Elimelech [Naomi's husband]*" (2:3).

I picture the writer pausing after recording that sentence, sitting back and quivering with awe and excitement at the realization that something big is unfolding. Aslan is on the move.

Boaz was God's instrument not merely to solve Naomi's financial problem (though he certainly did that), not only to again fill Naomi's house with the sounds of family (though eventually he did that as well), but to arouse in Naomi a new dream. 📖

In your life, how have you seen God visibly at work through other people to stimulate your own hope?

How God Deepens Our Desire

9. Listen to Dr. Crabb's further comments on what's happening to Naomi in the events of Ruth 2.

> 📖 Consider Naomi's words when she heard where Ruth "happened" to work that day. Immediately she recognized the hand of God. "He has not stopped showing his kindness to the living and the dead" (2:20).
>
> Two things require notice. First, the word she used that we translate *kindness* is the Hebrew *hesed.* It's a word that refers to a strongly bonded relationship where one party continues to be faithfully involved with another because it is the character of the first party to do so. Naomi no longer regards Shaddai as a power who could do something but does nothing. Now she sees His kindness, though her family is still dead. God could resurrect them. He hasn't. She continues to view God as kind.
>
> Second, she views that kindness as actually extending to

her dead husband and sons, to the "living *and the dead.*"
The dream surfacing in Naomi's heart crosses the borders
of this world. The better dream that is emerging out of the
debris of her already shattered dreams is not just about her,
about her life now and her life here. It reaches higher into
another world, an unseen one, and at the same time reaches
down into the depths of her soul where she discovers what
she really wants. 📖

Remember, however, the time frame involved in this development in
Naomi's life, as Dr. Crabb points out:

> 📖 Naomi endured ten years of darkness before God's hand
> became visible. We're forced to draw an unpleasant and dis-
> turbing conclusion: When the pain of shattered dreams
> helps us discover our desire for God, God seems to disap-
> pear. Or at least His absence becomes obvious. And then we
> feel our desire for God as throbbing agony. We discover how
> badly we long to know Him. *It is the frustration of our desire
> for God that deepens it.* Only by *not* revealing God to us, at
> least for a while—sometimes a long while—can the Spirit
> put us in touch with a desire that eventually displaces every
> other desire. 📖

How do you respond to the observations and conclusions drawn
from this part of Naomi's story? Record your thoughts and
impressions.

Addiction—or Deeper Tears

📖 People who find some way to deaden their pain never discover their desire for God in all its fullness. They rather live for relief and become addicts to whatever provides it....

All of us are trapped by addiction to a desire for something less than God. For many women, that something less is relational control. "I will not be hurt again and I will not let people I love be hurt. I'll see to it that what I fear never happens."...

More common in men is an addiction to nonrelational control. "I will experience deep and consuming satisfaction without ever having to relate meaningfully with anyone." 📖

10. In what ways can you relate to any of these indications of "addiction"?

11. Think carefully about the following words:

📖 When dreams shatter, we long to experience God's nearness in a way that dries our tears. Instead, deeper tears are released.

Perhaps that's why so few make any sustained effort to seek God with all their hearts, to discover how deeply they do in fact desire God. The discovery brings pain. We get in touch with a profound desire that we have no power whatsoever to satisfy. We find ourselves at the mercy of One who could provide satisfaction but may not, a Person we cannot manipulate, an unresponsive God who keeps whispering,

"Later." The stark truth is a hard one: Discovering our desire for God introduces us to a whole new world of hurt. When we realize how badly we want Him, He seemingly disappears.

But it's a hopeful hurt. It doesn't feel exactly good, but it does feel clean. Through our tears we actually can sing "Great Is Thy Faithfulness" and "It Is Well with My Soul." We can even sing "I Love You, Lord," not without an ache in our hearts but somehow through the ache.

A profound encounter with pain brings us to make a choice. Either we change or we sink into bitterness, despair, or hedonism. Either we accept the fact that life is *not* all about us and how we feel now and what happens here, or we push back the pain by living for the satisfaction of lesser dreams that might come true. 📖

As honestly as you can, describe your own journey in encountering any of the observations and experiences in the preceding paragraphs.

Discovering Our Desire for God

12. Dr. Crabb writes, "When we discover our desire for God, we can live for nothing less." How would you evaluate your sincere willingness to come to the point of living for nothing less as you move forward in discovering your desire for God? To what degree is "living for nothing less" an attitude that you truly want to attain?

13. In what ways, if any, are you afraid to reach the point of "living for nothing less"?

📖 But there's a problem, one I've already mentioned. Becoming aware of our desire for God seems to reliably generate severe frustration....

When Shaddai allows terrible pain to come into our lives, He is removing a satisfaction, often a legitimate one like the enjoyment of one's spouse, that keeps us happy and content whether we know God well or not. He is taking away good food to make us hungry for better fare.

But then He doesn't seem to give it. The table stays bare. Those who claim otherwise most often are feeding on their own resources or on their remaining blessings, mistaking them for God....

It is the frustration of our desire for God that deepens it. Only by *not* revealing God to us, at least for a while—sometimes a long while—can the Spirit put us in touch with a desire that eventually displaces every other desire. 📖

14. To what degree have you personally experienced the frustration mentioned above? If you've known this frustration (or know of others who've experienced it), how would you further describe it? (Remember that strong faith admits when God doesn't seem real; weak faith pretends.)

📖 We will not win the battle against addiction without discovering our desire for God. Therefore, if you want to know God, welcome shattered dreams. Nothing reveals our desire for Him so effectively.

But we must also discover God's desire for us. A *recognized* desire for God exposes our idolatry and sets us on a better path.

But only a *fulfilled* desire for God provides the power to consistently resist the lure of lesser pleasures and to stay anchored in Christ when life's storms rage....

How do we experience the reality of God? This is the most important question a Christian can ask....

I'm left wondering: What does it mean for you and me, in this day and age, to experience God? It's one thing to discover our desire for God. It's quite another to discover His desire for us, to know with absolute certainty when life is at its worst that His Presence is real, that He is with us, and that He cares. 📖

15. "How do we experience the reality of God?" Express as fully as you can your present understanding of the answer to this question.

The Elusive God

16. Read carefully through the following extended excerpt from *Shattered Dreams*.

📖 When we discover our desire for God, we're immediately introduced to a new kind of pain. We experience the terrifying dread that we will not find Him.

It was really much easier when we were satisfied with lesser things. One of my happiest friends is a successful businessman with an attractive wife who stays busy with clubs and shopping trips, three kids who are each athletic, bright, and good-looking, and enough money to take the family to the Bahamas for seven days one month and to hunt for a week in Alaska the next. He wonders why I struggle so much. He goes to church. He loves God. He can't figure out why I make Christianity so difficult.

Until we realize how badly we need God, how empty we are without Him, we can sing "Great Is Thy Faithfulness" without worrying whether God really shows up. We can enjoy a happy indifference to whether we discover Him.

For many people, things go well. They feel pretty good. The wonderful truth that God is faithful means to them that He will keep their lives moving along pleasantly. When their path hits a bump, they pray and things get better.

They know God can do something, and He does. Why does God seem to provide so well for the pleasantly committed and to withdraw from the seriously committed? It's enough to make us wonder if we've washed our hands of lukewarm Christianity in vain.

In Exodus, every time the Israelites complained, God blessed them. He straightened things out. Bitter water became sweet, meat and bread rained down from heaven when they told Moses they were hungry. But in Numbers, when they were farther along on their trek to Canaan, God changed tactics. Most often He refused to bless them. When they grumbled about manna, God gave them meat that produced serious indigestion. The next time they fussed about His inadequate provisions, He sent deadly snakes to bite and kill them.

Who wants to become mature? Answered prayer seems to be more frequently reported among younger Christians.

God, it appears, accommodates our immaturity not to

keep us there, but to give us a confidence in His Presence that will sustain the search for a deeper, more relational expression of His Presence. The farther we travel on our spiritual journey, the less responsive God becomes to our requests for a pleasant life. Things go wrong and God does nothing. He becomes the elusive God. He is inviting us to an experience with Him that is more fulfilling than an experience with anyone else.

Live long enough and important dreams will shatter. Things will go wrong that God will not fix. He could fix them, but He doesn't.

Then, when the pain of unmet desires puts us in touch with how desperately we long to discover the gentle Presence in our lives, we become more aware of His absence. From deep places in our being that we never knew were there when life was pleasant, we cry out, "God, where are You? Do You care? *Let me find You!*" 📖

What observations or reflections in this quotation can you most identify with, and why?

In what ways can you see that you have experienced the kind of pain spoken of in the above quotation?

Blocking Out the Noise

📖 We must begin our answer by appealing not to experience but to truth. The Bible is clear. God exists. He exists in heaven.

He exists on earth. He exists everywhere. Most importantly, He exists *in* us. That's where He is most personally and satisfyingly discoverable.

The life of the Trinity flows in our being (Colossians 2:9-10). Christ is in us (Colossians 1:27). The Spirit has entered us and taken up permanent residence (1 Corinthians 3:16). The Father and Son have made Their home in everyone who loves Jesus, and They promise to let us know They're there (John 14:23).

Our search for God is therefore an *inward* search. Silence and solitude are essential to discovering His Presence. We must block out the noise of life and become aware of our interior world if we're to find God. 📖

17. What does the term "inward search" mean to you—in practical, everyday terms—as you seek to know God?

Look up the Scripture references mentioned in the middle paragraph of the preceding quotation, and view each passage in the fresh light of what you've learned in this workbook. How would you summarize what these passages mean to you in terms of your own experience and responsibility?

📖 If we fail to be quiet enough to hear *all* that the Spirit is saying, we will be in danger of discovering our desire for God and never discovering His desire for us. 📖

18. What does it mean practically for you to "be quiet enough to hear *all* that the Spirit is saying"?

📖 If we're to encounter the divine Presence, we must enter the interior sanctuary of our heart and, like Jesus in the temple, become indignant over what we find. There is no way to God but through the rubble. We must go through, not around, whatever keeps us from Him. The process is what spiritual people call brokenness and repentance.

That does not mean, of course, that we should dwell every minute on what is difficult in our lives....

But we must let our souls live in a private monastery, in an attitude of contemplation that helps us see that all of life is sacred, where we remain alert to the Spirit's revelation of ourselves and God. When life gets tough and God does nothing, the Spirit is telling us that this world is not our home. He is whispering to us about another world and revealing Someone who is faithfully leading us there along the best path. And He is exposing the rubble that must be cleared away. 📖

19. What rubble in your life might need to be exposed and sorted through so you can move forward in the journey of knowing God?

A Bigger Dream

📖 Let me paraphrase Naomi's words when she heard that Ruth had caught the eye of Boaz. "The Lord has not discarded me. He has always been there, but now I can see His kind heart at work. My pain is still real. I've felt it keenly for ten years. But now something matters more. I'm beginning to recognize the shape of a dream that is bigger than every dream I have so far valued." 📖

20. Is this vision of a bigger dream also becoming *your* experience? If so, describe this bigger dream as fully and honestly as you can.

21. In quietness, review what you've written and learned in this week's lesson. If further thoughts or prayer requests come to mind, you may want to write them down.

22. What for you was the most meaningful concept or truth in this week's lesson?

How would you talk this over with God? Write down your response as a prayer to Him.

What do you believe God wants you to do in response to this week's study?

DISCOVERING GOD'S PASSION

THIS WEEK'S LESSON IS BASED ON

CHAPTER 11, "ABANDONMENT AND CONFIDENCE,"

CHAPTER 12, "HIS PASSION RESTRAINED,"

AND CHAPTER 13, "A HELL OF MERCY"

O ur journey continues…and Dr. Crabb reminds us that it's something quite different from the life-journey embraced by the secular
world and with a much different impact on the traveler's life.

📖 Satan's masterpiece is not the prostitute or the skid-row
bum. It is the self-sufficient person who has made life comfortable, who is adjusting well to the world and truly likes
living here, a person who dreams of no better place to live,
who longs to be only a little better—and a little better off—
than he already is.…

The Spirit's masterpiece is the man or woman who much
prefers to live elsewhere, who finds no deep joy in the good
things of this life, who looks closely in the mirror and yearns
to see something different, whose highest dream is to be

in the Presence of the grace-filled Father. It is the person whose life *here* is consumed with preparing to meet Him *there*. 📖

As you begin, remember again to ask for the Holy Spirit's help in hearing and obeying His words for you at this time.

Experiencing His Presence

📖 It is possible to meet God. He *does* visit people in this life. We *can* experience His Presence. Self-aware people want nothing more….

More than ever before in my lifetime, people are self-consciously hungry for God, for spiritual renewal, for deep satisfaction of the soul. And we are more in danger than ever before of managing our search and discovering a spirituality without Christ. 📖

1. As you think about what you've learned so far, what is harmful or wrong about "managing our search" for spiritual renewal?

How can "a spirituality without Christ" masquerade as a spirituality *with* Christ?

What passages of Scripture have helped most to convince you that we *can* experience God's presence in this life?

True Abandonment

📖 The search to discover God requires that we *abandon* ourselves, that we give up control of what matters most, and that we place our *confidence* in Someone we cannot manage. These requirements are as vital as they are difficult....

[T]rue abandonment, giving ourselves to God in utter dependence on His willingness to give Himself to us, pleads only mercy. It allows no room for control. It includes no claim on God that obligates Him to do anything. Only suffering has the power to bring us to this point. 📖

2. On a practical plane, what does this "abandonment" mean to you?

What examples of true abandonment to God have you seen in the lives of Christians you know? (If you can, include examples of dependence on God not only for material needs, but also for soul needs.)

To truly give ourselves to God, why is it necessary that we trust in His willingness to "give" Himself to us?

How would you describe your understanding and trust of God's willingness to give Himself to you?

3. From a survey of one or more of the following passages, find biblical statements that seem especially to address this topic of abandonment to God. List the significant phrases or verses, along with any personal

comments or questions—such as how the things you've learned help
you view these passages in a different light.

Joshua 1
Psalm 16
Psalm 130
Psalm 131
Proverbs 3
John 14

4. Dr. Crabb states that "only suffering has the power to bring us" to the
point of true spiritual abandonment. As you think about what you've
learned so far in the *Shattered Dreams Workbook,* explain your understanding of what he means.

True Confidence

📖 Confidence in God...involves an experience that takes
us beyond the realm of our five senses. It calls on our capacity to experience spiritual, not material, reality....

When in the middle of terrible pain we cry out to God,
He rarely grants an experience that, with our five senses, we
can recognize as God showing up.... But as we abandon
ourselves more to Him (What else can we do when we discover that He is all we want?), a confidence emerges, a sense
of His Presence, that only the awakened spiritual capacities
of the soul can identify. 📖

5. As you consider carefully the preceding quotation, what questions come to your mind? In what respects do you find yourself in strong agreement with these words?

How would you describe or illustrate "the awakened spiritual capacities of the soul" that Dr. Crabb mentions above?

Our Normal Reactions

> 📖 I wanted to throttle Him…to grab God by the shoulders, shake Him till He paid attention, then tell Him to do a better job of caring for His children.…
>
> I know my reaction is wrong. I know God is God and I'm not.… But sometimes it's hard.…
>
> Throttling God! The image is as ridiculous as it is insubordinate. But what's the alternative? Are we expected to experience God as unresponsive to our well-being and pretend we like Him anyway? Things that matter deeply to us don't seem to matter to Him. What are we to do with that fact? 📖

6. If you can, describe a situation when your feelings and thoughts were similar to the author's on the occasion he mentions above.

7. Dr. Crabb states that "what many call the Christian life is lifeless surrender to a system they cannot fight, coupled with an attempt to convince themselves they love the Judge." In what ways, if any, have you seen your own tendency to "surrender" in this way? How would such a surrender cause a person to miss out on experiencing God's reality?

Finding Solid Ground

8. As an alternative to such a surrender, Dr. Crabb describes this response: "Scream and holler until the terror of life so weighs you down that you discover solid ground beneath your feet."

    And what is this solid ground? He further explains:

    📖 The solid ground is not doctrine. It is not merely truth to believe. It is not recommitment and trying harder to believe and do right. It is *Him*....

    Solid ground beneath the pain of shattered dreams...is the realization that *it's more difficult for Christ to restrain Himself from making all our dreams come true than for us to watch them shatter.* At our moment of worst pain, Jesus' pain is worse....

    Once our feet touch the solid ground of His passion for us, we can neither dismiss Him as uncaring nor cringe before Him as a ruthless despot. 📖

    In an everyday sense, what do you think it means for us to "touch the solid ground of His passion for us"?

9. "Imagine what Jesus must feel," Dr. Crabb writes, "as He stands next to every bed in every hospital. With a word, He could cure every patient. What must He feel as He observes every divorce proceeding in every court?" As you understand the Lord's character, how would you answer that last question?

Dr. Crabb notes that in such a situation Jesus "could do something. Most often He does nothing. The mystery is why." He also states that our awareness of this restraint on the Lord's part can become "not a cause for complaint, but a sacred and appealing mystery." To you, what exactly is "appealing" about this mystery?

10. From a survey of any of the following passages, find convincing evidence of the Lord's "passion to bless." List the significant phrases or verses you see—along with any personal comments or questions.

Psalm 145
John 10
Ephesians 1
Revelation 2

Naomi's Story Continues

11. Think about these words as you prepare to read the third chapter of Ruth.

> 📖 Naomi's story offers a powerful illustration of what it
> means to abandon ourselves to God with confidence that
> He is there. It's a parable that may help us to depend more
> completely on God and to discover His desire for us. 📖

After reading Ruth 3, write out a concise outline of the events narrated in that chapter.

12. In the previous chapter of Ruth, we saw Naomi's growing awareness of God's work in her life.

📖 But, as is so often the case, when God began to visibly move in Naomi's life, He did not create a smooth path. There was more Naomi needed to learn before she could worship. Through the agony of shattered dreams, her soul was ripped open so she could discover her desire for God. Now she needed to discover God's desire for her. That's what happens next in her story. 📖

In Ruth 3, as "we meet Naomi again," writes Dr. Crabb, "she is a different woman." How so? Near the end of Ruth 3, Dr. Crabb finds another "telling phrase." He had earlier described it this way:

📖 If Boaz were to marry Ruth, both Ruth's and Naomi's financial problems would be over. But before he could marry her, Boaz had to overcome a legal hurdle stipulated by Jewish law. The obstacle was real. Ruth may well have been anxious. Would it all work out?

Naomi spoke words of wisdom to Ruth: "Wait, my daughter, until you find out what happens. *For the man will not rest* until the matter is settled today"(3:18). It is true that deliverance comes through a person, but it is also true that the person who delivers us must earnestly long to bring us joy. Deliverance always comes through love....

Naomi has discovered a good man's passion that lets her soul rest and releases her to be powerful in someone else's life. 📖

Dr. Crabb concludes, "In each of our lives...the deliverer is eagerly preparing to bless, unable to rest till He does." Have you sensed this restless, eager-to-bless love from God at this time in your own life? If not, describe any ways in which you may nevertheless be able to trust Him for it.

He Will Not Rest

13. Think about these comments from Dr. Crabb on the significance of this part of Naomi's story (as related in Ruth 3). For each section of commentary below, jot down your own responses, reflections, and questions.

> 📖 Picture what happened. Boaz, a middle-aged bachelor, wealthy, a devoted follower of Shaddai, wakes up one night at two in the morning and sees a beautiful foreign girl lying at his feet. Perhaps it was her delicate perfume that aroused him. He rubs his eyes, thinking it's a good dream, then looks again. There she is, dressed in alluring clothing and making a clear statement: "I am available to become your wife."
>
> He recognizes her at once as the peasant woman he'd met earlier. Ruth had caught his eye. Boaz had felt immediately drawn, both by her character (he knew of her loyalty to Naomi) and by her youthful beauty. Apparently his tasteful advances to her in the fields had struck a chord. Here she was, cleaned up and pretty, presenting herself to him.
>
> Boaz wanted Ruth. The writer allows no question about

that. He wanted to call the rabbi, exchange vows, and take her to bed. If I were writing a steamy novel, I would describe in lurid detail his sexual attraction to Ruth. The description would be accurate. But his passion, though including physical desire, is deeper, richer, more enduringly passionate than fleeting, easily satisfied lust. The inspired writer tells the story of a man who strongly desires a woman. The picture of Christ is hard to miss. 📖

📖 But there's a problem. The law stands between Boaz and Ruth. Jewish law stipulated that the nearest relative had the first right of refusal to marry his relative's widow and assume responsibility for the bereaved family. Boaz was related to Naomi (and so to Ruth), but there was another man more closely related.

Like an honorable lover refusing to enjoy the pleasures of sex until the covenant of marriage was sealed, Boaz withheld himself from Ruth. He actually moved away from her, giving her the noble gift of his absence until he could be with her without dishonor.

Boaz knew the law of the kinsman-redeemer. To marry a relative's widow and restore her to blessing, the candidate must satisfy three criteria. One, he must be a relative, the closest relative willing to assume the role of kinsman-redeemer. Two, he must have the means to pay the entire debt owed by the widow and her family. Three, he must have the power to remove anyone who wanted to remain on the widow's property after all debts were paid.

Ruth, at best vaguely familiar with Jewish law, was aware only that Boaz was withholding himself from her. She must have worried that he didn't really want her. She had discovered her desire for Boaz but was not yet confident of his desire for her. 📖

📖 I picture Naomi sitting on the floor of their little house, warming herself by the fire on a chilly morning. Ruth returns from her night with Boaz, still wearing her prettiest dress but no longer feeling beautiful.

"Naomi, what shall I do? I love Boaz and I think he loves me. But he said he can't marry me until some legal problem is cleared up. Oh, Naomi, I don't know anything about all those technicalities. All I know is that I want him. I don't want anyone else. I want *him.* Doesn't he want me?"

Naomi sits quietly. She knows. Her heart is at rest, quietly thumping with anticipation.

I've often wondered if it occurred to Naomi to suggest Ruth dress in an old rag, work up a sweat, and present herself the next night to the nearest relative. Maybe that would move them through the legal impasse.

Instead, with the wisdom of a spiritual director, she longs for Ruth to *abandon* herself to the heart of one who loves her, with *confidence*—in spite of his restraint—that his desire will find a way to bring them together.

"Ruth," Naomi says, "Boaz wants you more than you want him. He is withholding himself from you for a time at great personal cost. It is harder for him to keep his distance from you than it is for you to wait for him. Know this, that this man will move heaven and earth to find a lawful way to marry you. And that's what you want, a legal marriage that rests on an unshakable foundation. You want nothing less. Wait, my daughter. *The man will not rest* until the matter is settled today." 📖

The Spirit Speaks

14. Dr. Crabb offers the following statements as possible expressions of "the Spirit's words to us." As you're able to accept them in that light— as the Holy Spirit's words to *you*—record your response to each expression in your own words of prayer:

📖 [Y]our Heavenly Bridegroom is consumed with desire for you. 📖

📖 For reasons you cannot now understand, He is holding Himself back from filling your life with every imaginable pleasure. He could do what you're asking Him to do. 📖

📖 When He appears to do nothing, to leave you in your pain and provide no relief, realize this: *The Man will not rest till He makes everything good.* 📖

📖 In the mystery of suffering, enter the deeper mystery of His restrained passion. As the mother holds her baby still so the doctor can deliver the needed injection, so your Lord is allowing you to suffer for reasons you do not know. 📖

📖 Don't try to find comfort in explaining the reasons. Don't try to find the spiritual means to trust more. Enter your pain until your feet touch the solid ground beneath you, the solid ground of the restrained passion of Jesus. 📖

📖 I, the Spirit of Christ, will reveal His passion to you. Create space for Me to fill by waiting, by abandoning yourself to God. When I allow you to discover His desire for you, you will rest with confidence in His love. 📖

📖 Through the pain of shattered dreams, God is awakening us to the possibility of infinite pleasure. That is the nature of our journey; it's what the Spirit is doing. 📖

An Untroubled Heart

15. In the excerpts below, Dr. Crabb elaborates on the potential meaning for us when Jesus says, "Don't let your hearts be troubled." Once more, as you're able to accept these expressions in that light—as words from Jesus to *you*—read them reflectively, then record your prayerful responses to those that speak most to you:

📖 I know things are not now as you want them. I know many of your dreams are not coming true. I want you to understand that things are not as I will one day make them. I like neither the distance between us nor the pain you suffer.... 📖

📖 Until I come to bring you to My Father's house, I am devoting Myself to only one thing: I am preparing a place for you. And My Spirit, on My behalf, is devoting Himself to only one thing—preparing you to enjoy Me and all that I will provide.... 📖

📖 I have called you not to the secular journey where you must make everything in your life now as pleasant as possible. I have called you to the spiritual journey, to a process of enlarging your heart to desire Me above everything else.... 📖

📖 Do not be troubled by all the dreams that will shatter while you remain on earth. You will feel deep pain. But every sorrow you experience will be used by My Spirit to deepen your desire for Me. He will speak to you about Me.... 📖

📖 Listen for the voice. You will hear Him most clearly when suffering humbles you enough to want to hear Him, to know you cannot go on without hearing Him.... 📖

📖 This time of distance, when you will feel such disappointment both with your life and with yourself, will

awaken your heart to receive Me with great joy when I
finally come. I will not delay. I will come at exactly the
appointed time. My Father will give the signal. Listen for
the shout.... 📖

16. In quietness, review what you've written and learned in this week's lesson. As further thoughts or prayer requests come to mind, jot them
down.

17. What for you was the most meaningful concept or truth in this week's
lesson?

How would you talk this over with God? Write down your response
as a prayer to Him.

What do you believe God wants you to do in response to this week's
study?

WANTING
SOMETHING BETTER

THIS WEEK'S LESSON IS BASED ON

CHAPTER 14, "A STRANGE WEDDING TOAST,"

CHAPTER 15, "BUT LIFE OUGHT TO WORK,"

AND CHAPTER 16, "IT ISN'T ALWAYS GOOD TO FEEL GOOD"

W e dive deeper now into a more thorough exploration of themes you've seen earlier in this workbook. As you begin this week's study, ask for God's Spirit to give you genuine insight into these matters.

Naomi's Story Continues

1. Keep the following perspectives in mind as you read the final chapter of the book of Ruth.

   📖 In the last chapter of Naomi's story, we learn two lessons. First, the work of the Spirit will continue through every bump in the road, through every shattered dream. Second, there is one dream God will fulfill for us now, in this life, before we get to heaven, and its fulfillment will bring us joy. 📖

Now write out a concise outline of the events narrated in Ruth 4.

A Strange Wedding Toast

2. Dr. Crabb draws our attention in particular to a "strange wedding toast" offered in Ruth 4—the elders' words of blessing upon the marriage of Boaz and Ruth.

> 📖 Here's what the elder said about Ruth: "May the LORD make the woman who is coming into your home like Rachel and Leah, who together built up the house of Israel" (4:11). Was he hoping that Ruth, like Rachel, would be barren and, in her resentment over the shattered dream of bearing children, insist that Boaz have kids through her servant girl? Did he want Ruth to feel unloved, like Leah, and have all the children she could, thinking that one more child might finally win her husband's love?…
>
> Before the elder put down his glass, he added: "Through the offspring the LORD gives you by this young woman, may your family be like that of Perez, whom Tamar bore to Judah" (4:12). The first part of the toast was strange enough. This addendum is positively bizarre. Was he wishing Ruth to disguise herself as a prostitute to seduce her father-in-law and to bear a child by him? That's what Tamar did. Perez

was one of twin boys born to Tamar after she tricked Judah
into having sex with her. 📖

What are your reactions to these words of "blessing" spoken for Boaz
and Ruth's benefit?

3. Listen now to Dr. Crabb's further comments on this passage. Then
record your response to his words plus your further reflections and
questions.

> 📖 "May your wife be like Rachel and Leah." I read that as
> a toast to brokenness.... I hear the elder telling Boaz some-
> thing like this: "Boaz, you've married a lovely woman. I
> want the best for you. But even if the unimaginable happens
> and Ruth turns out to be as conniving as Rachel or as inse-
> cure as Leah, God will still be at work to bring about the
> good He intends. No matter how bad life may one day
> make you feel, remember something good is happening that
> you may not be able to see. Give yourself over to the God
> who is working out a good plan. Do not settle for rearrang-
> ing your world merely to feel better. Remember the twelve
> sons of Israel were born through the likes of Rachel and
> Leah."
>
> And when the elder added the words, "May your offspring
> be like Perez whom Tamar bore to Judah," I hear him saying:
> "Your life might turn into a mess. Trust God to bring good
> out of whatever happens. Boaz, things will go wrong in your
> life. Since Eden and until the Second Coming, things have
> gone wrong and will go wrong in everyone's life. You are

immune from no evil. Your failure may trigger even worse failure that will cycle into worse failure still. Look at Judah and Tamar. But their offspring became an ancestor of the Messiah. Give up your demand for blessing that will always help you feel good. When life falls apart, lose all confidence in yourself to put things back together. Yes, I know you're wealthy and powerful. But only God is the author of the truly good. And only the pain of shattered dreams can strip you of confidence in yourself to do anything truly good. Boaz, I wish you brokenness because I wish you joy." 📖

What Our Prayers Reveal

📖 We so easily pray for ourselves and the people we love that we will all be drawn closer to God. I wonder if we know what we're asking. Are we asking to enjoy His blessings with little interest in enjoying His Person?...

When someone shares his story of shattered dreams, our stomachs tighten with fear lest we should meet a similar fate. We dedicate our strongest efforts to helping that person feel better because we're terrified of ever experiencing deep pain that cannot be relieved.

Why? Why do we undervalue intimacy with Christ? Why does the prospect of becoming like Him and close to Him have less appeal than other good things? 📖

4. In your perception, what are the best answers to the "why" questions asked in the last paragraph of the preceding quotation?

The finest things this world can offer have no compelling appeal to a reborn spirit. They are as nothing compared to the joy of living in His Presence.

That's how God sees things. It takes some doing for us to see things the same way. It takes shattered dreams.

5. Here again we see the crucial significance of shattered dreams in preparing us to draw closer to God. What is your reaction to this concept at this time? Do you fully "buy into" it? Do you have doubts or some other form of resistance to it?

I realize that only in the experience of emptiness does God's Spirit confront us with the choice either to fill ourselves or to abandon ourselves to a God who leaves us empty for a long time and promises fullness later. I have come to believe that suffering is necessary to awaken our desire for God and to develop confidence in His desire for us.

I therefore pray for myself and the people I love that we will experience the severe mercy of shattered dreams, not because I want any of us to hurt but because I long for every one of us to experience the joy of knowing God's love.

I pray that each of our journeys will carry us into seasons of brokenness.

6. How do the words above compare to how you typically pray for your loved ones?

First Things or Second Things?

📖 Society—especially the government but also the church—
has taken on the job of producing more untroubled people
and fewer seriously troubled people.

Our method has been remarkably consistent: We work
hard to improve people's lives, to help people feel good by
seeing to it their dreams come true. We devote our energies
to improving circumstances—better homes, better families,
better jobs—and when bad circumstances cannot be improved, we work to improve people's ability to cope with hard
times. We want people, including ourselves, to feel good.

We focus on second things while God is working on first
things. 📖

7. What do you think Dr. Crabb most likely means here by "first things"
and "second things"?

In your life's most important arenas, how can you join with God in
focusing on His "first things" rather than the "second things" we more
easily embrace?

📖 It seems we are devoting our best efforts to one central
goal: making this life work better so we can feel better. The
unchallenged assumption behind our resolve is a delusion.
We assume life is *supposed* to work in ways that make us feel
the way we want to feel, the way we intuitively and irresistibly sense we were designed to feel.

We further assume that if there is a God, His job is to do what we cannot do to make life work as we want. We conceive of the spiritual journey as a cooperative enterprise where we pool our resources with God's to see to it that life works well enough to keep us relatively happy till we reach the world where life works perfectly and we always feel great. 📖

8. Rightly or wrongly, what have you assumed to be God's "job" in your life?

Counting on God

9. Dr. Crabb notes our tendency to think God should cooperate with us "to make life work so we can feel now all that He has created us to feel." Then he states, "There are two problems with that view":

> 📖 *One,* better circumstances, whether winning the lottery or saving your marriage, can never produce the joy we were designed to experience. Only an intimate relationship with Perfect Love can provide that joy. *Two,* in this life, we can never feel what God intended us to feel, at least not in full measure. To be completely happy, we must experience perfect intimacy with Perfect Love *and* every "second-thing" blessing that Perfect Love can provide. In this life, we have neither. God will provide both, but not till heaven. 📖

Notice the two *nevers* in the preceding quotation. Do you fully agree with the author on these points? Why or why not?

📖 It's hard to hear, but it is important to know that God is *not* committed to supporting our ministries, to preventing our divorces, to preserving our health, to straightening out our kids, to providing a livable income, to ending famine, to protecting us from agonizing problems that generate in our souls an experience that feels like death.

We *cannot* count on God to arrange what happens in our lives in ways that will make us feel good. 📖

10. For you personally, are the preceding statements indeed "hard to hear"? Why or why not?

📖 We *can* count on God to patiently remove all the obstacles to our enjoyment of Him. He is committed to our joy, and we can depend on Him to give us enough of a taste of that joy and enough hope that the best is still ahead to keep us going in spite of how much pain continues to plague our hearts. 📖

11. How exactly do you think we can count on God to "remove all the obstacles to our enjoyment of Him"?

12. What Scripture passages can you think of that relate directly to the main points of the two preceding quotations? How do these passages relate to the points Dr. Crabb is making?

The Spirit's Pull

📖 I know what it is to feel good when life works. For that I make no apology. We should enjoy God's blessings; the good things of life should generate good feelings. But I am coming to see something wrong that before I thought was spiritual gratitude: Those good feelings have become my basis for joy....

I can now feel the powerful undertow within me that has long been pulling me out to sea, into cold waters and uncaring waves. That undertow is an attitude insisting that life continue well enough for me to feel pretty good. When dreams shatter, I then feel alone, unloved, and desperate. And I resolve, more than anything else, to feel better. That resolve is the flesh.

But I can also feel gentle arms around me pulling me toward shore, inviting me to abandon myself to their strength, to believe with confidence that, despite what goes wrong and how bad I feel, they are guiding me toward deep joy. That pull is the Spirit. 📖

13. Think about both the "undertow" and the "gentle arms...pulling me toward shore" as depicted in the preceding quotation. Have you experienced either or both of these impressions? If so, describe those experiences in your own words.

📖 In this world, the dream of feeling as good as we want to feel *will* shatter.... Shattered dreams will create the opportunity for God to work more deeply than ever before, to further weaken our grasp on our empty selves.

They will also create the opportunity for bitterness and its children, defeat and immorality, to develop. Bitterness carries us farther from shore, into dark nights that never had to be.

Brokenness, on the other hand, allows us to relax in the arms that will bring us to shore, where a warm fire is burning and food has been prepared. 📖

14. In what ways, if any, can you see that God is further weakening your grasp on your empty self?

In what ways have you seen the tendency toward bitterness that this weakening can lead to?

In what ways have you experienced the brokenness that "allows us to relax in the arms that will bring us to shore"?

Flesh and Spirit

15. How would you explain the conflict in our lives between our "flesh" (our sinful nature) and the Spirit, especially as it relates to our experience of shattered dreams?

16. Dr. Crabb includes the following words in "a description of what the Bible calls our *flesh*":

📖 Without knowing exactly when it happens, we give up on God—not on His getting us to heaven, but on His making us whole, or at least a little more whole, in this life....

We begin to wonder if we have misread all the promises He made, promises about a peace that passes understanding, promises to anchor our souls with hope and lavish us with joy....

So we take matters into our own hands. We work hard to improve our marriage, to straighten out our kid, to make enough money to pay for the bare necessities. We want things to improve, and now it's clear *why* we want things to improve—we want to feel better. That's our bottom line....

Our misery drives us not to seek God, but to seek to feel better; not to please Him, but to use Him.

We come to a point where there is no more important fact in the world than that we feel bad and there is no deeper desire in our hearts than to feel good....

Look into your heart, study your interior world, and you will find that attitude. It's there in all of us. 📖

Which portions, if any, of the preceding quotation can you especially identify with?

17. Look over 2 Corinthians 4–5 and record your observations of Paul's responses to trouble in his life. How do you think they relate to what you've been learning?

A Fork in the Road

18. Dr. Crabb quotes a poem written by Columbine High School student Rachel Joy Scott a few days before she died in the tragic shootings at the school in 1999:

I'm drowning
in my own lake of despair.
I'm choking,
my hands wrapped around my neck.
I'm dying.
Quickly my soul leaves, slowly my
body withers.
It isn't suicide,
I consider it homicide.
The world you created has led to my death.*

Dr. Crabb then asks, "Suppose you had been a trusted confidante to Rachel, someone whom she asked to read her poem. What might you have said after reading it? More important, what view of life would have determined your response?"

He then suggests what we *might* say in such a situation if we more fully understood God's ways. As you read through each paragraph of this suggested response, think about your own life's journey and that of people close to you, especially anyone who might be hurting at this time. Choose one or more of the paragraphs to reflect upon, and record your thoughts and questions.

📖 Rachel, your pain is legitimate. You've discovered the part
of your soul that longs for what this world will never provide.
Your integrity has burdened you with the severe mercy of
realizing that nothing in this world provides true joy. 📖

---

* Rachel Joy Scott, quoted by Richard Roeper, "One year later, Columbine still offers no easy answers," *Denver Post*, 20 April 2000, sec. B, p. 9.

📖 You've come to a fork in the road. One path beckons you with the promise that life can work well, and God exists to see to it that things go well enough for you to feel pretty good. 📖

📖 The other path, the narrow one that not many choose, invites you to live in a disappointing world where good dreams will shatter and you will sometimes feel empty and alone, sometimes so empty and alone that it will seem like death. But this path promises the eventual discovery of a consuming desire within you for God and, far better, the thrilling discovery of His consuming desire to be intimate with you. 📖

📖 After many dark nights, you will taste the joy of that intimacy. You will not be able to describe it, but you will feel alive, hopeful, solid, even in the middle of continued anguish over hard circumstances. 📖

📖 Abandon yourself to God. He will seem at times cruelly unresponsive, callously indifferent. You will be tempted to manage life on your own, to do whatever you can to feel better. 📖

📖 But if you're quiet, you will hear both His voice and yours leading you to the narrow path. 📖

19. In quietness, review what you've written and learned in this week's lesson. As further thoughts or prayer requests come to mind, record them.

20. What for you was the most meaningful concept or truth in this week's lesson?

How would you talk this over with God? Write down your response as a prayer to Him.

What do you believe God wants you to do in response to this week's study?

THE BEST DREAM

THIS WEEK'S LESSON IS BASED ON

CHAPTER 17, "THE THREE LESSONS OF BROKENNESS,"

CHAPTER 18, "OUR HIGHEST DREAM—IF WE ONLY KNEW IT,"

AND CHAPTER 19, "A DREAM COME TRUE"

As you begin, ask for the Holy Spirit's help in hearing and obeying His words for you at this time, with these words from Dr. Crabb in mind:

> 📖 May I suggest that you set this book aside for a few
> minutes and pray. If your heart feels chilly and uninvolved,
> ask the Spirit to make you aware of a hunger for Christ that
> is stronger than your hunger for anything else. 📖

1. If you would like to, write a prayer such as the author suggests.

Naomi's Story Continues

2. Read again the final scenes of Naomi's story as recorded in Ruth 4:13-22. What impresses you most about Naomi in these scenes?

3. "Naomi's story ends with her feeling passion for God," writes Dr. Crabb.

    📖 She's no longer resentful, depressed, and empty, but quiet, joyful, and aware of more than she could see. This last episode of her life is recorded by the Spirit, I believe, to help us see the path to joy and to draw us to join Naomi on the journey.

    The book of Ruth ends with a simple scene. Picture yourself in the theater. The curtain rises for the last act. The stage is barren except for a rocking chair. A wrinkled but peaceful-looking old woman sits on that chair, holding a month-old boy on her lap. We watch as she looks down into the innocent eyes of the child with her eyes of love. Then, slowly, she lifts her gaze to heaven. She says nothing. It's as if we aren't there. No one is there. Naomi is in the Presence of God. We hear a chorus of women's voices sing, "Naomi has a son." She continues holding him on her lap, looking up. The curtain drops. And we sit....

    She's now an old lady. Her first grandson has just been born. She remains a widow. Elimelech is not with her to share her joy. Her son is absent. The child's father should be Mahlon. Instead it is Boaz, a kind relative but not Naomi's son. So many of her dreams are still shattered. God has done nothing to restore them. But He has surfaced a higher dream and is right now fulfilling that dream as Naomi holds Obed on her lap. 📖

Write down your responses to this description and commentary plus any further reflections and questions of your own.

On Her Lap

4. In this last portion of the book of Ruth, Dr. Crabb finds a final "telling phrase" that further shows how God has brought Naomi along on her journey to joy. The phrase is "on her lap" (4:16).

   It's a phrase that "suggests her participation in a much greater dream," he explains. However, we won't catch the excitement of Naomi's dream "unless we set it squarely against the backdrop of human misery. Bear with me as I arrange the set where Naomi is sitting."

   Dr. Crabb "arranges the set" by describing the biblical significance of the phrase *on her lap*. Read carefully the scriptural background he offers below.

   > 📖 The specific phrase "on her lap" occurs three times elsewhere in the Bible, all in Genesis. A brief look at those instances will reveal the climax to Naomi's story hidden in this final scene.
   >
   > *First,* Rachel, Jacob's wife, is barren and none too happy about it. She demands that Jacob sleep with her servant girl so that when a baby is born, Rachel can hold it on her lap. "Sleep with her," she instructs Jacob, "so that she can bear children *for me*"—literally, "on my lap" (Genesis 30:3)....
   >
   > Rachel longed to be part of God's story but wouldn't trust God to make it happen. In the pain of her shattered dreams, she took control....

Second, Jacob, now an old man, can barely see. Just before he dies, he holds his two grandsons Ephraim and Manasseh (Joseph's sons) on his lap. He turns to Joseph and says, "I never expected to see your face again, and now God has allowed me to see your children too" (48:11). In the next verse, the boys are lifted from Jacob's *knees*—literally, from his lap....

Jacob saw his highest dream realized in watching God move through his life and on through others to continue the journey to joy. When he saw not only his long absent son but also his son's children, he rested in the joy of knowing God was continuing to do him good....

Third, Joseph is in Egypt, years later. He longs to be in the Promised Land, but faces death in Egypt. We're told that by now he has seen "the third generation of Ephraim's children. Also the children of Makir son of Manasseh were placed at birth on Joseph's knees," literally, on his lap (50:23). With the children on his lap, he speaks his final words to his family: "I am about to die. But God will surely come to your aid and take you up out of the land to the land he promised." Then he adds, "And then you must carry my bones up from this place" (50:24-25). Joseph doesn't want to miss the party he knows is coming, a party that death would not prevent him from enjoying.

Joseph realized that his death was not an ending but rather another chapter in a story that would end well. 📖

With this biblical background in mind, how would you explain in your own words the significance of the phrase "on her lap" in Naomi's story?

5. "And now Naomi, as her life ends, is holding her grandson *on her lap,*" writes Dr. Crabb. "After her journey through shattered dreams, I hear this prayer flowing from her heart:"

> 📖 "O God, the path has been rough. I miss my husband. I miss my sons. The pain is still real. But you have given me a sense of Your Presence and the certainty that You have called me to be part of Your sovereign plan.
>
> "And I am tasting community as never before. Ruth is a wonderful young woman, Boaz is a good man, and this baby—well, I've never seen anything so beautiful. This is spiritual community, a community of people through whom You are working toward a higher purpose.
>
> "God, I am not now who I used to be. I was depressed, angry, and afraid of the future. Now I am content, grateful, and full of joy knowing You are here and You are moving. I am a transformed woman. My pain continues, but I'm anchored in hope." 📖

Write down your response to this imagined prayer of Naomi's. How much can you identify in your own life with these words?

Lessons of Brokenness

In chapter 17, Dr. Crabb points us to "three lessons of brokenness." Reflect on these as you see them summarized in the next few pages.

6. The first lesson:

> 📖 The good news of the gospel is not that God will pro-
> vide a way to make life easier. The good news of the gospel,
> for this life, is that He will make our lives better. We will
> be empowered to draw close to God and to love others well
> and to do both for one central purpose, to glorify God, to
> make Him look good to any who watch us live….
>
> The journey to God will always, at some point, take us
> through darkness where life makes no sense. Life isn't easy;
> it's hard, sometimes very hard. 📖

Which thoughts and phrases in the preceding "lesson" carry the most
weight for you?

How would you restate this lesson in a way that has the most personal
application to you at this time?

7. The second lesson:

> 📖 When God seems most absent from us, He is doing
> His most important work in us….
>
> The felt absence of God is a gift to gratefully receive.
> During those seasons of darkness He is doing His deepest
> work in us. 📖

In this "lesson," which thoughts or phrases carry the most weight for
you?

How would you restate this lesson in a way that has the most personal application to you at this time?

8. The third lesson:

> 📖 It isn't always good to be blessed with the good things of life. Bad times provide an opportunity to know God that blessings can never provide....
>
> Feeling good is not the goal. When we feel bad, we have the opportunity to do battle against the enemy within that keeps us from entering the Presence of God with no greater passion than to glorify Him. 📖

Once more, which thoughts or phrases in this "lesson" carry the most weight for you?

And how would you restate this lesson in a way that is most personally applicable to you at this time?

Looking to Jesus

> 📖 True obedience to Christ springs from a deep passion for Christ. But where does the passion come from? How do we get it? 📖

9. To your best spiritual understanding, how would you answer the questions in the preceding quotation?

📖 We look up. We see Jesus. He is screaming, hanging on a cross....

We keep looking, and we listen. We hear God declare, "It is enough!" We hear Jesus cry, "It is finished!" We hear the Spirit whisper to us, "Look now into the face of God. The veil covering His glory is removed. See Him and live!"

We see a smile. We hear a song. We realize, as if for the first time (though we've been Christians for years), that our deepest need, our deepest desire, is *not* for relief from current troubles. We don't even deserve relief.

Our deepest desire is for a kind of life only mercy makes possible, a life only grace provides. It is for life from God, life with God, life for God.

And we have it. We've had it since the day we trusted Christ to forgive our sins. But it took shattered dreams to put us more deeply in touch with what we already have. The pain carried us into depths of our heart that are still ugly, but the Spirit took us deeper, into the very core of our being, where Christ lives, where we are alive. 📖

10. With the preceding thoughts in mind, allow the Holy Spirit's voice to speak through any of the following passages, helping you look up and see Jesus. Feel free to write out your prayerful responses.

Hebrews 2:9
Hebrews 9:28
Hebrews 12:2-3
Hebrews 13:20-21

1 Peter 2:22-25
1 John 4:10
Revelation 5:4-10

First-Order Hope

📖 I realize the very best thing I can do for my newborn grandson is to be a grandfather who delights in the pleasures of God. Maybe the passion coming out of my soul for God will give him the courage to face his own deepest yearnings with hope that more than his stomach can be filled.

My eyes turn away from his. I look up. Tears blur my vision enough to see the face of God.

My heart swells with worship. I discover again how deeply my soul pants for God. Encounter with God, not holding my grandson, defines life. And because I know that, I long for God to reveal Himself to Jake, even if it requires shattered dreams to make it happen.

I still hope Jake stays healthy, does well in school, has lots of friends, meets a nice girl, marries, fathers beautiful kids, and leads his family into meaningful involvement with a local church. But those are all second-order hopes. My first-order hope for Jake is that he encounter God. 📖

11. As you think about these thoughts from the author toward his grandson, how would you express your highest longings for those you love most?

A Prayer in the Darkness

12. Dr. Crabb offers the following prayer as an expression that comes "in the middle of a dark night that has revealed the Son within us." Listen sensitively to these words. Choose one or more of the statements to reflect upon, and record your prayerful responses.

📖 Lord, I can feel within me the demand that You be a better friend. 📖

📖 I can sense my almost irresistible urge to turn to sources of pleasure that provide the relief You withhold. There are many. Some are people—my spouse, my kids, my counselor, my golf buddies. Others are activities like sex and busyness, or things like money and competence. 📖

📖 But none provides life. Only You, on Your terms, can satisfy my soul. 📖

📖 At this moment, though, I don't feel satisfied. I feel empty, desperate, alone. If I believed that there was a better friend than You, I would turn from You. 📖

📖 But I see the cross. I see Your holy wrath and my blaspheming arrogance and I know I deserve not relief but eternal misery. I deserve the emptiness of eternity without love or meaning. And I see Jesus bearing Your wrath so I can receive Your eternal kindness. I have no other friend like that. 📖

📖 How can I turn to anyone else? It would be insanity, foolishness. You are God. I am not. I abandon myself to You. 📖

📖 Like Jabez, I ask that you bless me. I ask that you satisfy the highest dream my heart can envision—an encounter with You. 📖

Learning from Naomi's Story

13. Early in the book, Dr. Crabb pointed to "one central lesson that Naomi's story teaches":

📖 Shattered dreams open the door to better dreams, dreams that we do not properly value until the dreams that we improperly value are destroyed. Shattered dreams destroy false expectations, such as the "victorious" Christian life with no real struggle or failure. They help us discover true hope. We need the help of shattered dreams to put us in touch with what we most long for, to create a felt appetite for better dreams. And living for the better dreams generates a new, unfamiliar feeling that we eventually recognize as joy. 📖

Following are a few phrases taken from the summary above. Think about how each phrase corresponds to something in your life. If something comes to mind, write it down. (To some degree you may

be repeating answers you've given to earlier questions, but this repeti-
tion can help deepen your grasp of the lessons God is teaching you.)

a. "better dreams"
b. "dreams that we improperly value"
c. "false expectations"
d. "true hope"
e. "what we most long for"

14. In quietness, review what you've written and learned in this week's lesson. Record any further thoughts or prayer requests as they come to
mind.

15. What for you was the most meaningful concept or truth in this week's
lesson?

How would you talk this over with God? Write down your response
as a prayer to Him.

What do you believe God wants you to do in response to this week's
study?

TRULY EXPERIENCING GOD

THIS WEEK'S LESSON IS BASED ON

CHAPTER 20, "THERE'S A NEW WAY TO LIVE—AND IT'S POSSIBLE,"

AND CHAPTER 21, "THE JOURNEY TO JOY"

I n our concluding lesson, remember once more to ask for the Holy Spirit's help in hearing and obeying His words for you.

The Exact Center

1. Read this excerpt as Dr. Crabb builds to a statement concerning Christianity's "exact center."

> 📖 For years we've presented Christianity as little more than a means of escaping hell. Knowing Jesus has been reduced to a one-time decision that guarantees the chance to live in a perfect, pain-free world forever.
>
> Christianity is about going to heaven, but that's not the center of Jesus' kindness to us.

Nor is it the opportunity to lead fulfilled, meaningful lives now. Returning to our Maker's manual and following biblical principles to make our marriages work and our kids turn out well and our bank accounts comfortably bulge is not God's plan for our lives....

Jesus revealed His highest dream for all His followers when in prayer He defined the true abundant life in these words: "that they may know you, the only true God, and Jesus Christ, whom you have sent" (John 17:3).

The exact center of Christianity is the opportunity it provides to enjoy God, to be more satisfied with Him than with anyone or anything else. 📖

Based on what you know of Scripture, how fully do you agree with this identification of Christianity's "exact center"?

What difference do you think it could make—and should make—when the true understanding of this "exact center" is embraced in your life?

What difference could it make as this "exact center" is embraced by your church?

Only Suffering

📖 If Luther is right—that only in suffering do we learn to fully delight in God's goodness—then it becomes imme-

diately clear why our enjoyment of God is so shallow.
We don't like to suffer. We see no value in suffering. We
arrange our lives to minimize suffering. And we believe
Christianity offers a God who will cooperate with that
plan. 📖

2. What value in suffering do you honestly see and appreciate?

3. Review some of the following familiar passages in a fresh way, in light
   of your thoughts and discoveries while going through the *Shattered
   Dreams Workbook*. How do these biblical teachings relate to your perspectives on suffering and life's hardships? In what ways do you view
   these passages differently than before?

   Psalm 119:67,68,71,75
   Romans 5:3
   2 Corinthians 4:16-18
   Philippians 1:29-30
   Hebrews 12:7-11
   James 1:2-4

   📖 So the question we must squarely face is this: Does
   knowing God really provide the pleasure our souls were
   designed to enjoy? Can we enjoy God more than anyone
   or anything else? Is it possible? 📖

4. What, more than anything else, convinces you that the answer to the
   above questions is "Yes"?

Only Worship

📖 The cure…for every form of slavery to something other
than God is worship. Not the dull worship of rote routine or
the shallow worship of contrived excitement, but worship that
creates deep pleasure in the One who receives it and the one
who gives it.

*Only a thrilling, soul-pleasuring encounter with God that gener-
ates more pleasure than sin will free us from our addiction to sin.* 📖

5. As you worship God, privately or with others, what do you seek most
   to know or experience? Express this longing in words as fully as you
   can, perhaps in the form of a prayerful plea to God your Father.

Your Journey to Joy

6. Mark or highlight any of the phrases in the following quotation that
   most strongly reflect your own genuine longings.

📖 Perhaps you're aware of how badly you long to experience
God. Many dreams have shattered in your life, important
ones, but you don't want to dishonor God. You don't want to
dismiss Him. You desire to know Christ as your best friend.

You want to enjoy Him and know His power to relate well
with others, to be a better friend, to parent your children more
wisely, to touch hurting people more deeply.

And you want to change, to find the strength to resist sinful urges, to persevere in your difficult marriage, to replace self-hatred and despair with an awareness of your unique value in the kingdom of Christ.

You long for an encounter with God, community with others, and real transformation within your self....

[Y]ou want to encounter *God,* to find in your relationship with Him a pleasure that exceeds all other pleasures, a joy that sustains you in every sorrow. 📖

Where do you think these desires come from? Why are they within you?

How Do You Think About God?

In the final chapter of *Shattered Dreams,* Dr. Crabb puts before us two core questions. The first is, "How do you think about God?" He points out three basic answers.

7. The first answer:

> 📖 The Bible reveals God as absolutely holy. The angels who continually surround Him cry out, "Holy, holy, holy is the Lord God Almighty."
>
> Paul introduces God to us in Romans as a holy God who is passionately furious at all that is unholy. His presentation of the good news of the gospel starts with bad news for us. God is a God of vengeance, of wrath, of retribution. He will

not allow the guilty to remain unpunished. The picture is
not one of a nice man; He is not presented as a warm and
loving father who likes His children and who sees to it they
all have a good time. 📖

What aspects of this description, if any, match your own perspective
of God?

8. The second answer:

📖 Our Christian culture has weakened our understanding
of the holiness of God by introducing too soon the idea of
grace....
   God means for us to obey His rules, we say, but if we
don't (and no one does, of course, not completely), He's
really quite understanding. That's our view of grace....
   We reduce the holy God of passionate wrath to a fatherly
God with strict standards. And we do it in the name of
grace. 📖

What aspects of this description, if any, match your own perspective
of God?

9. The third answer:

📖 But we're still uncomfortable with the idea of standards.
It restricts our freedom; it denies us the chance to be ourselves,
to express who we really are. So we dismiss God's standards by

attacking them as holdovers from legalism. God is the God of liberty. We're told to stand fast in the freedom Christ provides.

That freedom, we say, consists in our opportunity to find ourselves and become whole persons by following God's wise counsel, by listening to our inner voice. In His kindness, God has given us a lot of ideas about how to live. If we listen to them and practice them, we'll enjoy life as it was meant to be enjoyed. Things will go well for us. We'll feel good about ourselves and how our lives are turning out.

God has now become the helpful God of useful principles. 📖

Once more, what aspects of this description, if any, match your own perspective of God?

How Do You Think About Yourself?

The second core question the author asks in the final chapter is this: "How do you think about yourself?" Again he offers three potential answers.

10. The first answer:

> 📖 If you're looking for a quick boost to your self-esteem, the Bible is not a good book to read. You might especially want to skip the first three chapters of Romans. They reveal us as hopelessly arrogant, foolish enough to think that we're the point of things, that our happiness, our sense of well-being, matters more than anything else. 📖

What aspects of this description, if any, match the way you view yourself?

11. The second answer:

> 📖 In our Christian culture, we've weakened our under-
> standing of personal sin by talking too soon and too much
> about our longings and our needs. We want to feel good
> about ourselves, we long for enjoyable relationships, we
> desire effective and recognized ministries. *We* become the
> point and see nothing really wrong with it.
>
> Because we focus more on our longings than our evil, we
> see ourselves not as hopelessly arrogant, worthy of eternal
> misery, but as scoldably selfish, deserving of perhaps a slap
> on the wrist....
>
> We've weakened our view of sin by centering on what we
> long for to the point where, at worst, we see ourselves as
> deserving only a scolding. 📖

What aspects of this description, if any, match your view of yourself?

12. The third answer:

> 📖 We take it one step further. We may admit that our
> minor offenses warrant a reprimand, but we really believe
> that if someone knew what we've been through and the pain
> we feel, the scolding would give way to a sympathetic hug.
> We struggle and we make mistakes, but given our hurt,

given how poorly the people in our lives have responded
to our longings, our struggles are quite understandable.
If God loves us, He really ought to help. 📖

Again, what aspects of this description, if any, match your own self-
view?

Encountering God

Dr. Crabb then brings together, in various ways, these basic views we have
of God and of ourselves and shows what happens.

13. First:

> 📖 When understandable strugglers meet a helpful God of
> useful principles, they use Him to make their lives more com-
> fortable. They never encounter God as their greatest pleasure,
> they never enter into an other-centered community of broken
> people, and they never experience a deep change in their inte-
> rior being. Their experience of God is shallow.
>   They become spiritual narcissists, nutty people who live
> only to feel better. 📖

In what ways, if any, does this description reflect your own experiences, past or present?

14. Second:

📖 When scoldably selfish people meet a fatherly God
of strict standards, their encounter with God is never intimate. It breeds resentment and distance. They, too, never
encounter God as their greatest pleasure. Their approach to
community becomes appropriate and well-mannered, and
they turn into self-righteous Pharisees who congratulate
themselves on being better than others.

They become spiritual hypocrites, nutty people who
think of themselves as quite mature. 📖

In what ways, if any, does this description reflect your own experiences, past or present?

15. Third:

📖 But when arrogant people who know they deserve eternal
misery tremble before a holy God of passionate wrath, they
discover grace. They encounter the depths of God's kindness
and love, a kindness and love they find nowhere else. They
fall to their knees and worship Christ as their Lord and
Savior and as their truest friend, really their only true friend.
They know they don't *deserve* a hug, no matter how badly
they're hurting; but they get an eternal one anyway. That's
the grace that takes their breath away. 📖

Once more, in what ways, if any, does this third description reflect
your own experiences, past or present? And in what ways does this
third description reflect your longings for the *future?*

Those Who Truly Understand

16. In the final pages of *Shattered Dreams,* Dr. Crabb provides the following
    further description of people who deeply understand the true biblical
    view of God and themselves. As you've done before, read these words
    reflectively, choose one or more of the paragraphs to reflect upon, then
    write down your prayerful responses. How fully do these statements
    describe you?

> They enter into the community of broken, forgiven people
> who are hungry for all of God they can get. Nothing stands in
> their way—not shame, not the fear of revealing too much, not
> a desire to be well thought of. With abandon they seek God,
> alone and in the company of like-minded others.

> They're startled when they discover that their interior
> worlds are changing. They discover that they actually *want*
> to obey God. They find themselves caring less about their
> own reputation than about God's.

> They become spiritual people, not nutty but wise as they
> dream the dream of knowing Christ even better.

> And they welcome shattered dreams as friends. They
> enter their pain and discover an arrogant spirit that says, "I
> don't deserve this." They tremble in their unholiness before a
> holy God and discover how passionately they want to have a
> good relationship with Him. Then He reveals the new way

of grace, the gospel that lets them draw near to God and discover how wonderful He is. 📖

📖 But they learn slowly. More dreams must shatter before
they experience their deepest joy in Christ. 📖

📖 The journey continues, a journey through shattered
dreams to the exquisite joy of encountering Christ. 📖

A New Way

📖 A new way to live is available to us, a way that leads to a
joy-filled encounter with Christ, to a life-arousing community with others, and to a powerful transformation of our
interior worlds that makes us more like Jesus....
   I am praying for a revolution in the church of Jesus
Christ, a revolution that takes full advantage of the new way
of the Spirit....
   Pray with me that many will walk together in the new
way, that the revolution will begin. We can live beyond shattered dreams. 📖

17. Will you join the author in this prayer? If so, you may want to record
    your genuine expression of this request before God.
18. In quietness, review what you've written and learned in this week's
    lesson. Record any further thoughts or prayer requests as they come
    to mind.

19. What for you was the most meaningful concept or truth in this week's lesson?

How would you talk this over with God? Write down your response as a prayer to Him.

What do you believe God wants you to do in response to this week's study?

INTRODUCING NEWWAY MINISTRIES

*We have been released from the law
so that we serve in the new way of the Spirit.*

—ROMANS 7:6

With the release of *Shattered Dreams,* along with the writings of respected colleagues, I launched NewWay Ministries in 2002. It was birthed out of the passionate conviction that there is a new way to live—made possible by the New Covenant—and this new way of living must become better known. NewWay Ministries (NWM) joins with people who are excited about spiritual formation and authentic community to help ignite a revolution in how Christians live, think, and relate.

Let me introduce you to NWM by outlining its theological foundations, the essence of the new way to live, and the contribution we hope to make to the revolution.

THE THEOLOGICAL FOUNDATIONS

The Reformation was a reforming of the Christian theology of justification. It provided a clear understanding of how we receive life from God. In my years as a psychologist working with people who desperately want to change, I've come to believe that we need a second reformation, this one reforming our theology of sanctification. We know what it takes to receive life from God. But do we understand what is required to live the life we've received?

The good news that Jesus announced is not only that we've been forgiven, but also that we've been changed. There is new life within us that is stronger and better than the energy that drove us before we were converted.

That new life has four basic elements:

First, a new purity. We're now clean even when we roll in mud. The dirt is on us; the purity of God's life is in us.

Second, a new identity. We're no longer defined by our problems or sins or education or talents. No one is an alcoholic who happens to be a Christian. Now the person who compulsively drinks is a Christian who happens to struggle with strong urges to drink too much. The only label we wear is that we are Christ's ones, Christians. That's who we are; everything else is secondary.

Third, a new appetite. Our deepest and potentially strongest desire is for God—to know Him, to enjoy Him, to obey Him, to reveal Him. When a Christian sins, he is not giving in to his deepest appetite. Becoming like Christ has little to do with sheer moral effort and nothing to do with repairing psychological damage from traumatic experiences. It has everything to do with identifying, nourishing, and freely indulging our appetite for holiness. The route to personal change is release more than it is reform or repair. The latter two are the work of man. The former is the work of God.

Fourth, a new power. The Holy Spirit has moved in. Our hearts have become His home. The power is within us to live out the new life of purity, identity, and appetite that has already been gifted to us and implanted in our souls. We need a good theology about how to access that power. This new life, given to us according to the terms of the New Covenant, empowers us to relate to others in a new way. And doing so further stirs up the life within us so that our interior worlds become more like the interior world of Jesus. The community that's now possible is one in which we're known with no secrets. We are explored to help us see all that's inside; we're discovered to be alive with Trinitarian life; and we're touched by the Spirit through others.

NWM stands firmly within the borders of evangelical theology, but it highlights New Covenant truth and an understanding of real community as its distinctive foundation. Too often, our relational experiences fail to express and enjoy that foundation, but life can be different.

THE ESSENCE OF THE NEW WAY TO LIVE

Much of how we live is all about us. If we could see deeply into the motives, maneuverings, and messy emotions of our souls, we would admit that our bottom-line agendas are far more concerned with our well-being than with God's glory. And the self-centeredness we do see strikes us as reasonable and necessary.

When God planned the New Covenant, His intention was to recover His reputation that His Old Covenant followers had pretty well ruined. God's priority then, now, and always is His glory. New Covenant resources are provided so we can live lives that are all about God and not all about us.

The point is that God be glorified in us, not that He become useful to us.

The old life energizes a dad to want to straighten out his drug-abusing son, to be a good father who does things right. The new life empowers a dad to want above everything else to enjoy God and be abandoned and responsive and honoring to Him even when his son stumbles in the door at four in the morning, buzzed and defiant. Living the new way removes pressure from the dad to "do it right" and relieves the power struggle between father and son. And that opens up possibilities for better relating between them and for wisdom in better responding to a troubled child.

The old way is all about us and it draws on resources everyone has, whether Christian or not. The new way is all about God. Living it requires resources from God available only to Christians. Living the new way attracts outsiders to a life they can't have apart from Christ, but which they discover they desperately want.

THE CONTRIBUTION OF NEWWAY MINISTRIES

Our intended contribution to the revolution includes four distinct ministries.

1. LIBRARY

My earlier books reflected my commitment to biblical counseling. I focused on a biblical understanding of various life areas, such as marriage and manhood. Now, drawing on all that I've previously written, I am zeroing in on three topics:

- Encounter—what it means to experience God.
- Transformation—what it takes to become like Christ.
- Community—what real community is and what its role is in helping us know God and form spiritually.

My books *Connecting* and *Becoming a True Spiritual Community* (formerly titled *The Safest Place on Earth*) began the new focus by looking at the practice and power of community. *Shattered Dreams* and *The PAPA Prayer* directly address the most vital of the three topics, encounter. *The Pressure's Off* and *SoulTalk* lay the groundwork for understanding transformation. And *66 Love Letters* identifies the thread that ties together what it means to encounter God by knowing Him, what it means to be transformed by God, and what it means to relate like God in community.

2. Intensive Training

The School of Spiritual Direction (SSD) is a week-long intensive available to thirty students at a time. The school is an opportunity to understand and experience how the Spirit works deep in our souls to spiritually form us, and to learn and practice a way of following the Spirit in others to arouse and direct their hunger for God.

The objective of SSD is not to professionally prepare people for vocational ministry. It is to encourage Christians to consider the enormous value of spiritual direction and to equip a handful of selected people to engage in meaningful, powerful, soul-shaping conversations with folks who long to move through life's challenges into a deeper relationship with God.

I am persuaded that the absence of such conversations in our lives is significantly responsible for the all-too-common distance and shallowness in our experience of God. Paul speaks of a new way to live in Romans 7:6. He calls it the "new way of the Spirit." I understand spiritual direction to involve the supernatural work of relating to others in a way that guides them into the new way to think, live, and relate. This is what the gospel makes possible.

The NextStep School of Spiritual Direction is a week-long, hands-on intensive for thirty SSD graduates. The NextStep is an opportunity to focus on translating the teaching of SSD into conversations that matter through modeling, critique of videotaped conversations, and supervision. This is more an experiential time than a didactic time, a week of intensive and personal interaction in community.

The NextStep SSD mission is to more clearly understand—by watching, critiquing, and participating in spiritually directing conversations—how the categories of understanding presented at the SSD can inform our thoughts, guide our words, and stir holy passion as we interact with others.

Certificate in Soul Care: The Ministry of Shepherding provides relational opportunities for people, over time, to come out of hiding, to be seen as they are, to "look bad" in the presence of love, to live with no secrets and increasingly free from the power of shame, and to walk together with authentic companions into the amazing liberty of grace. The Certificate in Soul Care prepares people to engage in SoulTalk, to relate with

- vision-inspired confidence
- concern-motivated curiosity
- willingly sacrificial compassion

and to thus help form a community of people who listen to God and hear Him speak.

Certificate in Spiritual Direction: The Ministry of Healing provides relational opportunities for people, over time, to discern their self-obsessed energy, to understand the devil-inspired influence of background events that have shaped their patterns of self-protective relating, and to recognize those patterns in their relationships. As people experience brokenness over their self-centered ways of relating, the hope of the gospel stirs repentance that releases the life of Christ provided under the blessing of God's new covenant. Brokenness stirs repentance that motivates abandonment to

God, which in turn develops confidence in God's goodness. This releases people into a new way to live, the way of Jesus.

The Certificate in Spiritual Direction prepares people to release the passion of Christ into others as they relate to others with His wisdom. This passion/wisdom approach is designed to provide non-professional, relationally focused direction in becoming more spiritually formed.

3. CONFERENCES

In addition to many other teaching opportunities, NWM offers a complimentary weekend conference titled "Life on the Narrow Road: No Shortcuts, No Formulas, Just Life." During this conference, we look at the seven most important questions of life: Who is God? What is He up to? Who are we? What has gone wrong? What has God done about our problem? How is God's Spirit moving today? How do we follow the Spirit's movement in one another's lives? These are the seven questions God has answered to guide us on the narrow road and show us how to travel it to new life as we discover how to

- unmask the deception that makes the broad road look good.
- understand how real men and real women walk the narrow road.
- see why life on the narrow road has no shortcuts or formulas as we experience God and live like Jesus in every circumstance of life.

Together we learn how real change from the inside out develops as we discern whether we're on the narrow road to life.

4. INTERNET COURSES

NWM offers an Internet course titled SoulCare Foundations: A Model for Pastors, Counselors, and Friends. In conjunction with ChristianCourses .com, NWM offers this free, four-part, online curriculum in soul care. It is designed to introduce people around the world to the basic concepts of soul care that underlie psychotherapy, counseling, lay counseling, pastoring, spiritual direction, and friendship, and to provide training in the essential practice of soul care.

For more information please visit our Web site at
www.newwayministries.org.

THERE *IS* A NEW WAY TO LIVE.

Notes

1. Many have explained the shattered dreams in Naomi's life as God's discipline for leaving Israel. They say the family should have submitted to God's lesser discipline of famine by remaining at home. When they refused, God visited them with a greater trial. That may be so (we love to explain suffering; it makes us think we can avoid it). But Abraham and Sarah left the straight and narrow a few times to improve their lot, and God blessed them. Why not Naomi?

2. Jean-Pierre de Caussade, introduction to *Abandonment to Divine Providence,* ed. John Beevers (New York: Doubleday, 1975), 14.

3. Terese of Lisieux, quoted in Iain Matthew, *The Impact of God* (London: Hodder and Stoughton, 1955), 84.

4. Especially in this chapter, my thinking has been influenced by Iain Matthew in his excellent discussion of the writings of St. John of the Cross in *The Impact of God.* The first poem appears on page 10, the second on pages 23-24.

5. Matthew, *Impact of God,* 71.

6. Matthew, *Impact of God,* 12.

7. The phrase "our determined grasp of our empty selves" appears in Thomas Merton, *Contemplative Prayer* (New York: Image Books, 1996), 107.

8. I am indebted to Renald E. Showers for introducing me to these Jewish practices. His tract, *Behold, the Bridegroom Comes,* published by the Friends of Israel Gospel Ministry (P.O. Box 908, Bellmawr, NJ 08095), presents what this chapter summarizes.

9. A twelfth-century Cistercian named Isaac of Stella spoke of the dark night of God's felt absence as "a hell of mercy and not of wrath." Quoted in Merton, *Contemplative Prayer,* 102.

10. Rachel Joy Scott, quoted by Richard Roeper, "One year later, Columbine still offers no easy answers," *Denver Post,* 20 April 2000, sec. B, p. 9.

11. Adapted from selected verses in 2 Corinthians 4–5 in Eugene Peterson's *The Message* (Colorado Springs: NavPress, 1995).

12. This thought was suggested to me in a sermon, "The Day God Said Nothing," delivered by Dr. Don Sweeting, senior pastor, at Denver's Cherry Creek Presbyterian Church in April 2000.

13. *The Table Talk of Martin Luther,* edited by Thomas S. Kepler, translated by William Haglitt; (Grand Rapids, Mich.: Baker, 1952), 133-134.

14. J. I. Packer, introduction to *Meeting God: A Lifeguide Bible Study* (Madison, Wis.: InterVarsity, 1986), 9.

15. Augustine, *Confessions,* quoted in John Piper, *The Legacy of Sovereign Joy* (Wheaton, Ill.: Crossway, 2000), 51-57.

16. It's important to remember that our addictions are not the product of psychological disorder. They are not the expression of internal damage caused by difficult backgrounds. They are rather the fruit of the flesh, that natural tendency in all of us to fill our empty souls with some pleasure other than God. Obedience to God is a fruit of the Spirit's revealing the sweetness of Christ to our spirits so that we actually enjoy obedience more than sin.